Robert Hamill Nassau

Crowned in Palm-land

A Story of African Mission Life

Robert Hamill Nassau

Crowned in Palm-land
A Story of African Mission Life

ISBN/EAN: 9783744757379

Printed in Europe, USA, Canada, Australia, Japan

Cover: Foto ©ninafisch / pixelio.de

More available books at **www.hansebooks.com**

What can I do for you in this out of the way place?

Affec. your sister,
Mary C. Terrence

CROWNED IN PALM-LAND.

A STORY

OF

AFRICAN MISSION LIFE.

WITH ILLUSTRATIONS.

PHILADELPHIA:
J. B. LIPPINCOTT & CO.
1874.

"METHOUGHT that of these visionary flowers
I made a nosegay, bound in such a way
That the same hues, which in their natural bowers
Were mingled or opposed, the like array
Kept these imprisoned children of the Hours
Within my hand; and then, ...
I hastened to the spot whence I had come
That I might there present it,"—on her tomb.

DEDICATORY.

INSCRIBED TO

MRS. DR. WILLIAM C. THOMSON,

OF GLASGOW, SCOTLAND,

WHO DIED NOVEMBER 28, 1872.

I cannot thank her now, but I pray that, if consistent with His holy will, the Omniscient Elder Brother may cause her (whatever now her angel name) who bore on earth the name of Margaret (Frame) Thomson, to know that the completion of this labor of love, whose inception she first suggested, is not only pursuant of her wish, but responsive to foreign missionary interest and personal sympathy, centring from wide-spread sources around my wife's grave, and assuring me that grave was not wastefully made.

R. H. NASSAU.

PEEKSKILL-ON-THE-HUDSON, November, 1873.

CONTENTS.

	PAGE
DEDICATORY	5
INTRODUCTORY	9
GENEALOGICAL	13

CHAPTER I.
A PICTURE 15

CHAPTER II.
A HOMESTEAD . . . 17

CHAPTER III.
A CHILD 25

CHAPTER IV.
A SCHOOL-GIRL . . 33

CHAPTER V.
A TEACHER . 41

CHAPTER VI.
A MISSIONARY . 51

CHAPTER VII.
TO AFRICA . 65

CONTENTS.

CHAPTER VIII.
Corisco Girls' School . . . 82

CHAPTER IX.
A Romance 105

CHAPTER X.
A Wife, and the School 110

CHAPTER XI.
A Mother.—Return to the School . . . 150

CHAPTER XII.
Pioneering 188

CHAPTER XIII.
Little Paull 232

CHAPTER XIV.
In the Wilderness . . . 254

CHAPTER XV.
Journeyings Oft 291

CHAPTER XVI.
Fading Away 313

CHAPTER XVII.
Through the Waters . . . 332

CHAPTER XVIII.
Cairn-Stones . . . 355

CHAPTER XIX.
Cypress Leaves 373

CROWNED IN PALM-LAND.

INTRODUCTORY.

UNDER THE DAISIES.

"Though they smile in vain for what once was ours,
  They are love's last gift,—bring ye flowers, pale flowers!"

It is far away,—that grave.

Yet, looking across these brown November fields to-day, it seems near. As if I could touch it. As I did when, with two-year-old baby Charley's toddling steps at my side, I took—at his wish to "go mamma"—that sunset walk before each day's tropic twilight fell, and his little hands with mine gathered the white daisy-like flowers that humbly grew in the coarse, white sand, and laid them on her grave.

Only white flowers then. Gaudy tints hung from vine and branch over the path. They were not chosen. Their odors, like tuberoses, were too voluptuous for loveliness. Only white flowers and green grasses then.

But now, for the sake of the many who have thrown their fragrant thoughts about her name, that daisy monotone may swell into a harmony of sounds culled from the many-hued "alphabet of angels;" and I gather,—

> "With all the pale flowers of the vernal woods,
> White violets, and the mournful hyacinth,
> And frail anemone,"

cinquefoil and weeping-willow mourning for the dead; pine-leaves, mournfully musical, sighing pitifully for life so early ended; olive-sprigs and amaranths of thanks for the peace and rest found in the immortality "where we lay our burdens down;" roses, withered,—only memory recalling their loveliness; water-lilies, not purer than the heart that has at last by the sight of God realized His beatitude; tall reeds,—musical reeds,—recalling happy voices; and clinging, twining, friendly ivy; hopeful verbenas, and coreopses, and chrysanthemums, cheerful as the merry thought and sunlike spirit that shone no less even when the days were "cold and dark;" red sepals of pine-apple-blossoms, and leaflets of palms, feathery and graceful as the footstep that drew its lightness from an upright and perfect heart; and cross-bearing passion-flowers,—the cross of an unswerving faith; thoughtful pansies and forget-me-nots; submissive blue violets of meek regrets, and asphodels of regrets vain unless to purify; and red poppies and hyacinths, consoling with a faith in the developments of a future, and in the God who, though He makes pasts and has made futures, gives for actual duty only presents.

> "By all those token-flowers that tell
> What words can ne'er express so well."

†GENEALOGICAL.

MARY CLOYD (LATTA) NASSAU.

"Every family is a history in itself, and even a poem, to those who know how to search its pages."

1732.
*REV. JAMES LATTA, D.D.

Born in the winter of 1732, died January 29, 1801; Pastor at Chestnut Level, Lancaster County, Pa.; and his wife,

*MARY MCCALLA,

and their ten children, of whom eight survived them, viz.,

*Francis Alison,—Rev. F. A. Latta, Chestnut Level, Pa.; unmarried.

*William,—Rev. W. Latta, D.D., Great Valley, Chester County, Pa., to whom were born two sons and two daughters.

*John Ewing,—Rev. J. E. Latta, D.D., Newcastle, Del., to whom were born two sons and five daughters.

*Mary,—Miss Mary Latta.

*Margaret,—Miss Margaret Latta.

*Elizabeth,—Miss Elizabeth Latta.

*Sarah,—Mrs. Rev. Thomas Love, Red Clay Creek, Del., to whom was born one daughter.

*James,—Rev. J. Latta, Upper Octorara, Chester County, Pa., to whom were born one son and five daughters.

---

†See Sprague's "Annals" of Presbyterianism, vol. 3, names Latta, p. 199, and McCalla, p. 320.

14 GENEALOGICAL.

1769.
*REV. WILLIAM LATTA, D.D.

Born May —, 1769, died February 19, 1847; Pastor at Great Valley, Chester County, Pa.; and his wife,

*MARY CLOYD,
and their four children, viz.,

Mary Ann,—Miss M. A. Latta.

*Margaretta,—Miss M. Latta.

**James Francis*,—J. F. Latta, M.D., Chester County, Pa., to whom were born one daughter and two sons.

William Wilson,—Rev. W. W. Latta, Honeybrook, Chester County, Pa., to whom survives one daughter.

1808.
*JAMES FRANCIS LATTA, M.D.

Born May 8, 1808, died December 26, 1841; Great Valley, Chester County, Pa.; and his wife,

*LYDIA LEDLEY MOORE,
and their three children, viz.,

**Mary Cloyd*,—Mrs. Rev. R. H. Nassau, Benita, West Africa.

✝*Samuel Moore*,—S. M. Latta, died September 16, 1856, aged eighteen years.

*William James,—Capt. W. J. Latta, Eighth Regiment Penna. Cavalry; died October 5, 1862, aged twenty-two years.

1837.
*MARY CLOYD (LATTA) NASSAU.

Born February 20, 1837, died September 10, 1870, at Benita, West Africa; and her three boys.

"And I will establish my Covenant between me and thee, and thy seed after thee in their generations, for an everlasting Covenant, to be a God unto thee and to thy seed after thee."

✝ See Note, preceding page.

CHAPTER I.

A PICTURE.

> "And then I think of one who, in
> Her youthful beauty, died;
> The fair, meek blossom that grew up
> And faded by my side."

Two locks of hair.

One, fair and golden, cut when she——. No one can tell me now just when or by whom. Perhaps by a mother's hand. Perhaps in one of childhood's sicknesses, and laid away in this old family Bible of her maternal grandfather. Perhaps as a memento of happy youth, when that mother may have looked, in natural solicitude, to the possibilities of the future. One hand after another has preserved it from loss, hidden safely,—perhaps in this very Bible,—and there it has lain for a quarter of a century. While the light of youth that shines in these silken threads grew, beaming on the years of girlhood and womanhood, and—like the light of stars before the sun—has gone out in the glory of eternity, the little lock still lies here with the hue and coil of those little years, to tell of the form and features whose spirit gave it life.

The other, a heavy tress, in which the color of infancy has darkened, in a casket with the faded bridal wreath of buds from the orange groves of Corisco, cut off as a burden under Africa's fevers, before its mass had borne a single "almond" blossom.

How much the light-golden hairs could tell of the thought of the brain that pulsed beneath the wide temple, that spoke through the large generous mouth, or that glanced through the blue eyes under the high, wide, open forehead! The after-years, that darkened this tress to its ruddy auburn, only added to the vivacity that gleamed in those eyes when they were no longer a quiet, studious little girl's, but a sprightly woman's.

Each braid recalls a memory, and has a voice to speak for some special feature.

This, for the lithe form that, in spite of a forward inclination of head and shoulder induced by the close observation of near-sightedness, was taller than medium stature. *This*, for the graceful neck over which it played, tossed by the fresh western breeze that came with the swell of the Atlantic on Corisco's strand. *This*, for the white cheek,—never ruddy,—in whose skin's fair delicacy, even before tropic heat had played on it, the freckled footprints of the sun's rays had impressed themselves. And *this*, for the mobile lips playing with quick flow of words in animated conversation; or, from their quiet line of repose, springing into curved life in sudden repartee. And *this*, that played loose, either in accustomed negligence or in permitted enjoyment of its escape from restraint of netting or pin, recalls the agile step that on the sands sought with her native girls for shell, or coral, or weed, treading with no less lightness and elasticity than their own feet.

Lay them away again,—the golden lock in the old family Bible, and the auburn tress in the casket by the faded wreath. Their silent voices, though they recall a picture of the mortal lineaments, can not recall what has put on immortality.

> "Her memory is the shrine
> Of pleasant thoughts, soft as the scent of flowers."

CHAPTER II.

A HOMESTEAD.

1837–1842. In the Valley.

> "There were flowers beside the brooklet;
> There were colors on the meadow——"

THAT was a pleasant ride, one August day, when her two boys went to see the place where their mother had lived when younger even than they.

The cars had brought us through the valley of

the Schuylkill from Philadelphia and Norristown up into the Great Valley of Chester County. Resting there, about the middle of the valley at a small way-station, among connections of the Latta family, we shared the easy hospitality of a Pennsylvania farm-house of the kind that, with the refinements of education and the comforts due proximity to the city, unites rural true-heartedness and freedom from restraint.

The next day, with the family carriage and "old Mose,"—a relic whose age released him from the labors of the plow, but which better fitted him for safe driving by hands unskilled, or young, or timid,—we started on a pilgrimage to the various localities, within a radius of five miles, where Mrs. Nassau's infancy had been passed.

A pilgrimage to a Mecca. But whatever the sadness it might have for the older ones of the party, for the children it was to be as happy as had been their mother in those same scenes. Here, in the midst of "Chester's storied vales and hills," a painter-poet has laid some of the scenes of the "Wild Wagoner of the Alleghanies;" and, only a few miles distant, patriotism had suffered in the snows of Valley Forge. What a picture of loveliness, as we jogged along, gathering the view from either side! Under the burdened apple-trees of the orchard,—stopping under a neighbor's pear-tree to listen to a reminiscence of the Doctor, who "knew her from a child,"—winding from side to side of the valley as the land-swales followed the course of the errant stream. Those gently-sloping hills, the stone-walled roadsides, the low-roofed dairy-houses trying to hide themselves on the edges of charming meadows, the short, steep ascents and descents, till we came on our westward way up the valley to the Latta homestead. Up that steep ascent how the horses must have panted in summer! Down it, how the boys' coursing sleds must have sped in winter!

There had lived the Rev. William Latta, D.D., while pastor, for almost half a century, of the Great Valley and Charlestown churches. "He was a fine scholar, was skilled in the use of his pen, and was occasionally occupied in teaching. The General Assembly, in 1847, paid a tribute to his memory, by speaking of him as 'one of the venerable fathers of the Presbyterian Church.'"

The trees in the door-yard—those spruces and maples—he had planted. Sitting on the ample porch of the front door-way he could doubtless have looked over their top or through their vistas as their lines sloped down to the foot of the hill, and could see across and down the valley. But their tall tops and densely-interlaced branches, rioting in neglected wildness, shut out sight now.

The simple-hearted foreign woman, who boarded and lodged the employees of the adjacent stonequarry, kindly opened the house for us, and showed the neglected rooms where once courtesy, and talent, and patriarchial dignity of the ministry of a past generation had shed light on the now dusty walls.

The two boys saw, but felt none of these things. True, it was where their great-grandfather had lived, but, out o' doors were the trees to climb, and the hillside to romp on, and the quaint dairy-house at the foot, by which sped the brook that, though generations had come and gone, still sang the same song as it flowed " on forever, ever."

Then, a few miles east, down the valley, we passed the old stone church with its open, square vestibule. Its door was locked, but the new lecture-room, close by, was open. In the sisterhood of churches of that region, how that Great Valley Church has sadly lost its eminence! Once strong and vigorous and famous; now, as the children of the old families of the valley moved to the cities, carrying with them their ancestral wealth, their broad lands, passing into less cultured hands, were cut up into smaller farms for foreigners, often ignorant or irreligious, or others not of the once-dominant Presbyterian element. And the strong old church has become weak under an inevitable decay which Dr. Latta's able successors could not stop.

But the graveyard was there, with its precious record of the work of the past. And we entered it, while the boys played hide-and-seek in and around the benches of the lecture-room, with the daughter of a physician living hard by,—a little Mary, whose vivacity strangely recalled another little Mary, whose ancestors lay buried there.

There was Rev. Dr. Wm. Latta's pulpit-shaped monument covered by an open Bible, on whose two pages were carved the entire twenty-third Psalm. "The Lord is my Shepherd, I shall not want," was a promise of covenant grace his own ancestors had well proved. This tall obelisk is a memorial of one of his sons, Mrs. Nassau's father, Dr. James F. Latta,—a genial, ambitious, talented student and honored graduate of Dickinson College,—an enthusiast in his profession at the medical department of the University of Pennsylvania, a heart tender and loving and poetic, but brave for everything that was manly, and true for everything that was Christian. There, too, were the graves of Mrs. Nassau's mother and two brothers, Samuel and William.

Then we turned up a road by one side of the valley toward a rough-cast stone house, about five miles from the old Latta homestead. This was Dr. J. F. Latta's residence, prepared for his bride, Miss Lydia Ledley Moore, only child of Jonathan Moore, M.D., of Deerfield, Cumberland Co., N. J., who had been brought up in Philadelphia in the family of her paternal uncle, Samuel Moore, M.D., late director of the United States Mint, in the company of her cousins, Mrs. Mary Finley and Mrs. Surgeon-General C. L. Finley.

This was Mrs. Nassau's first home; not indeed her birth-place, for she was born in Philadelphia, during her parents' temporary stay there (as a relic visiting-card describes), at the "corner of Madison and Vine, near Twelfth Street," whence they had returned to the valley when she was a few months old. And that stone house, with the willows in front, was the home of her earliest infancy. The trees are the same,—her little hands had probably clutched the sweeping branches of these willows as did her children this day. They peeped down the deep, unfailing well, and twirled the handle to see the evolution of the rope, and drank from the bucket the ice-cold water, all as she had done. There were the fruit-trees, and perhaps some of those peonies in the back garden she may have plucked "in childish glee." But everything else of fence, or path, or adornment of window, cornice, or door was changed; and the denial of our request to enter farther than the front door probably saved the revelation of greater alteration in that early home. Here her affectionate parents had lived,— her father, devoted to his profession, successfully practiced his skill,—here her two brothers were born; and that father, from the effects of exposure in the beginning of his practice, had early died, when she was in her fifth year.

The widowed mother, with her three little ones and her own aged mother, remained for two years on the farm at the stone house, and then disposing of the property rented the "Academy" building. This was a select school located some five miles, up the valley, from Dr. J. F. Latta's house, and a mile beyond the Latta homestead. It was used as a dwelling successively by different persons, who, like Mrs. Latta, without having any connection with the institution, boarded the teacher, whose school-room occupied one-half of the first floor. It stands on the old Lancaster turnpike; a strong stone double house, with lindens and paper-mulberries in front. We entered what was once the school-room; half of it was partitioned off as a kitchen. We went into the room where she had sat as a day-scholar, and stood where her little feet had stood in the spelling-class, and spoke to the walls that had responded to the first literary utterances of a mind whose after-accomplishments gilded every life touched by her own.

Thus we lingered during two days, about spots so changed in outward form that some of them, like withered roses, had only their memories to make them beautiful, and in the evenings sat on the piazza of our hospitable friends' house, where, while the children played about the roots of the huge, ivy-clad sycamores, tales were told of their mother's childhood in that "Happy Valley."

In that brook down in the meadow,—shallow in summer, a torrent in spring,—divested of shoes and stockings she had waded, splashed the cobble-stones in its pebbly bed, and built mud-dams.

One of those cherry-trees in front of the porch had its story of climbings; for, even when she was no longer a child but a young lady at school, her heart had all the freshness and mirth of childhood, and on occasions, or in company where permissible, would enjoy itself unrestrained.

Of that cool dairy, where the water bubbled up as joyously as did the merry laugh that even in Africa never failed, she herself had often told me. The privations of our African home and table were often enlivened by descriptions, not regretful or complaining, of the luxuries of Pennsylvania country milk and cream, its generous slices of fresh wheat-bread and unstinted spread of sweet yellow butter. And among the plannings for that mythical time "when we should be sick enough to have to go to America," was a visit to hospitable Chester County homes and their appetizing bread and butter.

"—— like a just-departing child,
Who lingers on the threshold of his home,
Strive, with vague murmurings and lingering looks,
To store up what were sweetest to recall."

CHAPTER III.

A CHILD.

1842-1852. At Honeybrook.

> "Light, winged Hopes, that come when bid,
> And rainbow Joys that end in weeping."

CHILDREN make history; but it is mostly unwritten. Therefore, whether it be only as trifling as a feather, or as valuable as an Alexandrian Library, it is unknown or forgotten. And it passes away with those who loved,—and therefore would be most interested in its preservation,—as one by one they enter their graves. Childhood's thoughts presage its future. They should not be regarded as insignificant, unless they fail either to be recognized by every child as its own, or to serve as indices of opening character.

After his death some of Dr. Latta's poor patients, from force of habit and sure of a kindly word, continued to go to "the Doctor's house" with their minor wounds or other small ailments; and the physician's widow, under the stress of a sympathizing nature, would apply a bandage or give some simple remedy. Little Mary, or—as her relations called her—"Molly," sharing in this sympathy and desire to relieve pain, would assist. Doubtless in this slight beginning was laid the taste and tact and skill in therapeutic knowledge which, enlarging itself afterward by medical reading, enabled her, in Africa, to guard her own health and relieve the sicknesses of others.

Riding with her paternal uncle, Rev. W. W. Latta, one day, she startled him with a question whose defective theology must be laid to a child's logic and not to her Westminster Catechism: "Uncle, didn't God make all things?"

"Yes, Molly, all things."

"Didn't He make people?"

"Yes, all people."

"Well, uncle, what will people do when God dies?"

One day, while reading aloud, she came upon the word "*laugh*," in the middle of a sentence, a part of which might be something like, "love to laugh and play." She had been reading in the droning monotone of a beginner, hesitating on almost every word, and stopping to spell the larger ones. The looks of the word *laugh* did not suit her ideas of orthography, and she interjected into the reading a criticism,—letters, and words, and criticism being uttered without notice of punctuation, and in the same unvaried tone, as if they were all one long word:—"Love-to-l-a-u-g-h-but-it-ought-to-be-l-a-f-f-and-play."—Her face, meanwhile, as imperturbed and serious as if she were announcing a new discovery in philology.

Quiet Molly at the day-school would probably not be remembered among the mass of his pupils by her teacher (who is now an Episcopal clergyman); but she was a favorite among her young playmates. Once, when either neglectfully she had failed to write in her copy-book or heedlessly had blotted it, he required her as a punishment to carry the book around the room to each pupil and show the faulty page. She obeyed. But most of the children, particularly the boys, lightened the ordeal for her by keeping on at their own tasks, quietly refusing to look on her disgrace.

One of childhood's pleasures was to visit on Saturdays at the homestead,—enjoy the indulgences of aunts,—and ride with her grandfather Latta on his afternoon preaching services in the school-houses. The feet of life's travelers may have trod a long way between the termini of the journey, but life's track turns on itself and brings the grave near the cradle, so that the last words of the aged entering the one are often the first that were uttered when leaving the other. In the last weary year of her life Mrs. Nassau's memory turned brightly and lovingly to those days with her grandfather; I remember her recounting in detail the visits and rides and chats,—not forgetting the cakes that served as lunch on the way to meeting.

Calmness in danger was marked even in childhood. Riding with her uncle, who was driving a horse in whose acquaintance with railroad cars he had not confidence, as the carriage approached a train at a crossing, he said, with some anxiety himself, and to prepare her for any supposed alarm on her part, "Now, Molly, I fear we'll have a little trouble here."

"Why, uncle, perhaps it won't be as bad as you think."

In 1844, when Molly was seven years old, her mother, after occupying "the Academy" for a year, left it, and with her children removed to Waynesburg, Honeybrook P.O., some twenty-two miles distant, in the same county; where she built a home opposite the parsonage of the Presbyterian church, of which Rev. W. W. Latta was then pastor.

There the little girl's uneventful life was filled by childhood's joys and sorrows; roving with her brothers and cousins on their jaunts through the woods and meadows; with them jumping ditches, and mounting fences, and climbing trees. She bore conspicuously through all her after-life a scar that marked where, in falling from a tree-top, a lower limb had cut her under-jaw. But her cousins remember her not so much for her own merriment in those days, as for being leader and inventor of plans in which they found theirs. And often, instead of joining in their romping play, she preferred to sit down with an interesting story-book. Her studiousness was gathering that fund of information which, with a retentive memory and ready utterance, afterward made her a centre of attraction to children listening to her narrations.

Her widowed mother's self-reliance in the direction of her house and family seems to have impressed itself, so that on occasions when other children would have been discomposed or powerless through fear, she was self-possessed.

When she was about eight years old she was returning with a family party consisting, besides herself and Grandmother Latta, of some married cousins and their children. They were on the railway from the Valley to Downingtown, whence they were to proceed by stage to Waynesburg,—the present branch road thither not then having been built. In the confusion of the change at Downingtown, her aged grandmother, supposing her, like the Virgin's Child eighteen hundred years ago at Jerusalem, "to have been in the company," alighted, and little Molly was carried on by the train on its way to Parkesburg. She was immediately followed by telegram, and was returned by the next train to Downingtown and her distressed grandparent. The rest of the party had already left on the stage for Waynesburg, where they judiciously concealed the exact cause of delay from her most affectionate mother, and her uncle drove over to the station for her. She narrated that, when the train moved away with her, she recalling the localities on the road, and the fact that her grand-uncle, Rev. James Latta, was residing at Parkesburg, had felt at ease, determining to alight there and find her way to his house, and so had "just sat still in my seat" until the conductor, in making his rounds, had discovered her situation.

In after-years in Africa, on a two-months' journey at sea to England on the way to America, comforting herself for the discomforts of the voyage, she wrote in her journal, under date of August 14, 1863, an incident of this period of her life: "When I was a little girl and visited with my mother in Philadelphia, we always stayed at the Misses Hardie's. There was an old lady living with them named Miss Margaret ———, for whom I had little fondness, and who had little fondness for children. Observing my dislike of many kinds of food, she used to tell me, by way of reproof and warning, the sad story of a gentleman whom she had known. This gentleman had been used to say that of all things he would or could never eat fat pork or cold potatoes. The British took him prisoner, and he was confined in one of their dreadful prison-ships, and he was so reduced by starvation that he became thankful even for bits of salt pork and cold potato. I suppose I never made any reply to the story, but I know I thought in my own mind that cold potatoes were not very dreadful things; but as for fat pork or any other kind of fat I never should be brought to touching it. Yet here I am eating every day fat beef or pork as a relish to my baked potato. I take very little bits I can assure you; but still I like the fat for dinner with my potato. Poor Miss Margaret! She had her room in the third story, and I used to look with dread on the very stairs that led up to it. She is dead now; but the Misses Hardie are living in West Philadelphia, and I expect they will be delighted to see me for my mother's sake, if not my own."

At Waynesburg, she with her brothers and cousins were under the private tuition of Miss Maria Irvine, now Mrs. Rev. George Matthews of New York City. This protected period of life, which any child in a similarly privileged station can fill from its own history, occupied the eight years of girlhood, so formative for good or evil. The modest, studious little Molly had grown up under the careful, judicious, tender hands of governess, uncle, and mother, into the young girl of fifteen, intelligent, well-read, vivacious.

Orphanage might be called hereditary to Mrs. Nassau. Her mother, an only child, was fatherless in earliest infancy. And the same shadow of orphanage was about to fall on her daughter's life. In May, 1852, Mrs. Latta took Molly and her brother Samuel through Philadelphia on a western journey to visit cousins in Hannibal, Mo. There, while in the family of a distant connection, Mr. Meredith, Mrs. Latta was seized with dysentery, and, after an illness of two weeks, died peacefully June 25, 1852. The children received the care of their mother's relative, Clement L. Finley, late Surgeon-General U.S.A., then stationed at St. Louis.

In the following September Mary returned east to Waynesburg, where—though in the family and care of her uncle, to whom she afterward looked and felt as to a father—she was the nominal ward of Mr. David Buchanan, the executor of her mother's property.

The effects of this orphanage, occurring at the limit of her girlhood life, was felt in the immediately subsequent years, while that girlhood was rising into womanhood, when the judicious counsel and advice of a prudent mother are so much needed. She saw the need herself; and often in Africa referred to events in which she had sadly felt their want. A constant Psalm with her was the twenty-seventh.

> "Visions of Childhood! stay, oh, stay!
> Ye were so sweet and wild!
> And distant voices seem to say,
> 'It cannot be! They pass away!'"

CHAPTER IV.

A SCHOOL-GIRL.

1852–1855. At Norristown.

"Bear through sorrow, wrong, and ruth,
In thy heart the dew of youth,
On thy lips the smile of truth."

In November, 1852, orphan Mary took her place with other young ladies as a pupil in the Oakland Female Institute of Rev. J. Grier Ralston, D.D., LL.D., Norristown, Pennsylvania.

The impression received of her by her schoolmates differed on some points, according to their degree of intimacy, or as they saw her in the relations of classmate, playmate, or room-mate. A lady in Chester, Delaware county, Pennsylvania, sought me after a public missionary address and made herself known as a school- (not class-) mate of Mary Latta, and said that, though so immersed in the occupations of her household that she had forgotten even the names of some of her own class, she remembered Mary's face distinctly. Not being so intimate with her as were others, she was not impressed with a memory of her as a special lover of frolic, at least of tricks that were "mean," nor as confining herself to cliques, but as having kindness for all. She remembered her as a close and diligent student in the school-room. To Mary's room she and others used to go on Sabbath morning to study the Bible-lesson together. She spoke of her conscientiousness, and had, until I informed her otherwise, always supposed she was then a professing Christian; and had looked on her as one whom she would have supposed might choose a missionary life.

Another lady, during part of the school-course a classmate, who knew Mary more intimately, spoke much in the same strain, especially of the easy precedence that was taken in the recitation-room, but was aware of her not being at that time a professing Christian.

Another, who sat on the opposite side, but at the same end of the school-room, spoke of the "sunlight face" Mary bore as she entered the rooms; of her vivacity; and of the wonderful tales she invented for the amusement of the younger pupils.

The picture of her character, as reported by her mates, could not be true if it did not admit that this vivacity sometimes forgot time and place, and left a mark on the teacher's record-book. But fault was coupled only with truth and candor, never with subterfuge or malice.

Mary Latta's after-success in Africa as a translator of poetry showed her possession of musical taste, and she had an ear that enjoyed and commended some as distinctly as it condemned other music without being able to tell why; but she could not sing at all. This her school-companions well knew, and it often afforded them amusement in their recreation-hours, when, after others had been using piano or voice, she would say, "Now, girls, I am a-going to sing!" Thereupon seating herself at the piano she would improvise rhymes, singing and accompanying herself in a manner inimitable.

Her vacations were passed at her uncle's home, in Waynesburg, or with school-mates, visiting their homes (numerous visits at Abington, Pennsylvania, and one at Trenton, New Jersey, in December, 1853, being pleasantly remembered); and with her relations in the Valley.

On one of these visits to the Valley in company of two of her anxiously-careful aunts, the prescribed time for return to school had come. Not quite satisfied with the day's enjoyment, she wanted more. Another relation gave friendly connivance to a plan to accomplish that object. The railroad track passed only a few rods from the front of the house, and at the little way-station the train barely stopped before it would be again in motion. Her aunts were ready at the gate and anxiously urging against her apparent slowness. The slowness was necessitated by a search in the house for her watch, which, according to plan, was discovered just in time for her to see her aunts step on the train and herself left behind. Then back to her room to doff the city garb and don a dress that thorns could not spoil nor stains ruin, and in a trice she was up a cherry-tree, disputing its fruit with the merry robins. The after-confession of her *ruse* gave to her aunts as much pleasure as its successful consummation afforded herself.

One of Mary's room-mates has kindly permitted the insertion of portions of a letter (the only one in her possession of many received), written to herself during a vacation. It is characteristic, and —as intended—well burlesques school-girl extravagance of language.

"Waynesburg, April 12, 1854.

"My Lovely, Adorable, Charming, Darling, Dearest, Precious, Bewitching L—— (Did you ever peruse that enchanting work 'Mary De Clifford?'):

"Having finished a letter to Hannah ——, taken passage on the sofa to 'the land of Nod,' interrupted in my journey by a knock at the door; informed my aunt that there was a woman (I did not think her a lady) to see her; put on a hat of indescribable color, which one of brothers had cast aside as unfit for use, and which I had fished out of a dark hole, and decorated with ribbons, rosette, and a *feather;* started for the store in quest of paper; astonished the natives by singular headdress; came home again; went in the study, and that *woman* was introduced to me (imagine my surprise) as my cousin, Mrs. ——; whereupon I seized pen and ink and made a more hasty than polite retreat to the kitchen, as the only other place where I could find a comfortable fire (there comes my brother for me to commence him a fishing-net), wrote a letter to M—— H——; and now I am seated on a step of the stairs writing on a tall bench (at least I was when I commenced this sentence), being prevented from retreating to the study after my cousin of the forty-second degree had left, by hearing some one say they were going to wash the windows, which was my first disagreeable reminder that there was a kind of half house-cleaning going on in preparing for Presbytery, which meets here next week; but since I bestowed that long string of adjectives on your name, I have commenced a net for Samuel, eaten my supper, and removed to the room where they are all talking about funerals,—which is enough to give one the blues; and having no doubt pleased you by writing such a long sentence, and thereby reminding you of —— ——'s composition that you honored by reading, and having violated all the rules of rhetoric, and of everything else, it would be better to have a period somewhere on the second page.

"My head is never very full of ideas, and at present it is peculiarly empty, but as neither pen nor ink has the happy faculty of suggesting anything to say, and on asking some one what to put in a letter, she said, tell you there had been seven funerals, four on the other side and three on this; on inquiry, the line that divided the deaths proved to be the Welsh Mountain, which you need not take the map to find, as it would be too much trouble, though I ought not to think your inquiring mind would suffer any obstacle to "impede your search after truth." Aunt Mary Ann is telling a long story about some good boy that would not not fight, which I suppose is intended for the benefit of my brother Sam, who listens very patiently until she is done, and then asks 'how the man who makes those stories can manufacture such a variety.' . . . Now, L——, what in the world am I to say, and how are these four pages to be filled up? Oh, dear! you are not here to answer the question, and if you were there would be no need of an answer.

"I hope Mrs. Brown will have our matting down, and we can decide when we get there which curtain will be put up first, though I think your white one will look the prettiest. Then we must certainly have a towel-rack, and our spread is to be white. I bought three plates to-day, one common-sized tea-plate, and two smaller ones. Will you bring a saucer, if you think we need it? and a knife—and don't forget that Commentary, whatever you do.

"Imagine our being detained in Bible-class, and having to spend Sabbath afternoon in the study: 'Miss ——, how was the world created?' 'Out of the dust of the earth.' 'Miss Latta, what is the Sixth Commandment?' 'Multiply and replenish the earth.' I think, on the whole, we would have an exceedingly interesting time. . . . If you have given up the ghost when this arrives at W——, just send it back again, for no other eyes than yours are worthy to decipher these hieroglyphics. . . . Good-night, I am going to sleep on this.

"Another twenty-four hours have passed, and neither night-time nor the daylight had any more tendency to breed ideas than the sun's rays have to breed eyes. My thoughts rest ever most assuredly on my dearest L.——, and my earnest desire is to gaze with rapture once more on thy beautiful countenance. . . . Verily, I will corrupt your morals before long, and it is well that my paper is nearly out.

"Yours, most devotedly,
"MARY."

The accurate fac-simile of her autograph reveals a trait that, in dress and manner, appeared, in womanhood, as a freshness and charming unrestraint, but in school-days some would have called negligence or recklessness. Her room-mates remembered that, perhaps when dusting the room, or arranging the bed, she might, as likely as not, be found attired in her best dress.

On one of her vacation visits to Waynesburg there was a Sabbath-school picnic, attended by all the children of the church, and many others not connected with any church organization. Teachers with their several classes were to form in procession at a certain grove, and there was a friendly rivalry among the children to see which class should have the finest flags and banners. One unfortunate class, which either had no teacher to aid them, or were too poor to obtain any decorations, were, of course, wishing to share in the feast, but were in despair as to their personal appearance. Mary heard of it on the morning of the very day, and with the aid of one of her cousins concocted a gay banner that entirely filled the best wishes of that class. The fame of that banner was spoken of many years afterward, linked with the name of the good fairy who had sped to the rescue of the distressed little ones.

"Where'er I go I've a smile for all."

CHAPTER V.

A TEACHER.

1855-1860. Trenton. Chestnut Hill.

*" Dreamt out the scholar's dream, and then away
On troubled seas went voyaging with Care."*

HAVING completed the three years' course of study at Oakland, Miss Latta graduated in September, 1855; and in the October immediately succeeding, her energy seeking work, her taste for books and her love for youth selected a teacher's task as assistant in the Female Boarding-School of the Misses Beatty in Trenton, New Jersey, her attention being directed to that city by the residence there of distant relatives of her mother, and also of two or three of her Oakland companions. Beyond these, confinement to her duties prevented the making of new acquaintances; so that probably few in Trenton, other than her pupils, remember her year's stay there. Her very few new acquaintances were among the teachers of the Normal School, whose cultivated society she sought, and others, members of the Third Presbyterian

Church, under the pastoral care of Rev. Jacob Kirkpatrick, Jr., on whose ministrations she attended.

Some of those who saw her there as a faithful and regular worker in Sabbath-school, prayer-meeting, district-collecting, and other church work, may be surprised to learn that she was not then a professing Christian. Even had she been, her outward life could have shown to others in no respects a more consistent and conscientious walk. But to approach or be approached in conversation on personal religion was difficult. She remembered and ever spoke with affection of the faithful and judicious words of Mr. Kirkpatrick's dealing with her as a pastor.

In April, 1856, she was led to see the obligation of publicly acknowledging the Saviour whom secretly she loved. Circumstances prevented compliance with this duty until a year and a half later.

The pall of sorrow again fell on her. Her "dear brother" Samuel died in his eighteenth year, on the 16th of September, 1856, from the results of an accidental internal injury received from a playmate at school in Chester County, Pennsylvania. He had been her companion and favorite brother. To her younger and only remaining brother, "dear Willie," her affection partook somewhat of a mother's thoughtfulness; and her sisterly tendrils sought and received sympathy from, and clung to others.

Miss Latta closed her connection with the Misses Beatty's school about January, 1857, and, returning to her uncle's home, was for the next six months in various places for rest and recreation: in February, at her maternal cousins Finley's, in Philadelphia; in March, at Lawrenceville, New Jersey, to see her brother William in the semi-annual examinations and declamations of the Rev. Dr. Hamill's Classical and Commercial High School.

During the religious interest in her uncle's Waynesburg charge in the following summer, she took her stand for Christ; and on November 1 of the following autumn claimed, for the first time, her right to the Lord's Table. Her own record is,—

"*November* 9.—Yesterday week I united with the church;" though the entry on the session book of the Waynesburg church is made under date of November 17.

From this point began the happy two and a half years at Chestnut Hill, Philadelphia, in charge of a small school under the care of the Presbyterian church of Rev. Roger Owen, D.D. Its privacy, its infantile character,—a day-school, attended only by the children of the residents of "the Hill," —its somewhat parochial character, the responsibility resting with the church session, while the actual control lay in her own hands, fulfilled all the conditions of success for her special taste and adaptations. Her little pupils,—now the young gentlemen and ladies on the Hill,—as well as their parents, remember her most warmly.

A correspondence, from which I am permitted to make extracts, will best tell the story of her life at Chestnut Hill.

"HONEYBROOK, October 9, 1857.

"... The day I came home from Philadelphia, a letter came from Mr. Owen at Chestnut Hill, asking if I would be willing to take charge of a small school there. I had intended remaining at home this winter, and I hardly knew what to say or do; but finally I concluded it would be better to reply in the affirmative. I am now expecting a letter every mail containing particulars which will enable me to decide fully as to whether I go there or not."

A journal letter, to the same friend, begun at "Honeybrook, October —," and continued at "The Hill, November —," says,—

"Were I to give you the full benefit of the mood I am in to-night, I am afraid you would not thank me for writing. But, nevertheless, as the experiment is beginning to work a cure already, you cannot blame me much more than you would thank. . . . I am now, I trust, in winter quarters, and ere the first night is passed in my new home I want to talk a little while with you. I am in no light mood, but for the present you shall be troubled with few grave thoughts. . . . Last night and to-day I spent at Mr. Owen's." . . .

"CHESTNUT HILL, November 9, 1857.

"Oh, if you only knew how lonely I am, you would surely sit right down and make such good use of your pen, that a letter would reach me ere many days. . . . The family of Mr. H., though I would like to see more of the married daughter, seem to expect that I sit in the parlor all alone, while they occupy the sitting-room. It is so odd, —I never lived so before; but maybe I shall learn to love solitude after awhile. As far as I have been able to discover, there is no such thing as family-prayers, and that is the only arrangement or non-arrangement which suits me badly. Mr. H. is Episcopal, . . . the daughter a Baptist, and her husband too, I think; while, I am happy to say, I am a Presbyterian."

"November 11.

"I have ended my second day's trial of teaching here, and if it is not too soon to form an opinion, I think I shall like the school very well. There were seven scholars present to-day,—two of them boys not yet out of the alphabet. The younger is very stubborn, and has his tears stored up in a very convenient place for use; but I would be better satisfied if he did not feel the want of producing them so frequently. One of the little girls wriggles about as if quicksilver were an item—and a pretty large one, too—of her daily food; but then, she's so chubby, maybe she can't stand still. Mr. Owen is so very kind, attending himself to whatever might give me the least trouble; and I find his wife and sister-in-law very pleasant, too. The latter lady, Miss Lily McCorkle, was seated but two seats from me in the cars the day I came to Chestnut Hill. I wonder whether she considered me sufficiently dignified to take charge of her nieces. She asked me no questions and I volunteered no information. When the cars stopped at Germantown, she came and stated she was Mr. Owen's sister-in-law, supposing me to be Miss Latta. As I had nothing to say to the contrary, we kept up a little conversation whenever the cars stopped,—which was about all the time.

"I don't know the way from the depot to the church, but if you are once in sight of the church,—Presbyterian, and it is not far,—any one can tell you the way to Mr. H.'s . . . I have an indefinite idea that the contents of these sheets don't resemble each other very much. Which do you prefer? Do you know I have four places in my room in which to look for robbers before I go to bed,—five, counting a closet with shelves? It is very inconvenient; but as I didn't make the room, I haven't myself to blame. Our front door is actually just like the kind they have on mills; but if I want to look out I can shut the lower half and lean over, so that is quite a convenience."

"CHESTNUT HILL, November 12, 1857.

". . . The first hour after tea I generally try to do something useful, or that ought to be done. The occupation of the next depends on circumstances; and the last I do as I please. I have about three hours and a half or four of fluid-light, and I do wish I had something to do. Were I more of an adept in self-discipline I might study, but I don't take any particular interest in preparing lessons not to be recited. You know my resolution not to read any more novels this year; broke it lately, now (read one and a half) feel bad, and so on. Don't you think I deserve reproof? I wish you would bestow a little sometimes. . . . I had a stove put up in my room to-day, and it is one of the most excitable little things you ever saw. It heats and cools so quickly that I must get up every few moments to open or shut the door. I don't know exactly how to manage it, but I believe Mrs. H. thinks *that* the girl's business, and I am heartily glad she does. . . . When I first 'moved in,' I had to write on the window-seat (a high one), or make a writing-desk of my lap, as I did the first time I wrote—which was to you. Mr. H. supplied me with a table, and it's so little I have to put it in a little corner by the fire-place for fear it will upset when I sit close by it in writing. Before I left home I was telling them I wanted in my room a big easy-chair, an arm-chair, a rocking-chair, a lounge, and a footstool. Not having any of the five, I am very well satisfied without them; if I only had four pretty curtains that weren't made of paper! Don't you sympathize with me in my difficulties? I don't know what I shall do with that fire. It's rather under my management just now. I've tried to fix it for the night, but I reckon it won't stay fixed,—it will go out."

"November 15.

". . . I had not intended writing thus to-night, for I certainly felt in no sad mood when I commenced. I had been sewing on some charity work for more than two hours, and, after writing a letter of duty, wanted some little recreation. But it is Saturday night, and I may not wait to finish this; besides, you don't deserve it. . . . Do you not feel conscience-stricken in glancing at the several dates of my letters, and remembering you have not written me a word since the first of the month?"

"Chestnut Hill, February 1, 1858.

". . . I wish you could have come in the afternoon. I had much to say, but the children kept me from collecting my thoughts. . . . I am writing down-stairs, and the folks are talking about robberies, one having been committed next door to us a few nights ago. I am not as timid as many, but still I should feel rather uncomfortable to have any one enter without leave or license after honest folk are all abed, that is if I should hear them,—a doubtful case."

In the vacation months of July and August, Miss Latta was with relatives in Lancaster County, and in after-years spoke of having attended an interesting open-air revival meeting at Piquea in a grove of trees, some of which at least were growths on the same spot from trees under which Whitefield had once preached. Returning to her school, the journal continues:

"CHESTNUT HILL, October 27, 1858.

"Writing to you has of late been quite an unusual thing, but not altogether for want of thinking of you. The recollection of your last visit gives me pain, lest you should have thought I did not care as much to see you as formerly. The truth of the matter was, that Mrs. Ottinger being sick, and all of the nursing falling on me, I was tired out. At least I supposed myself very tired then; but I have learned since what real weariness of body is. Last week Mrs. Ottinger was sick again, and, besides teaching, I was chief nurse and housekeeper too. We had no girl, and I had not much help with the work. It seemed as if the last day of school—Friday—never would come; but it did, and by Monday my patient was much better. My uncle, with whom I make my home, has given up preaching for the present on account of ill health, and will probably spend the winter in the city. If so, I shall be in very often. My brother expects to be in Philadelphia, too, if he can get a situation to suit him. Should Willie be in the city, I should like him to be acquainted with you; and will you not try to lead him, to influence him aright? He is my only brother, and very dear to me."

Her uncle's residence in Philadelphia led Miss Latta there often, and she spent her vacations there with her brother William during 1859.

In the month of March, 1860, she had to leave her school temporarily to accompany to Jacksonville, Fla., her brother, who was threatened with pulmonary disease. His rapid recovery enabled her to return North in May. But her happy work at the Hill was not resumed, she being called in July hastily to complete preparations for the voyage to her longed-for work in Africa.

> "Not enjoyment, and not sorrow,
> Is our destined end or way;
> But to act that each to-morrow
> Find us further than to-day."

CHAPTER VI.

A MISSIONARY.

> " My soul is not at rest;
> There comes a strange and secret whisper to
> My spirit, like a dream of night, that tells
> Me I am on enchanted ground."

Miss Latta scarcely remembered a time when she had not thought of becoming a foreign missionary. And I cannot find, in the record of letters, or the testimony of acquaintances, a time, even in the extravagances of school-girl life, when she was not a Christian. Many children of the Abrahamic covenant, standing, even before their birth, in its precious stream of blessing,—carefully trained and conscientious in life,—cannot name the day when they first knew the Lord. Imperfect fulfillment of that covenant by parents or church-sessions, and sinful indulgence of delay by the baptized church-members themselves, may defer the claiming of covenant-rights until there come those "searchings of heart" that compel to duty. But their Christian birth-day even then should take a much earlier date than the formal sessional examination or the first communion season.

The story of Miss Latta's Christian and missionary thought properly belongs to *all* the previous eras of her life as child, school-girl, and teacher, and might have been left there in bright thoughts scattered here and there as we passed along. Indeed, in so doing the picture of *early* life would have been true. But I chose to gather in one bouquet, from all along the paths, whatever relates to the Christian and missionary aspects of her life previous to her departure for Africa.

When she was a child at Waynesburg, visitors to her mother's had seen her and been amused to hear her mother tell of "Molly's" liking for the negroes of the village, and of her talks even then about African missions. Herself had told me that she had felt a special interest, not in the companionship of, but in the endeavor to help the despised and neglected; and in any community, naturally found such among the negro population.

As she grew older, the going to Africa in 1849 of Rev. J. L. and Mrs. Mackey from New London, in her own county, and of Rev. G. W. and Mrs. Simpson, from her uncle's congregation, probably directed her interest toward that country. Her contributions of aid early went there, and her own name and her brother William's preceded her to Corisco; hers (as contained in an aunt's) being adopted by a native teacher in Mrs. Mackey's school, who still retains her Christian profession in spite of her husband's opposition; and her brother's, by a young man who died while studying for the ministry.

At Oakland, her school-mates remember her telling them she was to be a foreign missionary. Some regarded it only as one of her sallies of wit. At other times she was quiet and sad, and even dejected, and not until long after would give any reason to her companions, and then would admit only to her room-mate that the depressing thoughts arose from her neglect of religious duty. How seriously she thought may be judged by the closing stanza of verses composed by her for a school-mate's album. Instead of the usual hope of meeting in Heaven that even the godless express in parting, or other tender hours, hers was laid on the "faith" in a Saviour's blood:

> "Or, if God's dark-eyed angel should pause at our side,
>   To loosen, in youth, life's quivering cord,
> May we hope that through faith in Him who has died,
>   Our spirits shall rise to the courts of the Lord.
>
> "CLOYD."
> "Sept. 17th, 1855."

Sometimes a reckless feeling would respond to an inquiry from a sympathizing Christian school-mate in such a way as to permit her alarmed friend to think she doubted all religion. Her soul was fighting with itself, and was not at rest while it failed to acknowledge its Saviour.

A letter of Rev. J. Kirkpatrick, Jr., evidently one of a series, the others of which are lost, show how this conflict, under procrastinated performance of duty, was continued while at Trenton. It tells her own story as truly as if written by herself, and therefore I copy it almost entire. As a skillful physician, he was applying a medicine; from the adaptations of a medicine may be judged the symptoms that indicated it.

REV. JACOB KIRKPATRICK, JR., TO MISS MARY C. LATTA.

TRENTON, Apr. 28, '56.

MY DEAR FRIEND:

You know already why I have not answered your note of the 18th inst. before, so I will rest assured that you do not attribute the delay to any indifference to your spiritual welfare upon my part. With much solicitude I have waited for an interview with you. And yet, with the expression of your feelings now before me, I hardly know what it will be best for me to say in reply. You speak of one thing as "the test," and the cross which you have hitherto refused to take up, your "only cross;" now, dear friend, I tremble for you while you stand at that critical point, so near to the kingdom of God, yet standing still upon the very *probability* of sinking to a condemnation proportionately deep. You know it is a most fearful thing to fall from such a height. I will not dwell upon this most solemn consideration,—it is too painful.

May 5.—Three times, while writing the foregoing, I was interrupted and obliged to postpone it. Still, I confess that I could have finished this some days ago, but was induced to wait by the hope of soon having an opportunity of conversing with you. It seems to be manifest from your note that the " only cross" of which you speak, and of which you have spoken before, is the chief hindrance to your conversion; this supposition is confirmed in my mind by the acknowledgment that when you did write to your uncle it was with great reluctance, and only because of my urgency, and that under the consciousness of this you retained the letter after it was finished. Now let me say that I "urged" you, not because I thought it would be sufficient to communicate your feelings to him, nor because I thought the mere act of writing would answer any good purpose, but because I desired you to attain the spirit of self-denial which was requisite, and because I judged that the effort to write would *assist* you in acquiring that spirit. What I urged you to was the exercise of self-denial, for the sake of your own soul; and that seemed, according to your own acknowledgment, to be the proper test. What I still feel bound to do, my dear friend, is to press upon you the duty—the necessity—of humbling and denying yourself; and as long as you continue to acknowledge that that is your "cross," I must continue to urge you to stoop down and take it up, and bear it though you be bowed down under it. Ah! if Jesus had not taken up His cross what would have become of the world? What would have become of you? Consider the cross He bore, yea, the cross upon which He died. You "have not yet resisted unto *blood*, striving against sin," you are not required to, and can you not make so small a sacrifice for Him who shed His blood for you? What I refer to now is not writing to your uncle upon the subject,—that is a secondary matter,—but prostrating yourself in thorough humility at the feet of Christ, surrendering yourself without reserve to Him; denying yourself in every respect in which it may be necessary, so as to become wholly His, in truthfulness and devotion. . . .

You say you sometimes feel new confidence, but it soon vanishes. You cannot expect true peace to take up its abode in your breast, and remain there, while you confess that you "have refused to take up" your "only cross."

"Patient waiting" till God sees fit to give you

peace, let me remind you, is not incompatible with persevering, unceasing, and most ardent supplications.

You speak of a long-cherished desire to carry "the glad tidings" to the heathen; I am sincerely glad that such a desire has taken possession of your heart. Do you not regard that as a *special* call of God to become a true follower of Christ? . . . Be not desponding; you are "not far from the kingdom" of God.

After leaving Trenton, in the beginning of 1857, there must have been some correspondence with Mr. and Mrs. Mackey in Africa. They had been in this country on furlough in 1855, were at Rev. W. W. Latta's church, and Mrs. Mackey, just two years after her return to Africa, wrote,—

"EVANGASIMBA, February 17, 1858.

"MY DEAR MISS LATTA:

"We received the box about a month ago; and the variety and value of its contents make us feel that we are neither forgotten nor neglected by our friends at home.

"We have never before received a box so well suited to all our wants as this.

"Mr. Mackey wrote to Mr. Latta by the same vessel that brought the box, acknowledging its reception. I write this to yourself, having a pleasant recollection of meeting with you at your uncle's. The box in which I found your letter I gratefully accept as coming from yourself, and I *do* think that you have shown a great amount of ingenuity in selecting so many small articles, each one of which is of great use to us.

"The black sewing-silk was most seasonable, for I was just in want of some. The black coats in our mission often need darning, and sometimes a patch is necessary. . . . I astonished the girls yesterday with the counters. I told them that if they would recite their geography well, I would make their arithmetic easy. When they had done reciting, I laid them on the table. They admired their pretty colors, but could not contrive how they could count a sum in simple addition with them. When this was explained they seemed quite delighted in experimenting with them. . . . One of our best scholars among our largest girls is now teacher of the smaller girls. Her native name is Mabwami, and her English name is Mary Jenkins Latta. . . . I am glad to learn that your mind has been exercised on the subject of missions. If, in the providence of God, your lot should ever be cast among us, we would be most happy to greet you. I trust, in the first place, you have made a full, free, and unreserved consecration of yourself to the service of God, and then you will be ready to go wherever in His providence He may call you."

In the summer of 1857, during the revival at Waynesburg, before she had yet acknowledged the possession of Christ in her heart, she was earnestly seeking the conversion of others.

A response to some remark of her correspondent in the series already mentioned, in a lead-pencil note written from "Willow Grove," the home of a schoolmate near Abington, Pa., says:

"August —, 1857.

"No, I have seen nothing like insanity in you, unless it be your insanity in refusing to come to Christ as an able and willing Saviour. Why will you not come? Come now. In the sight of God there is none good, no, not one: and to you He says freely, earnestly, lovingly, 'Give me thy heart.' You must not refuse One who has done so much for you. . . . If your desire is to be at peace with God, let that desire absorb every other; do not think of what you have done, but of what you ought to do. . . . If you think my practice accords not with my precept, I own it. May our Father God grant that I be not a hindrance to you! I pray for you, I pray for myself."

"September 1, 1857.

"To-day commenced our protracted meeting, of which you probably heard me speak. Before the afternoon services were closed, one of the clergymen rose and appointed an hour at which he requested all to retire and pray for some loved one. I had two for whom to pray, and you will not doubt that I remembered you earnestly. You have been much in my mind through the day, and will be through the week. . . .

"*Thursday*.—It is not quite church time, and I wish to say a few words to you this evening. I fear you live carelessly for the very purpose of drowning thought; have you not told me as much? . . .

"*Friday*.—Yesterday all who felt any concern for the salvation of their souls were invited to remain. I could not stay; but last night they persuaded me and I remained. At least, one clergyman for whom I have great respect and affection urged me to do so, if I could consistently, for others might follow my example in turning away. Sometimes I feel as if I had given up all to Christ; if I really have, then all is safe in His hands; but doubts will arise. There are many who seem to be seeking the Saviour, but how much of it is excitement we cannot tell. But it matters little what others are doing, so long as we feel ourselves to be out of the ark." . . .

"Honeybrook, Chester Co.
"September 17, 1857.

". . . Do you remember asking me the last day in the woods but one, whether I really was going to Africa? My reply may not have been much to the purpose, but let me tell you now that ere another autumn has come and gone it is my wish to be on heathen ground. Doubtless I *may* have to wait, owing to circumstances of which I know not now, a much longer time; but such is not the desire of my heart, unless it be God's will.

"If it is not His will that I go at all, I trust I may be so convinced; but it is in reliance on His arm I would leave both home and friends, and with full faith on His promise, 'As thy day, so shall thy strength be.' I hope now that I am a child of God, adopted, through faith in Jesus, into His family on earth, and by the Saviour's atonement made heir to His kingdom in Heaven. If I am called to foreign lands, how much more gladly would I go knowing that you too had a personal interest in this great atonement." . . .

"HONEYBROOK, Oct. 9, 1857.

"How shall I tell you the joy with which I read the glad tidings of your new-found peace? Tears of heart-felt pleasure spring to my eyes, and I pause to thank our Heavenly Father for His abundant grace. . . . I hardly think that I said to any one that I expected certainly to go to Corisco, only that I wanted to very much. I wrote several weeks ago to Mr. Lowrie on the subject, but he either has not received my letter, or is not ready to answer it. At that time I was all impatience to go ere another summer should be passed; but, though my views as to becoming a missionary are unaltered, I trust I am willing to wait a longer period if such be God's will." . . .

"CHESTNUT HILL, Nov. 9, '57.

". . . You remember the last evening we spent together? Can you tell me or do you know why, of all the subjects mentioned, the one more important by far than any other was so passed over? I cannot think it was absent from your thoughts the whole time; it certainly was not from mine. Do not let it be so again. I was doubtless in fault; but to speak on religious subjects is to me yet a trial.

"Yesterday week I united with the church; but the day brought me little peace, excepting that which arose from the hope I was doing my duty. Since then, however, I have felt a firmer trust in God as my only Father, in Christ as my all-sufficient Saviour, and in the Holy Spirit as a sure Sanctifier. . . . And let me beg of you to abandon the habit of quoting Scripture lightly; it pains me to hear it, as you surely would be pained to hear from one you esteemed or loved. My brother Willie, in answering one of my letters long ago, made the modest request that I 'would stop lecturing.' Whenever you have the same request to prefer, it shall be attended to."

"Nov. 23, '57.

". . . The letter contained sad tidings, for it told of the death of John Newton's mother. The family are all in India, excepting John and Charley, and they, too, have not seen their mother for five years. . . . My very heart aches for her sons left motherless in a foreign land.

"I heard a missionary from Africa preach last night in the Episcopal church, and it was the first time I had ever left my own church for that of another denomination. Mr. Rambo, however, was a teacher of mine many years ago, and I could not resist the temptation. I stopped to speak to him after church, and he walked home with me, and sat a little while. I was so glad to see him."

"CHESTNUT HILL, Oct. 27, '58.

". . . What are you doing now? . . . Has God in any sense seen fit to lay His chastening hand upon you? You must believe in the perseverance of the saints,—we look at the good afar off, and it seems impossible for us to attain thereunto, but our present concern is not with the length of the road, but obstacles immediately in our path. True,. we must look to Jesus, but looking unto Him does not imply a summing up of all that is to be overcome. Grace will be given as manna to the Israelites, sufficient *only* for the day; but for *that* day an ample provision. Why ask more?

"I see Mrs. Ogden's name mentioned occasionally in the *Home and Foreign Record*. At one time I prayed earnestly that God would open the way for me without delay to enter upon the missionary work, but I am beginning to feel, as well as know, that God's time is always best.

"It is hardly necessary to inform you that this pen is not the best in the world. I hope your eyesight is not injured." . . .

Rev. Dr. R. Owen, of Chestnut Hill, to whose pastoral care her name had been transferred from Waynesburg, speaks of Miss Latta's coming to his study sometimes with questions of duty; and, in the conversation which would follow, he noticed her difficulty about religious talk. She listened but did not respond, except to assure him that " she liked to hear him speak."

In his Sabbath-school her work was marked by cheerfulness and faithfulness. And he remembers the joy with which she hastened to him with open letter to show him her appointment by the Foreign Board, sharing with him her joy "because it was too good."

That appointment by the Presbyterian Board of Foreign Missions, as a missionary to Corisco, had been applied for in September, 1857, but in those days of reaching Africa only by sailing-vessels, which had no proper arrangements for female

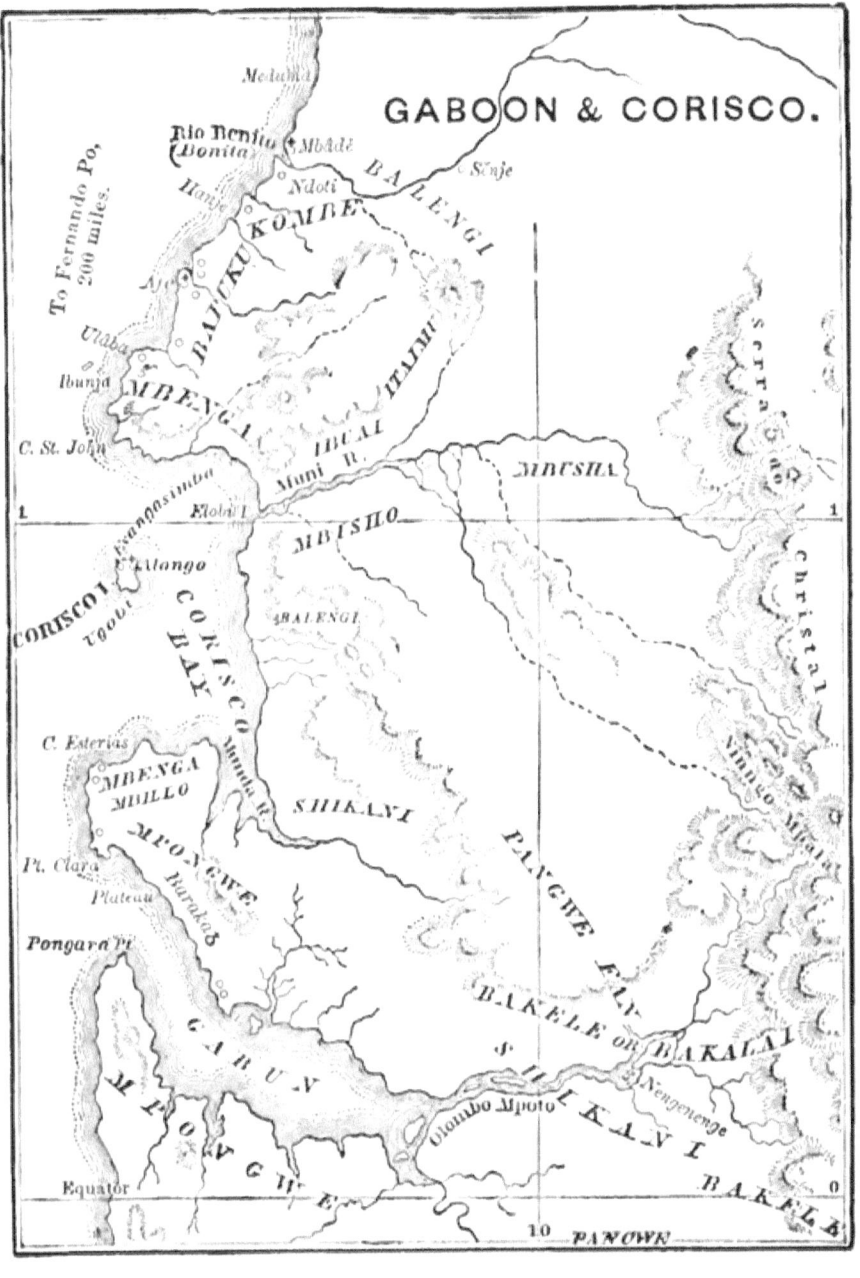

passengers without escort, she was delayed for company, and the appointment was not actually made until June, 1860; she, in the meanwhile, remaining at her school in Chestnut Hill. And in July, 1860, an excellent opportunity and escort presented itself, in the company of Rev. William and Mrs. Walker, of the American Board of Foreign Missions, returning to their station at Gaboon.

> "It is the voice
> Of millions starving for the bread of life.
> With gasping breath they send the cry abroad,
> 'Tell us, O Christian, tell us of thy God!'"

CHAPTER VII.

TO AFRICA.

August–November, 1860. Atlantic Ocean.

> "Go! may Jesus guide thy going,
> May He be where'er thou art:
> May His love, forever flowing,
> Cheer, refresh, and warm thy heart!"

Miss Latta sailed from New York August 1, 1860, in the brig "Ocean Eagle," Captain P. D. Yates. The passengers, besides herself, were Rev. William and Mrs. Walker and two Liberians, and, after leaving Monrovia, two Liberian girls, Waneta Alvareze, in Mrs. Walker's service, and Julia Goods, an orphan, taken by Miss Latta as her ward. From the following journal, and, indeed, from all of Mrs. Nassau's subsequent letters, I have purposely omitted sentences containing religious meditations and aspirations, assuming that their absence would leave no doubt on her missionary piety, and desiring to present especially the picture of missionary real-life not usually met with in formal memoirs.

MISS LATTA TO HER UNCLE'S FAMILY.

BRIG "OCEAN EAGLE," Aug. 21, 1860,
Atlantic Ocean, Lat. 37° 18′, Lon. 37° 18′.

This is not meant for a journal, nor even an apology for one; but if I do not write you a few lines occasionally, how will you ever learn anything about my voyage to Africa? It will be three weeks to-morrow since we left New York, and this is only my second attempt to handle a pen; so you will scarcely expect me to say much between this and Monrovia, our first stopping-place.

My industry depends on the waves. To-day we are becalmed,—not exactly, either, as the vessel moves slowly backward; we are drifting in nearly the right direction, as I understand the vessel heads towards the United States, Greenland, or some other such out-of-the-way place. There! I just missed killing a mosquito; partly from motives of economy, as he was resting on my page, and partly from stopping to observe his beautiful colors,—a bright crimson body and delicate wings of shaded brown. Some of the crimson, I am sure, was extracted from my little finger. The mosquitoes disappeared entirely after we had been a few days at sea; but some uncommonly large ones have been flying about of late, which had been put up at New York in the water-casks, and just released by the captain. Oh, how they do bite!

Now there is an appearance of rain, and windows must be closed; but no one thinks I am able to screw up the little round piece of glass in my stateroom, so I continue my writing, leaving Mr. Walker or the captain to attend to it. I did shut it the other night for the second time since coming aboard, and Mrs. Walker opened it for me in the morning, remarking, at the same time, she could neither open nor shut the window in her stateroom. Captain asked how it came to be closed, and I said I had fastened it in the night to keep out the sea when the vessel was rolling; but I only got laughed at for the explanation, the gentlemen thinking "a window Miss Latta had shut and Mrs. Walker could open would not keep out much water."

Steward says he knew it was going to rain, for his "*chronometers* have been paining" him several days; but the rain is still in the clouds.

They are "tacking ship," for the second time in the last half-hour, which will change our course a little; but the captain says the wind is "dead ahead," and he "don't believe it will ever be fair again." Excuse his want of faith, as he is not well, and our passage thus far has not been the most prosperous. We had head winds and calms for more than a week.

Three of the passengers are overhauling their trunks, and the fourth, after turning about uneasily in his berth for some time, has just turned out and put on his coat, preparatory to taking an observation of the weather, I suppose. There are but five in all. You shall hear something about them some other time; but to-day I am not in a particularly descriptive mood. There is likely to be sufficient spare time to say all that is worth saying, and much more besides, before we reach Liberia. A quick passage is not to be expected this time of year.

Friday, August 24. — Nothing of interest has happened to-day, and nothing is expected to happen. The wind and the sea and the ship and its passengers all seem in a peculiarly inactive condition, and I suppose I should be on the sofa if the tincture of cinchona had not been got out of the medicine-chest for my benefit. Mr. Walker kindly searched for and prepared it; all I had to do was to swallow the mixture,—and it *might* be worse certainly.

I believe I will go and read Mpongwe with Mr. and Mrs. Walker. That is the language at the Gaboon, but I only translate for amusement, never expecting to have any use for it.

Dr. Wilson gave me a grammar of the Benga language, spoken at Corisco; but it is dull work studying alone, as well as very slow. The conjugation of the regular verb *kalaka* (to speak), in all the voices, moods, and tenses, negative and affirmative, occupies some twenty pages; but, fortunately, there are few irregular verbs,—none given in the grammar. . . .

MISS LATTA TO HER BROTHER, W. J. LATTA.

MONROVIA, WEST AFRICA,
Sept. 18, 1860.

Since coming on shore this morning we have learned that a vessel leaves to-morrow for the United States, and whatever we may have time to write may reach you earlier than by the regular mail. The vessel came in yesterday, and is the one sent out by our government with the recaptured slaves. It had conveyed them to Cape Mount, a short distance north of Monrovia. Had we known of this before, we might have had letters ready, but we are thankful for time to write even a few lines home, that may assure you a little sooner of our safe arrival and good health.

We reached Monrovia on Saturday, September

15, just forty-five days from the time we left New York. We had no very rough weather, but I was sea-sick the most of the voyage; not sick enough to be confined to my berth more than a few days, but unable to write or sew much, or do anything else in a useful way. It was such an effort to write that I could not have sent you anything of interest in the shape of a sea-journal. I made the attempt several times, but was obliged to give up in despair.

The last week of the voyage I was not very well, but am better now, and think another day or two will cure me.

Mr. and Mrs. Walker were very kind all through the passage; took every care of me, and paid me every attention possible. I could not have had kinder friends than they have proved. Truly, God has been very good in bringing us thus far in safety.

Do you remember the young colored man who was pointed out to us as one of the passengers? He had the stateroom opposite mine, and the seat opposite me at table. I believe it seemed strange the first day or two to have him mingling with us all; but, if that impression did exist, it has so completely worn away that I can scarcely recall it. His father, Rev. Francis Burns, is bishop of the Methodist Church in West Africa; and to-day I write from the bishop's study, as we have been spending the day and dining with them. Mr. Burns is a veritable African in color, but his first wife was almost white; so the children are very light mulattoes. His second wife is very young in appearance; she is a mulatto, very lady-like in her manner, and seems to understand the art of making one feel at home.

When I have finished this letter it will, I suppose, soon be time to go on board; this is the second day we have spent ashore, but I expect to sleep on the vessel until I reach Corisco, in accordance with Dr. Wilson's advice (indeed, no one advises me differently), especially during the rainy season, which is not yet quite over. . . .

Rev. John Seys, one of the principal men here, is in the parlor, and I must go for awhile. There is a delightful breeze here from the sea.

Well, I have seen Mr. and Mrs. Seys, the first white persons to whom I have had the pleasure of speaking since coming to Africa. (Mr. S. is the agent in charge of recaptured slaves.) They regretted not being at housekeeping, therefore not able to have us spend a day with them; and I am sorry, too, for I liked them both very much.

And now, Willie, dear, I must say good-by for the present. I hope this will reach you before the mail. Give a great deal of love to everybody,— uncles, aunts, and cousins. I thought of you all very often on the voyage, and would like to see you for a little while now, if possible,—but that cannot be. I have had nothing yet to discourage me, except at times a feeling of my own unfitness for the work before me; but I must go on, trusting to God for all needful strength. I would not return yet, if I could; but it is rather early to be making assertions of that kind. Remember me in your prayers, as I always remember you. God bless you, and all my dear friends. . . .

MISS LATTA TO THE SAME.

Brig "Ocean Eagle," West Africa,
October 1, 1860.

Just two months ago to-day I bade you good-by in this same cabin from which I write. Does the time seem to be long to you? I hope you have not put off writing until you would have a letter from me, because then I will not hear from home till near the close of this year,—perhaps not until the beginning of next. Will you not try and write every month? Any letters that I inclose to you for others, you can read before forwarding; and this time I want you to take my letter for Uncle William to Aunt Moore to read, before you send it to him. If uncle is in the city, give it to him first, of course; let aunties see it, too, if they are in Philadelphia.

I wonder where you all are, where you all will be through this winter? The days must be getting cool now; but it is hard for us to realize that. We had some very hot days at sea, but have not suffered from the heat since reaching the African coast,—indeed, the rain has been our principal trouble for the last two weeks.

The sea was quite rough yesterday; and to-day there is so much motion that I can scarcely write, but it does not make me sea-sick, fortunately. A week's stay in Monrovia cured me, and gave me a good appetite, so that I am ready to eat almost any time of day. The sweet potatoes we get here are the best I ever tasted; they are very white (one kind), and more mealy than any potato I ever saw at home, whether Irish or sweet. They have, besides, yellow ones (about as good as ours), and red, which I have not yet seen.

My other letters, which you will read, will give an account of my stay in Monrovia. We left there last Wednesday,—reached Bassa on Thursday, and stayed until Saturday. I did not go ashore, as the bar was bad and sharks very plentiful. While we were at Monrovia a Krooboy was killed by a shark,—bitten right in two. Captain Yates asked our head Krooman, "Who got the body?" and was told, "Shark got half, we got half."

Oct. 11, Cape Palmas, W. A.—I am writing to-day from the Episcopal Orphan Asylum at Cape Palmas, at present under the superintendence of our old teacher, Rev. J. Rambo. It is very pleasant to be here. Mrs. Rambo is a sweet woman, and very kind; and I was very glad to see any one I had known in America. This is the first time we had been entertained by white persons since leaving home, and I enjoy it even more than I had expected. There is here, besides, a Miss Ball, teacher of the school, making three missionaries at this place; and there are others at stations not very far distant.

This is the third day I have been ashore, but I go on board every night as a matter of prudence. Mr. Walker goes to take care of me; but Mrs. Walker sleeps on land, as it is so much pleasanter than being rolled from side to side in the vessel. The rolling and pitching of the ship does not disturb me, as I seem to have bid farewell to seasickness since our arrival at Monrovia. Mrs. Walker does not mind sleeping in the vessel so much as she does going back and forth in the boat,—being a little timid.

The last day we went ashore at Sinoe, it began to rain before we started for the boat, or rather before the boat reached the landing, and we did not get off until nearly dark. We waited awhile until the rain came down more gently, and then two native cloths were wrapped around me, a handkerchief tied on my head, and a new velvet and oil-cloth hat put over that. Mr. Payne, into whose house we had gone to wait, lent me the cloth and cap from his store, and I left my bonnet behind for the captain to bring next morning. Mr. Walker tied his handkerchief over the hat to make it keep its place, Mr. Payne not appearing to have thought about my unusual allowance of brains,—skull,—or something else. A big Krooman took me in his arms and carried me to the boat, and the captain held a large umbrella over me, so that I did not get much wet; and then our men began to row. Wind and tide were against us, and we had the bar to cross, but it was not a bad one. Fortunately, Mrs. Walker was not with us, for we had rather an unpleasant time. On reaching the bar, or just after crossing it, the Kroomen rowed for nearly half an hour without making any sensible progress. One time, when the men changed oars, I thought the boat was getting ready to capsize; and again I was a little startled by a large sea striking us. But I cannot say that I felt any fear,—indeed, we were in no danger that we knew of. We were an hour and a half in reaching the ship, and when I walked into the cabin Mrs. Walker began to laugh and cry. She had not expected us, and Mr. Walker had wanted me to sleep on shore, but I preferred going to the ship. Had we capsized, sharks would have been the chief trouble perhaps. However, a merciful God watched over us; and without His care we could not be secure at any time,—with it we should never fear. . . .

Cape Palmas, Oct. 15.— . . . The Ocean Eagle will sail in a couple of days, and I may be in Corisco in three weeks from to-day, or even sooner. . . .

MISS LATTA TO THE SAME.

"Ocean Eagle," West Africa,
Oct. 22, 1860.

It seems scarcely possible that only a week ago we mailed our letters home, and now we must begin to write again for the next month's mail. In a few days we will be at Cape Coast, and I must leave letters for the steamer there, which you will be glad to receive, I suppose, though the date be not much later than the last.

We are anchored off the coast some twenty miles below Cape Palmas, and the natives have been bringing palm-oil on board to trade with the captain. I made the acquaintance to-day of "King George," but was not much overawed at being in the presence of royalty for the first time. His majesty came on board early this morning with some of his men, and did not leave until after dinner. Mr. and Mrs. Walker and myself dined first, then the mates, and finally the "king" with one of his "head men." His back was towards us, so I cannot inform you whether he used his knife or his fork, or either. His dress was different from any I have yet seen. A cap of dark cloth, pointed at the top and decorated with several colors, and drawn on like a night-cap and confined by a long band under the chin. A cloth cloak, with sleeves slightly flowing, reached from his neck to his feet; the sleeves were trimmed with a ruffle of the same. The coat was cut something like a sacque, and, being fastened only at the neck, disclosed a dirty white shirt, or something I took for one. Around his waist was fastened a very pretty red cotton cloth that fell a little below the knees. That is the manner in which the cloth is worn by the most respectable, but many wear only a small piece fastened around the loins.

King George was brought into the cabin and introduced by the captain; after shaking hands with us all, he took a seat at the upper end of the small apartment. Another man followed and sat down near him, after giving us each a shake of the hand.

After a little conversation in broken English, I was going on with my sewing when I heard the king trying to attract my attention by calling, "My fren, my fren" (friend). I turned to him, when he partly closed his hand, raised it to his mouth, throwing back his head a little, at the same time saying something I did not understand. I smiled and said, "I no hear," meaning I did not understand; though I must confess the action spoke pretty plainly for itself. The other man laughed and said, "Whisky." I told him, "Oh, that be bad. I no have whisky. *I* no drink it." Then added, "You want drink?" "Yes, ma'am." "I give you water." He laughed, and said, "No, no." So I informed him that was all I had to drink myself, and could give him nothing else. In talking with them, we have to imitate their manner of speaking as much as possible, or they could not understand.

The natives are continually wanting you to "dash" them,—that is, make a present of some kind.

Here come the hot biscuit and tea! I have been sharing the table with the plates and mugs for some time.

October 23.—Good-morning, dear Willie. Our vessel is still at anchor, which does not mean at rest, but rolling from side to side; and the more quiet I wish to be, the more apparent that motion becomes. While reading, sewing, or eating, I am not much troubled by the rocking, but when I attempt to use my pen it is a little unpleasant,— not much after all.

This morning we had cakes and lemonade,— limeade rather. Our drinking-cups were cocoanut-shells, nicely prepared by Mr. Walker—after he had taken out the meat—for our use. The fresh nuts are very good, though not quite as soft as I had supposed they would be, after hearing that they could be scraped out with a spoon. Occasionally you might get one that could be eaten in that way, but it must be quite young. Mr. Walker intended putting a handle on mine to make a dipper of it, but cannot supply himself with materials very well on board ship.

Do you remember the cups we sometimes had at home?

Fruit is not so plenty as you may suppose along the coast, as some attention must be paid to its cultivation, and the natives seldom take that trouble. Some of the colonists have a great variety of fruit, but the most of them little or none. We are out of Liberia now, and I do not know that we shall go ashore again, except at Cape Coast, before reaching Corisco. . . . Don't be troubled if letters do not always come when you are looking for them. The Corisco mail is sent by boat some distance to meet the steamer, and occasionally arrives too late. In that case two months would go by without your hearing from me. . . .

MISS LATTA TO THE SAME.

EVANGASIMBA, W. A., Nov. 19, 1860.

Most probably a sheet of note-paper will hold all that I ought to write to-night, but——

Nov. 20.—Well, Willie, dear, you will see I did not make much progress in my letter last evening, and now Dr. Loomis tells me that we must hurry with our letters for the mail.

We reached here last Friday, November 16, after a voyage of exactly three and a half months. The next day the vessel left for Gaboon, and I suppose Mr. and Mrs. Walker are home by this time. We were sixteen days in coming from Cape Coast, a distance that might have been made in a week without any difficulty, and indeed in less time, with favorable winds and current. That tried our patience a little, especially when we were three days in coming the last forty miles. We ought to be very thankful, however, for such a pleasant voyage as ours has been. A little time we suffered from the heat while crossing the Atlantic; and on the coast we were several times kept close prisoners in the cabin by a day of heavy rain; but our ship was a comfortable one, and we have not had any severe storms.

One tornado, which came before we were quite ready for it, sent the ship pretty far on one side, and tore one of the sails into so many pieces that it was past mending. The mate stood ready to cut away the ropes attached to the foremast if necessary, but it was not done.

One of the Kroomen cried out, "I am dead, I am dead!" and another, "O, I shall never see my mother any more!" But we did not hear of that until the storm was over, not understanding their language.

The stools moved from one side of the cabin to

PLANTAIN-TREE.

the other without any apparent exertion on their part. Under the berth in which Mrs. Walker's girl slept were a number of wooden pails, for trade with the natives. A nest of three or four rolled out, and Wana started after them with more haste than carefulness. The buckets rolled into the captain's stateroom, and Wana, stooping at the door to seize them quickly, was, by a sudden lurch of the vessel, pitched headlong into the captain's berth, while another lot of pails came rolling after her with all possible speed.

As I stood at the cabin door watching the storm and hurrying sailors, the head Krooman threw me his old blue flannel shirt, to preserve it from the rain. The tornado was not a severe one, and soon over; if the ship had not been so light, and the sails could have been taken in in time, there would have been no trouble. I knew there might be danger, but prayed to Him who ruleth the winds and the waves, and He kept me from all fear. God has indeed been merciful to me in all my way, even until this present time.

". . . it will be sweet
That I have toiled for other worlds than this."

CHAPTER VIII.

CORISCO GIRLS' SCHOOL.

1860-1862. Corisco.

" Yes, the tiny coral insects, by their slow but constant motion,
Have formed those lovely islands in the distant, dark-blue ocean ;
And the noblest undertakings that man's wisdom hath conceived,
By oft-repeated efforts have been patiently achieved."

THE missionary force which Miss Latta found at Corisco was distributed at three localities: at Ugobi,* on the southern end of the island, Rev. C.

---

* The following rules for the pronunciation of the Benga words as they occur in the following pages are equally applicable to all the dialects of Equatorial Africa.

1. Give their English sounds to all consonants except *g*, which is *always hard*,—as " Tanganyika."
2. Give the vowel a the force of *a* in ah! or father,—for example, " Baraka," " mwanga;" give the vowel â the force of *a* in law or saw,—for example, " malânga," " tândâkâ;" give the vowel e the force of *e* in they, or of *a* in fate,—for example, " Nengenenge," " ejaka;" give the vowel ĕ the force of *e* in met or every,—for example, " mbâdĕ," " nyĕngĕle;" give the vowel i the force of *i* in mach*i*ne, or of *ee* in seen,—for example, " Benita," " ikenga;" give the vowel o the force of *o* in bone or own,—for example, " Alongo," " konongo;" give the vowel u the force of *u* in rude, or of *oo* in moon,—for example, " Ujiji," " ukuku."

De Heer, with his Benga boys' school; at Evangasimba, two miles distant, on the western side, Rev. and Mrs. T. S. Ogden, stated supply of the church; C. L. Loomis, M.D., and Mrs. Loomis, superintendent during the absence of Rev. J. L. and Mrs. Mackey in America; and Miss M. M. Jackson, in charge of Mrs. Mackey's school-girls. Messrs. Loomis and Ogden were building a commodious frame house only a few hunded feet from the Evangasimba house, and distinguished from it by a name "Itândiluku" (Sister-love), which the natives contracted to "Maluku" (Sisters). At Alongo, three miles farther, on the northern end, Miss Jackson's brother-in-law, Rev. W. Clemens, and his mainland boys' school.

Writing from Evangasimba, on November 20, 1860, to her brother, Miss Latta continues:

"I am staying now with Dr. Loomis and his wife at the principal station, but will be in Mr. Ogden's family as soon as their new house has another room completed. Dr. Loomis is very kind and thoughtful. I like him very much, as I do all the other missionaries. Miss Jackson, with whom I am to be associated, is rather quiet, but very kind, pleasant, and lovable. I have not yet

---

3. Close *every* syllable with a vowel,—as " Bo-lo-ndo," " bwe-a-kwĕ."

4. Accent (with an exception not necessary here to mention) the *next to the last* syllable,—as " Evangasimba," " uvăndă."

commenced on any of my new duties, as they wish me to rest a short time.

"The first night I was here several red spots appeared on the back of my hands, which I supposed to be the bite of some insect, and congratulated myself that they gave me no uneasiness. Sunday morning Dr. Loomis observed them, and asked me what I thought had caused them. When I told him, he said, no, it was a mark of fever; but he was glad to see them, as they showed the fever was coming to the surface. He said the spots might appear and disappear half a dozen times before I would have an attack. They were about the size of a three-cent piece, or smaller, and were gone the next day, except a purplish spot that had marked the centre. Doctor says, 'Let the fever come; do not be troubled about it;' and I am sure I am not troubled in the least. If it comes, well; if it stays away, perhaps better. I am very well now, and I know that if careful I shall continue so as long as it is the will of my heavenly Father that I should." . . .

Opportunities for sending mails were rare, native boat-crews expensive and difficult to be obtained because of tribal quarrels; so that casual opportunities of passing trading vessels were used. Miss Latta's slight knowledge of medicine soon came into use for herself and others. Though the presence of Dr. Loomis was a great advantage, she had come to the country with a well-selected chest of medicines from her brother's employers, Ellis & Co., Philadelphia, and with prescriptions from Dr. Clement L. Finley, which she herself could fill out.

MISS LATTA TO HER BROTHER, W. J. LATTA.

Corisco, Dec. 26, 1860, 9 p.m.

This writing at night is one thing I had resolved never to do if it could possibly be avoided; but at the present time I am scarcely breaking my resolution, for I do not know what other opportunity I shall have to get letters ready for the "Homer." A boat leaves for Gaboon, where the vessel is lying, early on the morning of the 28th, and I shall have no more time to write to-morrow than I have had to-day, and it was only yesterday evening we received the word.

This may reach you before the letters sent by mail last week; and, if so, you will be spared some anxiety. I was sick with the fever all last week, and had to beg hard to be allowed to put in the few lines I added to the close of your letter. Miss Jackson wanted to write them for me; but I knew that would alarm you needlessly. It was my first attack of fever, and not very serious. Dr. Loomis was very sick when I was taken, and Miss Jackson not at all well; but she was able to attend to me and prepare my medicines. I followed Cousin

Clement's prescription in part, but could not adhere to it strictly, as Miss Jackson could not find the bottle of comp. cath. pills. I sent to Mrs. Loomis for some; but she gave me something else which did as well. Thursday afternoon I was carried up here to Mrs. Ogden's in a hammock, as we had intended moving the girls' school the beginning of the week. The station is near and connected with Evangasimba.

Mrs. Ogden was not well, and went to Gaboon on a visit the day we moved up; so Miss Jackson was nurse and housekeeper, besides having charge of the girls. Now that I am pretty well, she keeps house, and I keep the children. I have just let five of them go to bed for the second time tonight; they kept up such a talking that I made the larger ones put on their dresses and come down into this room for a little while, till they would be tired and sleepy enough to let their tongues rest. As this is a new house, and not yet completed, I am not yet settled in my own room. As soon as the boards are laid on the floor above, I can move in and leave Miss Jackson sole occupant of this apartment. The house is frame, no ceilings, and no plastering; but we hope to cover the sides of our rooms with paper as soon as it arrives from America. Parlor, dining-room (a very little one), study, and sleeping apartment are all on the first floor. The house is raised on posts some eight feet from the ground; it is thought to be healthier.

I have amused the children sometimes telling them about my brother Willie when he was a little fellow, and they all think he must be something remarkable. Behâli, one of the little girls, begged me to tell you that you are her "biggest friend," and she would like you to write her a letter. Several of them were in my room a few weeks ago, looking at some pictures, when Matuku, one of my favorites, said, "Eh, mamma, I want to see my friend Willie." When I showed them your photograph, they were very much pleased, except one child, who said, in a disappointed tone of voice, "Eh, mamma, I thought Willie wore frocks." Perhaps you will not be much flattered by the admiration of my children; but they are pretty fine little girls for the most part. They all call me "Mamma Latta;" and I am quite proud of the title. Here comes Miss Jackson; I must not write much longer now, because I ought to be to bed and rest. We rise at six, have half an hour to dress, and then the bell rings for prayers. Breakfast at seven. I told this to some one before,—was it you? We dine at twelve, or a few minutes after, and take tea at five. The bell rings for worship again at half-past six; and then some one must keep the girls until eight, their bed-time. The rest of us retire when we please. . . .

A change was made in the school arrangements by the marriage of Miss Jackson, in January, 1861, with Rev. W. H. Clark, of Gaboon, and their transfer to Alongo. Mrs. Clark, writing from Alongo, February 12, 1861, to Miss Jenny W. Baird, of Washington, Pa., says:

"You are perhaps aware that, by the 'Ocean Eagle,' another young lady assistant was added to our number, in the person of Miss Latta, from Chestnut Hill, Pa. She is a *dear, sweet sister*; but I fear her strength will prove insufficient to her cares in this trying climate. She is now feeble, and it is not quite three months since her arrival. The girls' school was removed to the new building, a short distance from Mr. Mackey's, which was built by Mr. Ogden for the girls' school; and it is now under his care. That station is manned by Mr. and Mrs. Ogden and Miss Latta."

Years later, Mrs. Nassau wrote, of an experience at this period, thus:

"Shortly after my arrival, one of the young girls asked me about the shirts she was sewing, and I replied, 'I don't know any more than you do.' She opened her big eyes very wide indeed, and said, in English, 'Mamma, you don't know shirts?'

"'Yes, Matuku; I don't know shirts.'

"'Mamma, what will you do?' (Sewing shirts was one of their constant occupations.)

"'Well, Matuku, I suppose I must learn.' And

I have long ago learned the mysteries of collars and gussets, and yokes and bands."

Miss Latta took up her work cheerfully,—not unmindful of its responsibility, but with a light-heartedness that threw aside anxiety, and a bravery that overcame trouble. On the death of Mr. Ogden, May 12, 1861, she disbanded her school, to aid, with young Charity Sneed (Mrs. Ogden's Liberian assistant), in the care of little fatherless Spencer, and in the household arrangements of kitchen, payments of natives, etc. In paying employees, and in buying native provisions, all sums are reckoned not in money, but in goods,—*e.g.* beads, crockery, hardware, cloths, etc.

MISS LATTA TO MR. W. J. LATTA.

Corisco, West Africa.
Maluku, June 10, 1861.

Where do you find time to write me such good, long letters as you send me every month? Why, the mere sight of this, my extensive sheet, is almost enough to bring on a small fever. No, I feel better now, after taking the scissors and clipping off a few lines at the lower end. . . . Willie, you ought to make some inquiries in regard to my children (your little nieces), my occupations, etc., because I never know what to tell you would be particularly interesting. One piece of information I can give you: no letters came for me last mail, and I was disappointed; but it is the first time that I have been disappointed, so I should not complain. They are looking for a vessel at Gaboon, which may have our mail on board. I wish it a speedy passage.

We are hoping Mr. and Mrs. Mackey have sailed; but we cannot look for them before September, I suppose. It will be a joyful day in the mission when we can welcome them back.

Mrs. Ogden and I am still at this station, but we have not taken back the girls yet, on account of the continued sickness of Mrs. Ogden's babe. He seems better now, and I informed her at dinner that I was ready for the school to commence again next week, if she would be ready. Of course, I could not expect any assistance from her in the care of the girls. One of the men has come to recite; please excuse me a little while. Willie, do you know that Corisco snails are destitute of any sense of honor? A woman brought me some snails several weeks ago, which I bought, as the shells were pretty, and deposited them on the porch. The next day, when I went to take a look at my purchase,—would you believe it?—they had all crawled away; money gone, snails gone! That same week a woman brought a pineapple to sell, for which I offered her a small article. While I went to get it she sold the pineapple to Ibolo (the native who buys for Mrs. Ogden), and then asked me to give her the article for "a dash" (present). When I tell you I gave it, you will not be disposed to think very highly of my trading faculties.

I do not get tired of Corisco, of the trees that never lose their green, or of the natives who are always black, but I *do get tired* of writing the same things over and over again to so many different individuals. Mr. Walker told me if I wanted to write a book, I should do it the first year,—I would find so much more to say. Well, I don't want to write a book; and, besides, the year is almost ended; it will be nine months on Saturday since the stormy day we anchored off Monrovia.

June 11.—Here are Mrs. Ogden and the baby, come to pay me a visit; so I don't know how I shall talk to you and entertain them at the same time,—that is, in a sensible manner. You must go and see Mrs. Ogden when she goes home; she will be in Philadelphia for a time. I think you will like her very much, if she should be cheerful as she sometimes is; but her heart is heavy yet from the great loss she has sustained.

Perhaps she may tell you how troubled she used to be at times, because there was no fresh meat to be had, and I would not eat salt beef and mackerel. Chickens are scarce now, and the natives will bring a little one, not fit to kill, and ask the price of a good-sized fowl. You tell them it is not worth so much, but they reply, "Oh, it will grow!" Suppose you buy it with the understanding that it is to grow; perhaps it lives, perhaps a snake will kill it, or it may wander off to town, and never wander back again.

Sometimes we have a young kid, and that is pretty good, only I should prefer it without the slight flavor of mutton. We have several goats, but each mother-goat has two or three young kids the greater part of the time, so that they are not worth much for their supply of milk. As I have learned to prefer coffee without milk, and I don't like puddings, I rarely miss the milk. It would be good with mush; but mush is good seasoned with salt, if one only thinks so.

You must call Aunt Margaretta's attention to this letter particularly; let me think if I can recall any more inconveniences for her benefit. Our butter is soft, but not so soft as to drop off the knife, as it sometimes did on shipboard, when we were not careful. The last Mrs. Ogden got from the store-house was sixty cents a pound, but it usually is fifty cents. Our flour is almost done; but, if the supply is exhausted before another ship arrives, we must live on our corn-bread. Sugar is also nearly out, but I shall only miss that in limeade, not being fond of cakes, custards, or preserves. As the lime-trees are not bearing very plentifully just now, perhaps I shall be so fortunate as not to miss the sugar at all. Mrs. Ogden makes corn-coffee for me every day, as I thought the other did not agree with me very well. You might think the other missionaries could use molasses to sweeten their coffee; but the only cask of molasses (syrup, I believe) that is on hand went to work on its own account before it was opened, and it is too sour to sweeten coffee; otherwise, I believe, it tastes very well, and Dr. Loomis says I will like it; but we have not had any yet. My dear Willie, have I said enough about provisions for one letter?

One of my scholars (I have but two now) is waiting to recite his lesson. As he doesn't know English, and I don't know Benga (though I can pronounce it tolerably), you may imagine what progress a dull pupil would make.

A youthful missionary is often placed in situations where inexperience is tried in responsible offices, and tender women bear and do what might appal strong manhood. Within a year after her arrival at Corisco, Miss Latta, under stress of duty, shared, as nurse and assistant in surgery, in a scene whose remembrance, though her part was acted bravely and efficiently, she never willingly recalled. Her work was increasing as the missionary company was diminishing in strength and numbers. She attended to the remnant of her school; and then, mounted on the mission Yoruba pony "Charley," would visit her native friends in the villages, or recreate herself by a call at Alongo, on her dear friend, Mrs. Clark, who, in July, 1861, was about leaving for a furlough in America.

The rebellion had broken out in America; Miss Latta's brother had enlisted as lieutenant in the Eighth Pennsylvania Cavalry, and the stress of patriotism and sisterly affection were added to her mission work. The destructions by the "Alabama" and other cruisers made the reception of supplies and even of letters thenceforward for years irregular and scanty.

MISS LATTA TO LIEUTENANT W. J. LATTA.

Corisco, W. A., July 30, 1861.

I fear if I tell you I do not love to write short and hasty letters, you will be tempted to doubt my veracity, for here is another of that kind. There is a vessel in Gaboon expecting to sail tomorrow for New York; and should she sail tomorrow, the boat leaving here in the morning will not take my letter in time.

Mrs. Loomis is still very sick, and Dr. Loomis, I fear, may have a bad attack of fever. Other missionaries are pretty well.

The American mail came to-night, but letters that I expected from you have probably been sent out on the "Ocean Eagle." I received letters from Aunt Mary Ann and you, dated March, which would have reached me just two months ago if sent by mail; but they had been put on a schooner at the Mission House, and were four months on their way.

You do not know what a disappointment it is when the mail brings me no letter.

Oh, my brother, I wish there was peace at home! If it were not that I trust in the goodness of God, I should feel much troubled about you; but I know that "He doeth all things well." Still, I cannot help wishing some word had come by this mail. War had not commenced at the last dates, but it may be raging now.

MISS LATTA TO HER AUNT, MISS M. A. LATTA.

CORISCO, W. A., July 30, 1861.

Your letter, of March 22, made its appearance this evening, and if it had come by mail you might have been reading the reply to-night.

Letters are so frequently delayed from one cause and another, that you must never think it strange if you get no answer for a long time to some things you wonder I should neglect.

In the first place, now I do thank you very much for the aprons and the dark dress that I learn are on the way for my children. You could not please me better than by sending such things to my numerous family. I am glad the dress is dark, as Julia is rather hard on her clothes and I like her to look respectable,—at least if clean clothes would make her so.

Mrs. Clark has gone to America. Mr. Clark accompanied her to Fernando Po, where she was to take the steamer, and meet Mr. and Mrs. Bushnell of the Gaboon Mission.

You wonder I wanted new things so soon. Well, they will not reach me until I have been here nearly a year. Some things I gave away and some I sold,—not as a money-making speculation, but because others needed them more than I did, and they would not take them as a gift.

I don't know what to say about quilts. The children use them. Not very large size; but any you would make would be too good to give them. I generally prefer spreads for myself. I sleep under a blanket the most of the year, occasionally two.

To compensate the loss of frequent sight of each others' faces, tied as the mission company were by their local duties, they would let scarcely a day pass without sending pupils as messengers with letters and notes of salutation, or exchange of some dainty received from American homes or purchased from some chance native opportunity.

MISS LATTA TO REV. WM. CLEMENS.

MALUKU, Aug. 5, 1861.

Your boys have come, and I put aside a very uninteresting letter I am trying to write to America, to send you a few lines.

Thank you for your care of "Polly;" I don't know what we should have done with her while Mrs. Ogden was sick. We have not heard from Evangasimba this morning. Mrs. Ogden was down there yesterday afternoon. Mrs. Loomis still had fever, but her pulse was 109; lower than it had been, though not so low as at one time. Dr. Loomis said it was malignant or continued fever, which lasts from seven to thirty-five days, and that she had passed the first crisis.

I had a short note from Brother De Heer on Saturday night; he was not at all well; but we have heard since that he preached yesterday. His boys have not been over to-day.

Dr. L. was not out yesterday. Ibǿpe took charge of the meeting, and it was conducted as a prayer-meeting. Ibolo would not take charge. Andĕke was absent, and Ubĕngi was the only other one present who could read. Ibǿpe, Imunga, and Ubĕngi spoke; they all lamented much that a Sabbath should have come on which there was no white missionary able to address them; and one of them remarked it was probably a judgment from God on Benga Christians. All seemed to feel a desire that religion might be revived in their midst; and Ubĕngi proposed that they should have a prayer-meeting in the afternoon, if the bell did not ring for Sabbath-school.

In the evening monthly concert was held, and

Andèke conducted the exercises. Many of the young men were present, and the meeting was quite interesting. I suppose they met for prayer in the afternoon, as there was no Sunday-school in the church.

Mrs. Ogden and the baby are well. I am contented and happy in my work; but very unfaithful to the souls committed to my charge.

After a protracted illness, Mrs. Loomis died in the middle of August, 1861. The mission was reinforced by the landing, on the 12th of September, of Rev. J. L. and Mrs. Mackey, Mrs. G. M. McQueen, and Rev. R. H. Nassau, M.D. The latter two were located at Maluku; the former two resumed their work at Evangasimba; and in October Dr. Loomis and Mrs. Ogden, with her baby and Charity Sneed, returned to America. The girls' school was enlarged in the number of pupils. Miss Latta entered on the second year of her mission life. The young ladies of a Sabbath-school class at Washington, Pa., had supported Ijule, a most interesting pupil of the school, while it was in Miss Jackson's (Mrs. Clark) care, naming her, for their teacher, "Jennie Baird." Ijule had been removed by her parents; and Miss Baird's class wrote to have the name and support given to another child.

MISS LATTA TO MISS J. W. BAIRD.

Corisco, W. A.
Itàndiluku, Dec. 19, '61.

Our letters must be ready in less than an hour, and I do not like the mail to go without an answer to the one you sent Mrs. Clark. I am trying to write in the midst of my little flock.

It is after evening prayers, when the larger girls study a hymn for Sabbath, and the small ones are taught, sometimes orally, and sometimes called to recite by myself. The hymn this week was "Rock of Ages," and, though this is only Thursday night, they all know it, having learned it in part before, I think.

Mrs. McQueen, Mr. Clark, and Dr. Nassau are writing in "the big house" (as we say), and all seemed a little surprised that I should make an attempt to write while taking care of the girls. I told the children I was going to write to a lady who liked to hear about girls; and so they are all on their good behavior, that I may send a pleasant report of my children.

The one we have chosen to take the name of "Jennie Baird" is a little girl of a bright, happy temper, and a favorite with all. Her native name is Elungu, and she seemed quite pleased with the new one, though she keeps forgetting it all the time. She is just beginning to read and talk English; but we hope she will be one of our best scholars, as she comes from a good family. You would like to hear her talk English. Sometimes she puts her arm beside mine and says, "Give me white; you take my black." When I asked her what word I should send, she hesitated, and the others began to answer for her, "Elungu sews good;" "Elungu is a good girl;" and one little child said tell you that "Elungu is a velly (very) little girl."

She is about eight years old, and sews better than most girls in America of her age: she can make her dresses very well when the work is basted, excepting gathering the skirt. To be sure, she has been longer in school than many of the other little ones.

A younger sister came a few weeks ago, and it was quite pretty to see the motherly way in which Elungu took the little one around for the first few days. Jennie Baird (Clark) is back in school, and very anxious to stay, but we fear she will not be with us long. Her father has betrothed her to a polygamist on the island of Elobi, and the man says she must go to his home soon. We are all very sorry, especially as Ijule herself is so much opposed to it; but "the things" have all been paid, and I suppose there is no escape. It is a sin and a shame! . . . We have twenty-three girls in school at present. Tell the young friends they must pray that God will bless the dear little girl they have chosen to support; and I pray that they may give their own hearts to the Lord, who rules over all.

Within a year Ijule was dragged away by three drunken men,—her father, uncle, and betrothed. A maddening scene, that burned itself into memory. More than nine years afterward, when Mrs. Nassau was in her grave, Ijule was brought to light as a Christian inquirer in a manner that shamed our weaker faith, that had given her up for lost, or that looked upon her education as wasted.

In January, 1862, came one of those events which test strength, and which revealed Miss Latta's calmness in danger, decision, and versatility of resource.

Ukuku means a departed spirit (plural, *mekuku*). It also means a secret society, into which all males are initiated at puberty, whose proceedings may not be seen by females, nor its laws disobeyed by any one under pain of death,—commuted, occasionally, to a heavy fine. Its decisions are uttered as an oracle from any secluded spot by some man appointed for the purpose. On trivial occasions any man may personate Ukuku, and issue commands for his family. On other occasions, as in strikes to raise prices, this society lays its commands on foreign traders, and other white men. Sometimes representatives of the fraternity from several tribes discuss inter-tribal difficulties.

The Ukuku of Kombe, a tribe forty miles north of Corisco, was angry at the spread of Christianity there, and came to Corisco to consult with the "sons of Belial" there against our work and schools. It came in a company of forty or fifty men, on the evening of January 10, filing in front of the Maluku school-house, and the children fled in dread to hide their faces in their bedroom.

The next morning two old Benga men from the village of Esowĕ, who were respectively father and step-father of two of the girls, hastily came to the front yard, and entered the house excitedly. Instead of coming in deliberately, sitting down, arranging their persons, and then awaiting the salutation, "*Mbolo*" (May you live to be old), they, without seating themselves, said, "*Ndakiya mwan' ame*" (Call my child). This being a demand, and not a respectful request, as would be indicated by the usual addition "*wĕ?*" (please), it was not complied with promptly. The elder of the two started to go through the hall to seize his daughter. They were induced to sit; and then they told the excited rumors that were flying of danger to our house, and their desire to remove their children from that danger. The children were brought, and the father unceremoniously marched off with his, without the courteous intimation, "*Mb' 'alandi; wĕ?*" (I am going), or even the final word, "*Mbi valindi*" (I am gone).

VILLAGE OF ESOWE, CORISCO ISLAND.

Mrs. McQueen and Miss Latta were both present; the latter had acted as interpreter during the conversation, with her rapidly-acquired knowledge of the language, and now interfered with the stepfather, induced him to sit again, represented the foolishness of the fear he was impressing on the child's mind, laughed at Ukuku with an audacity that amazed him, flatly said (what for a native to say would be death), "*Ukuku a ndi momo, pa*" (Ukuku is only a man), added some entreaties, and enforced them with a small gift, until the man himself laughed, and went away satisfied, leaving the child in her hands.

About noon of the same day, just as school was closed, another cry of fear was raised,—the children scattered in all directions. Some immediately returned after the first paroxysm of fear; others were apprehended and brought back by the more faithful of our native assistants; others had fled to their villages. Miss Latta rose from a couch of weakness to meet the trying circumstances, and, gathering the returning children, locked them in her own room, partly for retention and partly to gratify their own wish to escape the light of day and Ukuku's face. While at dinner, three women, belonging to a man who had three girls in the school, came and demanded their children. These being safely locked up, Miss Latta told them she would yield them only to their father. They reviled her, but the dinner was proceeded with. Presently their husband came, in blustering, drunken haste. Miss Latta knew him well, and hinted that when drunk his vanity was manageable. He drew a long knife and plunged at our dog that had sprung at him. The dog was bidden down, the angry man appeased; Mrs. McQueen adroitly invited him to the table at the best seat, and his plate was heaped with yams, and bread, and chicken, and plantain. He became voluble, friendly, and witty; dismissed his women; requested to see his two younger children; with a face terrible in passion ordered them to remain at school; passed his knife across his own throat as a threat of what he would do if they disobeyed, and handed them back to Miss Latta.

Before she had been two years on the island, the mission was indebted to her for valuable assistance in unraveling some knots in the incomplete Benga grammar. Though she did not know as many *words* as older missionaries, she knew as much of the idioms, and could at that time talk almost as well as any. Outside of the school her interest was drawn especially to the women, slaves, and children. The common phrase, as they entered the public reception-room of the Maluku house, was, "*Mbi ma viyandi ka yēnē Mama Lata*" (I have come to see Miss Latta). The mission force was still further reduced, May 20, 1862, by the departure of Rev. Messrs. Clemens and De Heer to Gaboon, for America; the former to find an ocean burial on the way. Some portions of the Corisco work suffered by their absence. But the girls' school continued to flourish; no change in Miss Latta's work or position being made by her change of name to Mrs. Nassau, on September 17, 1862, as she entered the third year of her African life.

> "There blend the ties that strengthen
> Our hearts in hours of grief,
> The silver links that lengthen
> Joy's visits when most brief."

CHAPTER IX.

A ROMANCE.

1862. Corisco.

> "Responds,—as if, with unseen wings,
> An angel touched its quivering strings;
> And whispers, in its song,
> 'Where hast thou stayed so long?'"

ANCESTRAL associations, similar in birth, station, culture, and family covenant blessing: early co-residence in State and town: paths of life that had often approached in curves parabolic, or crossed in lines eccentric during academic training, by town, on streets, and at public gatherings: only names known while yet there was no acquaintance, until a passing introduction, by what people call chance, on the eve of her sailing to Africa; almost the entire conversation at which could be comprised in, "I shall see you again in Africa:" hands that worked together in mission-house and church: feet that together led the merry schoolgirls, and with them romped the Esowĕ beach, or clambered Ugoni's tangled path, or raced on Kâmbâ's sands, or clambered Upe's gnarled trees, or exulted in excursion to Leva, or Alongo, or Ugobi, or Elwĕ: tastes consonant: dispositions unlike, not contrary, and therefore complementary: loneliness that sought in all these one of God's compensations for what had been left in dear homes six thousand miles away: sentiments that found congenial soil in the beauty of tropic light and leaf and flower: respect and deference born of characters tested by storm, wild adventure, and trying ordeal: two lives twining like tropic convolvuli in a common dependence that was unrecognized—unless to woman's finer intuitions—until one said,—

"I was not playing. But perhaps presuming. I had heard your affections were engaged in America. Will forgiving the presumption imply forgetting the presumer?"

"You were misinformed. And the forgiveness is as you please." So the little three-cornered note replied,—

"Yours,

"MARY."

The school-girls did not receive the announcement with satisfaction. Looking on betrothal from their heathen stand-point in woman's lot, it meant to them surveillance, restriction, and an end to personal liberty. One of them, with too full a knowledge of heathen ways, looking upon it as an expression by their loved teacher of an *intention* in reference to another, and not as a contract between two, asked curiously, as if it were an intrusted secret, "And does Dr. Nassau know?"

In others jealousy was aroused. Judging their teacher by the measure of the little love they had seen in their own villages, they imagined that the affection plighted was just so much to be abstracted from themselves.

Her native female friends in the villages were disposed to object. One of them made a formal call at Maluku, and in a set speech warned her of the trials of married life, asking her whether she did not know how much accustomed men were to beat their wives. The laugh that could scarcely restrain itself courteously till the speech was done, and then resounded through the house as her best response to such dismal warnings, seemed to the prophetess of evil a strange fatuity that was explicable only by a native's usual reference to "*utaŋ-ŋani's*" (foreigner's) incomprehensible ways.

But all were soon satisfied when they found that instead of losing one friend they had intensified another. And they were not slow, in their knowledge of human nature, to point requests for small favors by "*o nyanga ya Mama Lata*" (for the sake of Miss Latta), and to add unnecessary assurances of their own love for her.

During the mail's delay of several months, until the 17th of September, 1862, waiting for responses of welcome from respective friends in America, the prospective ceremony was made—like everything else in the missionary life, even things which in civilization would be secluded in the sacredness of home privacy—a test, in frequent conversations with natives, to mark the dignity and honor that Christianity put on marriage in contrast with the entire absence of contract and almost of ceremony in heathenism.

To the same end, on the eve of the day, messengers were sent all over the island to the headmen of the villages to notify them of the "white man's" wedding that was to be held in the church on the next evening.

A German botanist, Herr Mann, a Christian gentleman who was staying with the mission at the time, exercised his skill and taste in the selection and arrangement of flowers and orange-blossom wreaths. The Rev. William Walker, of Gaboon, made the usual tedious journey to Corisco to perform the ceremony.

The native employees of the several stations drew on their monthly earnings wherewith to indulge in new suits of a shirt and five yards of calico to grace the feast, provided by Mrs. McQueen, that was to follow.

Just after sunset, the low-roofed bamboo church of Evangasimba was filled with several hundred curious spectators. Some of them had seen the ceremony performed for native Christians in private houses, but only once before had they witnessed it in the church and for missionaries. On the dark forms of some, and on the brilliant-colored cloths of others, the dim light from a few impromptu lanterns made of tin cracker-boxes, aided by the rays of flaring candles, contrasted strangely with the civilized dress of the missionary pair, who, under the shadows of the limes, and cocoas, and oranges, and guavas that arched the front door, had awaited a signal to advance to the brighter light of the pulpit kerosene-lamp, where Mr. Mackey had meanwhile been improving the occasion by some preliminary religious services.

"It was the time of roses."

CHAPTER X.

A WIFE, AND THE SCHOOL.

1863-1864. Corisco. The Sea.

"'Go, little boat; go, soft and safe,
 And guard the symbol spark!'
Soft, safe, doth float the little boat
 Across the waters dark.
  The river floweth on."

THE Maluku house, though the same that Mrs. Nassau had occupied for two years before her marriage, was invested, as she entered the third year of her African life, with the new interest of *Home*. It was a story-and-a-half frame house, thatched with palm-leaf (*ngonja*), forty feet square, exclusive of the veranda on two of its sides. It stood on a crest of a slight ridge of somewhat sandy soil that sloped from the rear of the house westward to the sea by a path which lay through a portion of native forest. But the elevation of the house was sufficient to give a view of the sea from the back veranda over the tree-tops.

It stood on iron posts, so as to raise the first floor some six feet above the ground, kept damp by frequent rains. In a portion of the ground space was a low platform, where, on Monday mornings, sat Mrs. Nassau, keeping in order her noisy little subjects, as they dabbled their clothes in the wash-tubs arranged along the edge of the platform, or on benches around.

The wide, overhanging eaves, extending nine feet from every side, afforded protection against sun and dashing rain.

On a small porch at the front door would be found sitting every morning, when the first bell was rung at 6.30, a company of women and children and a few men, offering for sale cassava (manioc, tapioca root), sweet potatoes, yams, eggs, chickens, fish, and the fruits of the different seasons. They were part of the company at morning worship, as their marketing was not attended to until after worship. In the large "*Ikenga*" (public reception-room), into which the front door opened, these purchases were made in barter by pipes, soap, plates, basins, knives, beads, cloths, fish-hooks, etc. These village people had certain seats assigned them, the school-girls theirs, and a special settee for Mrs. McQueen, Mrs. Nassau, her Liberian ward Julia, and little Timothy, who had been intrusted in her care by his father, licentiate Ibiya. In the dining-room, which was also sitting-room, Mrs. Nassau would pass a large portion of the mornings at her sewing-machine over the clothing of the girls; there they would come to get their dresses fitted. A constant phrase, as one and other dropped in, was, "*Sâsâ, mama, bestaka ituma jamĕ*" (Please baste my sewing). All the natives readily coined verbs from ours when their language had none to suit. Over the bureau, in the corner in which the school sewing was kept, was a looking-glass; and many unnecessary visits were made to the room with questions, the time occupied in receiving an answer to which was filled by a dressing of their crispy locks in front of the mirror. At her feet were always some who preferred, instead of the play in the yard, to chat with her as she sewed.

In the study were quite an array of shelves and bottles of medicines, where those whom she reported as on the sick list came, as to a dispensary, awaiting their turn as they sat on a low lounge covered by a brilliant-figured chintz, sent to Africa as a relic of her girlhood. The wooden walls of the bedroom were attempted to be enlivened with a wall-paper of "Hobson's choice," its principal feature being a blue vine with blue leaves and blue grapes. A small room, partitioned from the side veranda, opened into it, and was of great service; for when Mrs. Nassau was too weak, or the weather too stormy, to take the girls to their sewing out in the school-room, she could lie in her own room and give all necessary directions to the busy fingers almost within reach in the little room. There the evening hymn was taught before the girls retired. A door communicated from the room to the up-stairs, where they slept, so that any little one could readily be reached at night, if necessary. In the rooms up-stairs were mats made of the leaves of the pandanus (screw-pine) for eighteen children. Natives did not use beds; even in their own houses did not have bedsteads, only a low frame to raise the sleeper above the clay floor. This frame was not necessary on our dry, broad floors. For covering, the children had a sheet of cotton cloth, and, in the cool-dry* season, a quilt. Under a single quilt were put two children of such a size and disposition as that the feet of one should not tyrannize over the other for the occupancy of the whole. *Age* was often a subject of quarrel. "*Mbi nd' utodu wa*" (I am the elder) was offered as sufficient answer when any one had to be called to account for unkind imposition. When the disparity of age

---

* The seasons at the Equator, on the African West Coast, are four,—two rainy, covering seven months; and two dry, occupying the other five. They correspond, in *time* only (not at all in character), with the four seasons of the temperate zones: viz., the "early" rains corresponding to autumn; a short, hot, middle-dry, during our midwinter; the "latter" rains corresponding to spring; and the cool-dry comprising our summer.

The alternating land and sea breezes, blowing for twenty out of every twenty-four hours, moderate the heat, the mercury marking, *in the shade*, not above 90° Fahr., but never as low as 65°.

was great, advantage would be taken of it, and every older girl was put in charge of some younger one, of whom she was expected to take care. Being thus dignified with the position of monitors, they did take care of them; in consideration of which the younger carried water from the spring, and did other errands for them. This consideration was none of Mrs. Nassau's arrangement; but it was allowed as a universal custom of the people. In that dormitory would terminate the last of Mrs. Nassau's daily labors; after their sewing half of the day, their oversight out of school-hours, their verses in the evening, she put them to bed at night. Silence then was the law when she removed the light. It was the only time of day peculiarly her own, or when letters could be written undisturbed. That silence being broken, a monitory rap of her knuckles against the door at the foot of the stairs preceded the calling down of the delinquent who failed to regard it. Delinquents during the day were sent to a quiet retreat in a little room up-stairs (called "*tyogo*," prison, but which was prison-like only in its isolation), which was occupied at night by those of her pupils who by age or good conduct were called "big girls." There they kept their chests, purchased by their own needles, in which they treasured the few garments or pieces of crockery they were amassing for their prospective marriage. These were permitted to sit up an hour later than others, without surveillance, reading, or sewing, or looking at pictures in the "*Ikenga.*"

Down in the rear of the house, at the foot of the slope, near the forest, Mrs. Nassau recreated herself in a little garden, where were planted American seeds,—enormous cucumbers, ordinary-sized radishes, excellent corn, small watermelons; and of native produce, ginger, chillies (Cayenne pepper), and eschalots (a kind of onion). In the cool of the afternoon it was her amusement to hoe, weed, or plant cabbage, cauliflower, asparagus, or other such seeds as always persisted in not growing. Yet the invitation, "*O 'ka o mwanga*" (Come to the garden), was responded to, though the seed-planting were fruitless of other benefit than the exercise.

In the rear of the Maluku premises were gathered, at Mrs. Nassau's wish, from the premises of our own or other missions, more than two dozen kinds of tropical fruit-trees, indigenous or imported from the exotic gardens of the French at Gaboon, and of the Spanish at Fernando Po. These included the oil-palm, cocoa-nut, grenadilla (a fruit-bearing passion-vine), plantain, banana, pine-apple, tamarind, orange, lime, lemon, rose-apple, papaya ("pawpaw," not the American fruit of that name), sour-sop, mango, Avagado pear (vulgarly called "alligator" pear), cacao (chocolate), bread-fruit, elola, guava. The bread-fruit was her especial pride, for hers was the first one on the island (introduced in October, 1861) that succeeded in growing. She rejoiced in literally standing under the shade of her own "vine and fig-tree." The leaves of the bread-fruit are fig-leaf-shaped, three feet long, with deep digitations in a width of twelve or fifteen inches. The vine was an acquisition from the French Plateau garden.

The branches of the few trees in that portion of the rear yard occupied as the girls' play-ground were made rather ragged by their frequent climbing. The destruction to dresses, and the danger to legs and arms, were represented to Mrs. Nassau; but she had not forgotten that once she had liked to climb trees, and, being willing to help mend the dresses, she accepted the risk to the legs. The children enjoyed the fun, and they always landed on their feet. There were so many things indecorous in heathen games and plays that had to be forbidden, that the largest liberty was given whenever their own amusements could be allowed.

In the girls' *mwidi* ("compound," premises) was located their kitchen. The four or five largest girls were admitted (missionary point of view) to the dignity of cooking for the rest. Whether the labor required was compensated by the honor was sometimes doubted in those girls' view. Each one had the duty for a week, and was assisted by a younger, chosen by herself. The little fag really did the work, but the elder had all the responsibility. That responsibility lay in the wearing of the key of the cupboard that contained the daily supply of fish, plantains, bananas, salt, *mevândâ*, and *ngwĕsĕ* (two forms of preparing the (manioc) cassava.) Those two girls were each week excused from their sewing and from school earlier than the usual hour, in order to attend to their cooking.

The path in the rear of the house wound past a garden of eddoes (tania, koko, an *Arum esculentum*), cassava, plantains, and sweet potatoes (a white variety), down to a little cove by the sea, where Mrs. Nassau and Mrs. McQueen sometimes went in their bathing-dresses, and where the girls were taken to wash regularly every Saturday, and sometimes on other days.

Joy at the arrival of the mail on the 1st of January, 1863, as the little company of Corisco missionaries were enjoying New Year's quiet celebration at Alongo, was shadowed by Mrs. Nassau's receiving news of the death of her brother in a Washington hospital, from disease contracted in Virginia swamps just after his promotion to a captaincy. She bore the affliction with her usual calmness when under trial. With characteristic thoughtfulness of others, when she discovered the contents of her letter, she made no demonstration by which the good news of others should be marred; but quietly rising left the company, making only a sign for her husband to follow to another room.

Mrs. Nassau was constantly adding to her knowledge of the native language, and using that knowledge in the translation of hymns. Some that reached America too late for the edition of 1864, are now issued in the edition of 1873. One of these, the translation of "Christian, see the Orient Morning," was written about this time while sick in bed, detained from church on a Sabbath morning. It was correct as she wrote it, no alterations being made by the native interpreter, to whose criticism it was subjected. That copy was lost. She re-wrote it, but less perfectly. The original copy was years afterward found, and the issue of 1873 was a combination of the two.

Mrs. Nassau's first mainland experience was in a boat journey with the two members of the Mainland Visiting Committee, in March 6–10, 1863. At that early day, though deeply interested in her Corisco pupils, she often wished for removal to the mainland. The journey was to Hanje, forty miles north, in the limits of the Kombe tribe. The Lord's Supper was administered for the first time there. A woman was baptized, and on the return two native Scripture readers were located at Aje, eight miles south of Hanje, in the Bapuku tribe.

Mrs. Nassau was the first white female missionary who had been seen among the tribes north of Corisco, and probably the first white woman. (The few captains' wives who accompanied their husbands on that coast never went ashore.) She was a great curiosity to the people, and especially to the women, who were permitted to handle her feet and hands, and unroll her hair as she sat on a broken canoe under the shade of a tree near the beach.

In spite of a most drenching rain, on approaching Corisco on the return, she was so delighted with the view of the wide work on the mainland, that the longing for it was not satisfied until we were permitted to go there two and a half years later.

MRS. NASSAU TO HER SISTER-IN-LAW, MISS M. H. NASSAU.

Thursday night, May 14, 1863

... Our mail is brought by a French steamer from Fernando Po to the Gaboon; but the commodore, being somewhere up the coast, must have his missives first, while missionaries, officers, traders, and common folks in general must wait.

Well! ours came on the 11th. As we were sitting in the evening in our little parlor, listening to Hamill reading aloud "Hypatia," we were interrupted by the welcome letters.

What did they contain? Pleasant words of love and remembrance,—interesting comments on what had been thought and said and done in the last month; and some very good news, but not quite enough of it. . . . You can understand how anxiously we look for the mail sometimes when only half satisfied by a former one.

You see I am writing nothing, but it is because I am not in a writing mood,—got tired of it this morning.

Many thanks for the school dresses that we have had, and for others perhaps on the way. They will be very acceptable; but we are getting on quite comfortably.

We are all seated at the round dining-room table getting ready for the mail.

Good-night. Much love to my new and dear relatives. I love to read and hear the kind messages you all send to me, whom you have never seen, in this far-off land.

In furtherance of the project of a mainland station, permission for which had already been asked of the Board, the Mainland Visiting Committee, in a journey of superintendence of the out-stations in July 9–17, 1863, made a voyage to the Bonita River, fifty-four miles northward, and entered it some eighteen miles. A naval surveying party had entered its mouth; white traders had often visited it, and one had gone up about fourteen miles; Rev. Wm. Clemens had gone beyond, to certain rapids at Sĕnjĕ; but the committee went farther, to a fall ("*ivova*") called Yovi, remarkable not for its height, but for the body of water coming over, and for the terrible power of a whirlpool in its basin.

When I returned that Friday, 17th of July, from that journey, Mrs. Nassau met me with a question, whose shadow we had dreaded, and therefore had resolutely put away. Now it had to be faced and answered in a single hour. Should she go to America? She had previously shut her eyes to growing weakness, and refused advice not to attempt a fourth year on that West Coast. But a combination of indications made all the little missionary company at both Corisco and Gaboon say, "She ought to go."

A boat had been awaiting Mr. Mackey and myself with important letters from Rev. W. Walker, of Gaboon. He had found an English bark, the "Moultan," of the firm John Laughland & Co., Glasgow, about to sail from Gaboon on the 23d, and had sent us word; Rev. W. H. Clark had decided to take this opportunity to return on furlough to America; there was some doubt about the fitness of such a vessel for an invalid lady. A steamer could have been selected, but our mission, under the war-straitened treasury in America, was taught the closest economy. Mr. Clark's company supplied escort: I had no reason in ill health to leave my work. Every point had been discussed during the two days while my return was awaited. Mrs. Nassau was to go. The impromptu lines she handed me, dated "Tuesday night, July 14, 1863," had conveyed her assent. They may have been suggested by Mrs. Sarah B. Judson's "We part on this Green Islet, Love;" and are the only verses I am aware of her having written in Africa:

> "We part, my husband, yes, we part
> 'Mid hopes, and fears, and pain;
> 'But we shall still be joined in heart
> And hope to meet again.'
>
> "We part, my husband, yes, we part;
> And I go forth alone,
> With timid, restless, yearning heart,
> From my beloved one.
>
> "We part, my husband, yes, we part;
> And you on Manji's isle,
> With lonely and with saddened heart,
> Will miss one loving smile.
>
> *   *   *   *   *
>
> "We part, my husband, yes, we part;
> But God, *our God*, is *Love;*
> And we must rest upon His heart,
> And look for light above.
>
> "We part, my husband, yes, we part;
> But well the chain is riven,
> And we shall still be joined in heart
> On earth, and one in heaven."

God gave a strange ability to endure.

The time to prepare was short,—Friday, Saturday, Monday. Mrs. Nassau rose from her bed and helped in directing, or in using, the sewing-machine. The journey was not as in this country. The simple style of dress worn in the mission home would be *outré* in England, and some preparation must be made for it, and for the change of climate. She was relieved entirely of the care of the children by the smaller ones being sent to school both morning and afternoon; and the larger ones assisted Mrs. McQueen both day and night with their needles; in which work some former pupils were hired to assist.

Oatmeal, fresh vegetables, and native *belola* wine were gathered to add to the ship's stores; cocoa, and a few delicacies for invalid taste were obtained by our kind Gaboon friends, Rev. I. M. and Mrs. Preston, from the French Plateau store; a barrel of sweet potatoes and a hundred oranges from Mrs. Walker; prepared rusk, and one of our own goats, "Epepa," to give milk at least part of the way; dried raspberries and cakes from Mrs. Mackey; and a six-gallon jug of fresh water from the Baraka spring.

On Tuesday, July 21, at 10 A.M., Mrs. Nassau left Corisco in the mission sail-boat "Manji," with the baggage, and manned by six skillful Benga oarsmen; stopped at Cape Estinas, twenty miles distant, at midnight ; slept for a few hours ashore ; off again at 7 A.M. of the 22d, and reached Baraka at sunset. Mr. Clark followed in the " Draper," a smaller boat, and arrived, wet and exhausted, four hours later.

A delay of the " Moultan" two days in completing her cargo, gave a desirable rest from the fatigue of the boat journey.

The ship was not intended for many passengers, and they were to provide their own bedding. The only two extra state-rooms were still in confusion when we went on board, at 7 A.M. of Friday, the 24th. As sails and other things were being taken out of the room that was assigned Mrs. Nassau, a batch of bread, dark as ginger-cake, ready for baking, was observed in the wash basin! It did not augur well for the prospects of the journey. Captain G—— promised fair. But, the privations of that voyage! His heartlessness became, in the latter part of the nine-weeks' voyage, cruelty.

As I returned ashore, the sails were flung to the morning land-wind of the cool-dry season. And as shortly after my " Manji" went out the Gaboon's broad mouth, on the north bank, toward Corisco, the " Moultan" stood out to sea on the south bank.

By the departure of Mrs. Nassau and Mr. Clark, our mission white force was reduced to four,— Rev. J. L. and Mrs. Mackey, and Mrs. McQueen and myself. We two continued the girls' school, using native aid in the teaching.

As if with a prophecy of the future, a "cry for help," that became more terribly true seven years later, was sent to America by one of those lonely pickets at the front: "*Won't somebody stir up the* CHURCH? *It is not the* BOARD'S *fault. We are weak and 'weary and faint.' The words of Mrs.* E. C. Judson, 'I have come from a land where a beautiful light,' etc., *are becoming true for us. This is no economy of money or life. While we toil with work that cannot be made less, we fall before assistance comes; and then the assistant, taking up the burden, himself unassisted, falls in his turn. Two are better than one. Our native helpers are good, but themselves are a care. Why don't the reapers come to the vineyard?*"

On August 1 arrived at Corisco letters that had come from the "Moultan" by the pilot-boat that accompanied it down the Gaboon.

MRS. NASSAU TO HER HUSBAND.

BARK "MOULTAN," Gaboon River,
Friday, July 24, 1863.

. . . Oh, these partings! oh, these partings! . . . But you are away; and soon I will go; and then the long months will come, and we will pray for each other.

While you were up the coast there was a verse

that was such a comfort to me: "To him that overcometh will I grant to sit with me in my throne," etc. Well, when I felt fretful, or impatient, or sick, and when I wanted you back so badly, I would remember that "to him that overcometh" was the promise made. Then I would ask myself, overcometh what? Why, whatever might be trying just at the moment, whether small or large. And so I tried to "overcome;" and I think those long days you were away from me perhaps were for my own good. . . . I do not believe I shall suffer much on the voyage; every one seems very kind; the captain brought me a soft pillow, and the steward got a coat to throw over me, and both say I must let them know if there is anything they can do.

The captain and Mr. Clark are having a slight religious talk, but I do not understand the drift of it. Now it's done.

I don't know how that ginger-cake is getting along in my room; but I told Mr. Clark there was a batch there.

I am sitting up on the seat on which you left me lying, and writing on the broad window-ledge.

Of the discomforts of the voyage, from the loss of the goat on the fourth day, to the actual rationing of food, the diet on fare that might suffice for able-bodied men, but not for delicate invalids, and the self-denial that would choose the social privations of second- and third-rate accommodations to save the church's treasury, only a portion was recited in her letters, and then only as a matter of history, not as complaint.

The captain's fair exterior changed to positive rudeness. He monopolized the only cabin there was besides the small saloon, occupying it as his bedroom, so that others could not use it when he was drunk or napping. The first evening of the voyage he spoke very piously, and assented to Mr. Clark's wish for morning and evening prayers and Sabbath preaching. But the crew detested his hypocrisy, and never came, and by the end of the fifth week the religious services had been so often postponed and interrupted by his various excuses and obstacles, that they were broken up entirely, and the announcement made that "the Koran was as good as the Bible, and a Hindoo as safe as a Christian." The two mates, Messrs. Kerr and Monroe, were invariably attentive and polite.

MRS. NASSAU'S SEA-JOURNAL TO HER HUSBAND.

BARK "MOULTAN," Friday, July 31, 1863.

. . . I have not been able to sit up since leaving Baraka. I tried it yesterday for ten or fifteen minutes, but the motion of the vessel was too much. Our fare is good, I suppose, for ship; but if I had not some extras with me, it would go pretty hard. . . .

August 1.—Three years ago to-day I sailed for Africa, and three years ago I saw my brother for the last time. He was the last, my darling brother! A day or two ago must have been the third anniversary of our meeting. May God grant that our next meeting be not far off! Father, mother, and brothers are gone, but my husband is more to me than all; more than any earthly friend has ever been. . . . This morning before I was up the waves came into my berth. The steward had closed the window the evening before, but Mr. Clark opened it for me at bed-time. I called for the steward, who screwed up the window, and scolded at the same time about its having been opened. I sat in my wet night-dress in the soaking berth, and took it all very meekly. Fortunately, my day clothing was so disposed of that none of it got wet. The bedding has been out drying to-day, but the mattress is not dry yet. I don't know what I am to sleep on to-night. . . .

August 3. *Monday.*—Yesterday was the Sabbath,—a pretty comfortable day. . . . To-night I had for supper cocoa and a roasted sweet potato, —my best meal to-day. I ate but a little pea-soup for dinner. I feel pretty well this evening. . . .

Wednesday, August 5.—"There is a good time coming." The steward got out some hops,—hops imply yeast, yeast implies bread or biscuit. We have had nothing but pilot-bread as yet, of which

I have eaten a little. We shall have pudding tomorrow, too. I don't know what kind; but all our desserts heretofore have been some kind of fruit,—very nice. I hope it will be fruit-pudding; we had a good one on Sunday. Dessert only comes three or four times a week. Thursdays and Sundays we have chickens, always boiled,—and I can't eat them. One morning we had stewed kidney, canned, and that I was able to eat. Salt beef, pork, and pilot-bread is the regular supper. But the best thing I have had was a piece of Epepa's liver, fried. She choked herself on a banana the first week out, and we had her liver fried for supper. You will say I think too much of my eating; but I can't help it here, where it is so hard to get what I can eat. Yet it is a nice vessel, and everything on board well ordered. The cooking is all of the cleanest, and there is a wonderful amount of scrubbing done all around. The steward is very kind, and gets everything I ask him,—which is not much. . . .

Tuesday night, August 11.— . . . I asked the cook to-night what his wife did without him. "Ah! she breaks her heart all the time," was his reply. The captain has had a short attack of fever, and we were debarred the privilege of his cabin several days. He is about as usual now, and the cabin is thrown open to us. That pudding last Thursday was veritable *plum*-pudding, full of currants,—

light and good. Yesterday I commenced "Life and Epistles of St. Paul," but the book is so large that I cannot hold it long without wearying. It is hard on the eyes, too, in a reclining posture. I am very much interested, and feel so sorry that I should have forgotten so much that it seems like a new book. There are many hours of every day in which I can only lie still and sleep or think. I try not to set my heart on any of my plans, but if God spares my life and yours, you know I will try very hard to come back to you in a year. . . .

Friday night, August 14.—Just three weeks to-day since we sailed. This morning I felt worse than I have at all before, perhaps because we were nearly becalmed, and directly under the sun. . . . I have been at the table to-day, the first time since I have been on board. It was quite an effort to make up my mind to sit up and eat, but I got along very well. We had bread two days ago for the first, and have had it fresh both days since. The steward bakes it generally in the shape of biscuit, and they are pretty good. . . . We were in sight of the Cape de Verdes to-day ; and, after some forty-eight hours of uncertain winds and weather, we have caught the northeast trades. . . . We spoke a vessel yesterday from Buenos Ayres, and one to-day from Macao. No news from them, of course. . . .

Saturday night, August 15.— . . . Will you please give Andekĕ, with my kind regards, a copy of

Spurgeon's Sermons that is in the parlor? Read first a sermon entitled "Comfort for Feeble Saints," and another on the text, "And the arms of his hands were made strong by the hands of the mighty God of Jacob." It is a long time since I read either, but I remember liking both very much. . . .

Tuesday night, August 18.— . . . We are having a good wind, and the captain said at supper-table this evening that two weeks of such sailing would bring us to anchor. I shall be glad if we are so highly favored, for though I am in no special hurry to reach America, yet I am not likely to gain any strength while at sea. I am getting very thin. Yesterday morning my back and limbs ached so much more than usual, and were so sore, that I got some brandy from Mr. Clark to rub them. It was rather inconvenient to lie in such a narrow berth and rub my own back; but I felt easier afterwards. Lying down so much on not the softest places does not help one's bones. . . . I do not look forward half so much to my arrival in America as I do to the prospect of leaving it a year later. . . . You must write all that is done in regard to the establishment of Scripture-readers at the mouth of the Bonita. I suppose I can hear at the Mission House what they wrote about your being sent there; but I want to know what the mission letter said, and what you and Mr. Mackey thought of it. . . .

Tuesday, August 25.—Upon inquiring the day of the month, Mr. Monroe insisted upon it that it was the 26th; and Mr. Clark could not tell the day of the week, though I was sure it was Tuesday. After my date was written, our young mate found he had made a mistake. Mr. Kerr, the first mate, is very kind and pleasant, all that I see of him; and he and Mr. Clark have some long talks on deck. The captain we do not either of us like, though he lets us alone. He is ungentlemanly.

. . . How much I want to hear you sing! I did not think I should miss your voice in that way so much as I have done. But I miss you most when the time comes for my last prayer at night. It is a precious privilege to pray for each other, but still more precious to pray *with* each other. . . . Sometimes it seems to me as though the prayer would be answered, for I feel such a sweet peace after asking it of God.

Last night the rain came in, and would have wet me pretty well in my berth if my white spread had not been pretty thick. I drew the spread double over my shoulders where the water fell, and when it got about soaked I pulled up a dry part. The shower did not last long, but it made me uncomfortable, although I did not get wet. When I said at the breakfast-table the rain had come in, the captain replied that the seams of the vessel would soon swell; and that was all the consolation I got from headquarters. However, I know we are far better off than many passengers have been in American vessels.

Of course, our fare is not equal to that of the "Ocean Eagle." When Captain Yates gets to Corisco tell him I often sighed to be in one of his vessels. I hope you may never have to go home by way of England, especially before the war is done. I never felt hardly before against the English; but it does seem strange how any persons can be so stupid. I hope the first news we shall hear will be that the "Alabama" has been taken.

Friday night, August 28.—Five weeks to-day since I left you, —— ——! . . . In my thoughts I limit our separation to one year, although I know there is not much possibility of our meeting in that time. Or, rather, I say to myself, in a year I will try to leave America. And so, on the 25th of this month, I said, Well, one month has gone and eleven are left. . . . We have been almost becalmed for a couple of days. . . . I drink *belola* in my water. . . . I am obliged to continue the quinine every night.

Mr. Clark is very kind in all he can do, but in the matter of health I have to rely altogether on myself. But I try to be patient, and hope for the best. God rules all things for our good.

I want to be in Corisco,—that means principally

you. How I should like to walk with you again around the yard, and see the new leaves that have been put forth since I left! Which tree grows the best? Which do you think will bear fruit first? Is the rose-apple alive that was transplanted at midday? Write me about all my especial pets. . . .

Monday night, August 31.— . . . God keep me from loving you too well! I do love my Saviour best. . . . We are still becalmed, or making only about a "knot" an hour, sometimes less. I try to "commit my way unto the Lord," and to trust only in Him. . . .

Thursday, September 3.— . . . This morning the captain went off to a vessel sailing in company with us, and spent the day. About dark he came back, bringing two English papers, with later news from America than any we had seen. Of course, their papers would give all there was against the North; and, if we may believe them, the South are doing wonders: "New Orleans is taken!" "Washington and Baltimore in danger!" And the rebels threatening Harrisburg! . . . I do not like to feel bitterly against the English, but I wish I was out of one of their ships.

We have sailed very little for some days, but as I am not seasick in a calm, it is easier for me to be patient than it might be in other circumstances.

If the flour lasts I can do pretty well, but we never have enough to hurt ourselves. I have two cans of cocoa yet unopened, and the sweet potatoes are not done, so I get along very comfortably. I enjoy the oranges very much now, but for several weeks could not eat them. A number have spoiled, and I do not think any of them will keep long.

The rats are very bad, and disturb me almost every night in my stateroom. Several times the rats have awakened me with their feet on my head, and at other times I suppose it is imagination. I do not rest well, or I should not be so much disturbed by them. Two nights ago a young rat got in my pitcher, and floundered around until I woke. I got up to see what the noise might be, and, finding the youngster, covered up the pitcher with a towel, to prevent his escape. He was very soon quiet, and I thought he was drowned; but the little rascal kept his nose above water until morning, when Mr. Clark threw him overboard. I would not have slept comfortably if I had known he was in such an unpleasant fix all night. . . . Do try and take care of your health. Mr. Clark said yesterday you would work till you got sick, and then come home for me. He was not putting the two together, as your *intention*, at all. I answered more quickly, "I am sure I hope not. I don't want Dr. Nassau to come home for me." Neither do I; but I should be very much pained if I were to find on my return (if I live) that you were needing to go to America. . . .

Saturday night, September 5.—Last night I cried for you, my husband. It was not the first time; but I have not shed tears often since leaving Africa. God is good, and watches over me, and I suppose I could not expect to feel well and cheerful all the time. . . . Yesterday and the day before I had a bad headache. Our diet is not nourishing, and the butter is done, and rice and canned potatoes are the only vegetables, excepting my sweet potatoes. The bread is good, but we are served out a certain allowance; and this afternoon I actually suffered from hunger from dinner- until tea-time. The rusk have moulded, but the cocoa lasts.

I must not forget to tell you that, on reading the papers yesterday, the news was not half so bad as the captain reported at first. He must have heard it on the other vessel, and had not read the news himself, for he was very quiet yesterday, saying nothing on American affairs. The subject is rarely broached at the table. I have only spoken twice when it was, but I have always been vexed. New Orleans is *not* taken; but the rebels were up in Pennsylvania. The latest date was July 3, and I am quite anxious to know the result of the fighting in my own State. If the rebels are not soon driven back, it will be a burning shame.

I should not have said above there "I *suffered*" from hunger; but I was really hungry.

Writing you has put me in better spirits than

when I commenced. The captain of the vessel that our captain visited has his wife and three children along with him. The captain told Mr. Clark this morning, when he was proposing to go on board again, and he asked if we could spare some oranges. Mr. Clark appealed to me, and we sent nine, just the half of our stock. . . . How are the children getting along? I hope they are learning nicely; and I do hope sister Bella is there to assist in the care of them. I am sure they will love her.

Do you know we never named any child for Jennie Frank Nassau, as she requested? Give her name to Ikwele, unless you have some other preference. She is one of your favorites. Are the papayas going to bear this rainy season? Mr. Monroe, the second mate, says that on a voyage from China to England their captain took a number of flowers, and nearly all lived. How have Mr. Mackey's yellow sweet potatoes succeeded? And how have the eddoes, sent by Mr. Mann, grown? . . .

Thursday night, September 10.—See, it is five days since I wrote you; but we have had cold winds and some rain, and I have not felt well. . . . Our flour is nearly done; and what is left they must be saving for "duff," as we have only had soft bread once this week. I think we had a little stale on Sunday evening, but do not remember about that. Yesterday half of the raspberries were stewed for me, and they are very pleasant. I have persuaded Mr. Clark to eat a few; but we shall make them last several days. I did not bring them on the table, but ate them with some of Mrs. Mackey's cakes to-day. Her cakes are keeping nicely. Last night I had some oatmeal porridge, made for the first time, and another dish to-night. I hope it may last until we get to Cork, as I enjoy it very much more than pilot-bread. The sweet potatoes were finished yesterday, and I shall miss them very much. I have not felt feverish for some days, but I think it safer to continue the quinine in small doses. It seems to me I might feel pretty well on land. . . .

Monday morning, September 14.— . . . We are still within about a week's sail of Cork, and have been for the last seven days. . . . For several days we have had E. and N.E. winds, and I have stayed in my berth most of the time just to keep warm; dressed, of course. Mr. Clark is always kind and attentive.

Thursday, September 17.— . . . There is now some prospect of our reaching Cork on Monday. . . . This is quite a month of anniversaries with me. Three years ago to-day I first set foot on African soil at Monrovia. The 3d was my brother Willie's birthday, and the 16th Samuel's. My brother Samuel died on his eighteenth birthday; the only sad one among the days to be remembered. The happiest is September 17. . . .

Our fare has been rather better this last week, and we have every morning now a good hash, made of pilot-bread and salt meat. That, with rice, makes as comfortable a breakfast as any hungry person need want. We had rice and peas for dinner,—something very extraordinary to have two vegetables at one meal. My appetite is improving rapidly. . . .

Saturday, September 19.— . . . To-morrow we expect certainly to be off Cork, and I am so glad it will be in time for this month's steamer to Africa. . . . The jug of water is not empty yet, and I have used none other for drinking. It has been a great comfort. . . . God has been good to us thus far. Let us thank Him. . . .

The arrival at Cork just in time for the outgoing African mail-steamer closed the sea-journal at the above point. It was continued by the next month's mail.

MRS. NASSAU TO HER HUSBAND.

BARK "MOULTAN,"
Firth of Clyde, Sept. 24, 1863.

At last we have a steam-tug fast to the old "Moultan," and after all our delays and uncertainties there is every probability of our being in Glasgow to-morrow.

My first letter to you I closed on Saturday, and Sabbath morning a pilot came on board from

Cork. Mr. Kerr went ashore, took our letters with him, and came back after dinner bringing a quarter of beef and a bag of potatoes; but, most important, our orders for Glasgow, instead of to Leith.

Now, would you have eaten the provisions? I thought best to do so, "asking no questions for conscience' sake." Roast beef, boiled beef, beef hashed and stewed have been the various changes,—and three times a day. Once we all had steak; but since then the captain has kept the steaks for himself, not offering even me a piece. A supply of liquor came aboard at Cork, and the captain has been drinking more than is good for his temper ever since. Yesterday morning he would not wait until Mr. Clark had made my chair steady at the table, but called to the steward and began helping the plates as fast as he could without any blessing. He added, as Mr. Clark took his seat, "Would to God you had gone ashore at Cork!" When breakfast was nearly done, he began asking Mr. Clark about the bill that had been made out for the voyage before we left Gaboon, and made some unpleasant remarks about the "dollar down at four shillings two pence." Mr. Clark said the matter of exchange was to be settled when we learned what it was at Glasgow. "I am looking after my own interest," said the captain; "you know I get half cabin freight." How glad I was to get away from the table! . . . I shall be willing to hurry through the country, and be off to America just as fast as Mr. Clark chooses. He has proposed that we go by the Cunard line, and take second-cabin passage. At the beginning of the voyage I would scarcely have consented to go in the second cabin, but there is no doubt that the fare will be good, and my pride has worn away by sea-sickness. . . God has been very good to me, and I do hope I shall have learned some lessons of patience from some of the discomforts on board of this ship. It would be truly a blessing to say, with St. Paul, " I have learned in *whatsoever* state I am therewith to be content." . . . Mr. Kerr brought me an apple, too, the first I had seen for three years. . . .

Tuesday morning, Glasgow, September 29.—Our vessel arrived in Glasgow near midnight on Thursday, September 24, and we had decided to go by the Cunard line on Saturday if possible. We met, however, with such kind friends that we were prevailed on to stay and take to-morrow's steamer. Mr. and M/s Thomson have done more to make us pleased with Scotland than ever the captain did to prejudice us against the country; and I am still proud to say that my ancestors were partly Scotch.

After our voyage on the " Moultan," the atmosphere of kindness seems so pleasant and rests me so much that I dread the sea again. . . . I told you we arrived near midnight of Thursday, and we took a cab to a house that Mr. Kerr said he knew to be a quiet and respectable one. The next morning, after not a very good rest, I went to the small parlor, and found Mr. Clark, who had been gathering information from the newspapers. After a hearty breakfast of beefsteak and rolls had been served up to us in a private parlor on my account, Mr. Clark went out on business. In a few minutes he came in bringing me a paper of plums and pears, for which I had been longing. Afterwards he went out to make arrangements about our leaving that night for Liverpool, and to see Mr. Laughland. I remained alone, sitting very close to a small fire that had been made for me in a grate. Your afghan was thrown over my shoulders besides. I was thinking Glasgow a dismal place. . . . While I was sitting on a low stool, looking, I've no doubt, very dismal, the servant came to the door saying that two gentlemen were inquiring for "Mrs. Nassau," and straightway ushered them in. I was in a momentary maze, but had not time to wonder much, for as I rose one of the gentlemen stepped forward, held out his hand, and announced himself as "Mr. Thomson, of the Calabar mission." He introduced the other gentleman as his uncle, Mr. George Thomson, and handed me a note from Mr. Clark. As I looked up from the note, Mr. T. said they had called to ask if I would not go with him to his house during our stay; Mr. Clark had been unable to come with them, but would meet me there if I were willing to go. I answered, "Oh, I would rather go with you than stay here."

They had learned through Mr. Laughland of our expected arrival, and on seeing by the paper that the "Moultan" was in port, they sought out Mr. Clark and myself and brought us to their house.

On reaching Mr. George Thomson's I was introduced to his sister, Miss Amelia, who keeps house for him; and the kindness of all made me very much at home. The next day their niece, Miss Jessie Thomson, returned from a visit in the country, and she is the only other member of the family. They have been almost too kind.

The first day, while we were still expecting to leave by the night train, Mr. Thomson ordered a cab and took me a drive through their park around a very pretty part of the town. Before evening I found that Mr. Clark was willing to remain until the beginning of this week, and I said I too should be very glad to stay. Miss Thomson went out with me that afternoon (Friday), and I bought a very pretty dark-brown wrapper. I have also bought a warm shawl, which I hope will last me for best and traveling through the winter. I do not want to get a cloak for one winter only; it would not seem right. . . .

ROYAL HOTEL, LIVERPOOL,
Wed. morning, Sept. 30, 1863.

Here we are at our last stopping-place, having arrived about six o'clock this morning. We were expecting to leave Glasgow at 4 P.M. yesterday, but it was finally decided that we should remain until evening, and go by the night line at 9 P.M. We took a first-class car, partly on my account and partly because we could bring with us a larger amount of baggage free. I had rather advised taking a second- or third-class, but even in the most comfortable car I was quite tired when we reached the end of our journey. There were seats for six in the compartment that we occupied, and a gentleman who rode with us for a short distance showed Mr. Clark how to arrange the portmanteau and cushions so that I could lie down quite comfortably.

Mr. and Miss Thomson have given me a cordial invitation to visit them on my return to Corisco, and to make my arrangements to remain for a few weeks, in order to see something of the country. It was my first experience of kindness shown me as to a *missionary*, and it made a deep impression. (I should except my visit at Mrs. Berrian's, in New York; and perhaps my visits on the Liberian coast.) The American question was discussed pretty freely, and they seemed glad of information on some points, but I heard nothing unpleasant.

Mr. John Laughland called on us two evenings ago, and was very pleasant. A Mr. Clark, of the Botanical Gardens, sent me a beautiful bunch of flowers. It has rained almost every day since we reached Glasgow, and Sabbath morning it was far too stormy for me to attempt going out. That was a disappointment, too; but I was able to go through some rain in the afternoon. We went to hear Dr. MacDuff, the author of several books in our mission; but I must confess to being disappointed,—only a little, however. The sermon was very beautiful, but the first part was almost too full of figures. . . .

Mrs. Nassau's full, cheerful, sprightly pages of her journey to New York, and short stay in the United States, are marked by the same kind receptions and tender welcomes that began so brightly at Glasgow; then at Liverpool at the embarkation, September 30, on the "City of Baltimore," on the Inman line of transatlantic steamers; at the landing in New York, October 13; at the Mission House, 23 Centre Street, New York, by the secretaries of the Board, and in letters there awaiting her from four different homes; the glad return to her loved uncle's in Philadelphia; the hearty affection and sympathy of her new parents and brothers and sisters at Lawrenceville; the rare skill and judgment of her Christian physician,

Dr. C. S. Bishop; all these, with the social privileges, as much as medicine and food, contributed to rapid restoration to health and strength.

At Corisco, the mission work had gone on as successfully as the few hands there could direct. The Spanish had proceeded on a shadowy claim made years before, and in February, 1864, built a large and handsome mission-house, called "St. Ignatius," near the village of Esowĕ, on the line of the path between Evangasimba and Ugobi. On May 6, Rev. George Paull's arrival on Corisco added a fifth to our missionary company. But on the 23d of May it was again reduced to four by the temporary return of Mr. Mackey to America.

After the birth of her Willie, on February 28, 1864, Mrs. Nassau kept a constant look-out on the shipping news for an early opportunity to return to Africa, her home, and her chosen work. Before her babe was three months old the arrival of the "Greyhound" at New York from Africa excited her hopes and plans for a passage by it.

MRS. NASSAU TO REV. W. H. CLARK.

1638 North 15th St., Philadelphia,
May 13, 1864.

My ship-letters per barque "Greyhound" came this morning, and I wish to make some inquiries immediately, although I expect to hear from you in a day or two. If possible, I wish to return by the "Greyhound." Does Captain Yates sail in her? Mrs. Preston wrote me from the ship that he would not unless his wife wished to accompany him. Please find out for me as soon as you can. If "our Captain Yates" does not go, who will? Will the Board send Mrs. Clemens by this opportunity?

Mrs. Preston made no complaints of the accommodations, and I presume I could get along if the vessel be considered sea-worthy.

I am much better than when you saw me, and do not like to lose a good opportunity.

Please let me know *right away* the first things you can find out. I am hoping to take the babe with me. Dr. Nassau leaves the final decision of the question with me, and I want to take the child. He will be eleven weeks old on Sunday.

Would the Board rather I should wait till something more definite is heard of the movements of the Spanish? . . .

This is a hurried letter, but you can let them read it at the Mission House. The "Benga Primer" came. I am much pleased with it. I am getting strong enough to have my teeth attended to now, which will be all that could delay me. I want to go if I am able.

MRS. NASSAU TO HER HUSBAND.

LAWRENCEVILLE, N. J.
HOME, Mond. night, May 30, '64.

Little Willie is asleep, asleep in his grandpa's cradle, and I will say a few words to you. A short letter must do you for this time, for I have been in a continued hurry and bustle for the last two weeks, and in two weeks more I may be on the "Greyhound" bound for Corisco. Baby and I are coming to you, . . . and I have engaged a woman to go with me. She is twenty-four,—a native of Sierra Leone,—and asks three dollars a week. I tried to get an older woman, but I could not. . . . The wages are high, but I may as well spend the money on our child as give it away.

Wait on the beach,—do not come off in the boat,—and wear a hat, that will look more *fatherly!* We talk a good deal to baby about going out to see his papa, and he seems much pleased with the prospect. . . . Bring my little colored children down to the beach,—I love them the more now. . . . The boxes you sent came the week before I came to Lawrenceville. If I had had your last letter, of March (which came May 28), I would have saved more than I did for Dr. Bishop. Will you not put up a box purposely for him, and have it ready to send by the "Greyhound?" I gave some to Mrs. Gallagher and Mrs. Boyd, some to Kate and Aunt

Margaretta.... Sister Bella will tell you of my visit here. It is like home. I love them all *so* much. Brother Joseph is at home, too, and I was so glad to see him.

I have bought a cradle for Willie, and will get a little carriage for him. I want to bring some things for our black children too.... God spare our little one's life to return to America! He is to be Aunt Lizzie's boy, with your consent, when we give him up....

... I was at Princeton to-day, and saw the door of your room in the Seminary. The students are all gone, so I was not able to invite any to go to Africa.... I was saddened at the thought of the Spanish being on Corisco. If we leave there, I think I do not vote for Gaboon. You said once you thought you could get along better with the colonists in Liberia; but, I want what you want, except Gaboon, or even that.

> "For my secret heart is taught the truth
>   That makes Thy children free;
> And a life of self-renouncing love
>   Is a life of liberty."

CHAPTER XI.

A MOTHER.—RETURN TO THE SCHOOL.

1864, 1865. At Sea. Corisco.

" Casting upon the common things of earth
A brightness, born and gone with infant mirth."

" Mother, with thine earnest eye
Ever following silently."

Uncertainty marked Mrs. Nassau's preparations for return to Africa by the "Greyhound" until within a few days of its sailing. Not an uncertainty in her intention, nor in readiness of baggage, but as to whether the small accommodations could admit her. There was room for only one more passenger, and Mrs. Clemens (whose going was still uncertain) had the precedence of right to it. Mrs. Nassau finally received word from the Mission House that she could not go. But in the very last days her former Corisco friend, Dr. Loomis, interested himself personally, vigorously, and even manually in inclosing from the ship's cabin an extemporaneous room, and a telegram summoned her joyfully to embark.

A happy company of returning and new missionaries that set sail in the "Greyhound" on June 16, 1864. Besides the captain, P. D. Yates, and his wife, there were, for the Lutheran mission in Liberia, Rev. Mr. and Mrs. Rice, and Mrs. Kistler, each with her infant; for the Episcopal mission at Cape Palmas, Rev. Thos. Burrows; for the Gaboon mission, Mrs. Rev. I. M. Preston; and for Corisco, Mrs. Clemens, Rev. Mr. and Mrs. De Heer, and Mrs. Nassau and babe and nurse.

MRS. NASSAU TO HER SISTER-IN-LAW, MISS M. E. NASSAU.

BARK "GREYHOUND," Aug. 23, 1864.
Tuesday, Off Guinea Coast.

We anchored off Monrovia Monday evening, July 25, and sent a few notes ashore to our friend, hoping to receive invitations to come off the next day, the anniversary of Liberian independence.

Mr. James (Hon. B. V. R. James) was up the St. Paul's River, but Mrs. James wrote a few kind words of welcome, and the most of our company decided to spend the day on land.

As it was a misty afternoon, the Kroomen did not meet us as far out as usual; but soon after we came in sight the canoes came steering towards us, full of more than half-naked savages. Several wore their shirt and large cloth in a bundle on top of their head, and came on deck almost nude. Except a little strip of cotton cloth, for the sake of decency, they had nothing to encumber them as they climbed up the ship's side, and presented themselves with a "How do, mammy?" to our new lady passengers. Mrs. Rice and Mrs. De Heer ran away at first, but soon returned to make acquaintance with some real Africans. After reaching the deck, some of the exquisites put on a shirt and large cloth, and paraded around conscious of their superiority.

Willie showed no fear, and was willing to go to any of them, which the other babies would not do at first. Finally, your aspiring nephew got hold of one of their big black fingers, and found it much more to his taste for biting on than his rubber ring. . . .

On Tuesday morning all went ashore but Mrs. Kistler, Mrs. Preston, and myself, and we enjoyed very much a quiet day on board, with more room to move around in than we had for more than five weeks. . . . As I was not on shore, I cannot tell you much about their great day; but all the company came back in fine spirits,—the new-comers delighted with their reception and entertainment. Mrs. Rice said, "Who would have expected to see such style on the coast of Africa?" . . . They went to the Representatives' Hall, and heard the orators of the day, and then divided for dinner.

The next day Mrs. Preston had one of her hard headaches, but the rest of us went off. Mrs. Clemens had not stayed ashore the first evening; she held Willie in her lap from the ship to the beach. It commenced to rain before we reached the shore, and we found the landing rough, too. One man jumped out and tried to hold the boat, while another caught up Mrs. Kistler and waded off to dry land with her. Her silk skirt got a wetting in salt water as a wave came up and carried us back to sea. It was some minutes before the waves subsided enough to let us come up to the beach again, and I feared Mrs. Kistler would worry about Harry; but, at the second or third trial, they landed us all. The rain was falling fast, and we all went up to one of the Kroo huts to wait awhile. The people crowded in, and Willie was passed around and praised by the natives. One woman, I think, wanted to let him nurse, but I pretended not to understand; not because she was black, but because I did not know how old her child might be. When the rain slackened a little, we started up the hilly, rocky, grassy path for Mr. James's. Monrovia streets are the worst I have seen in Liberia. (That is the first moral reflection; you can stop and study it at your leisure.)

About half-way up we met Mr. Crummell, a colored Episcopal clergyman, and on inquiring whether Mr. Kistler had been heard from, he said he had seen him but a few minutes before, and would bring him to us. On second thoughts he took Mrs.

Kistler with him to meet her husband, and the rest of us waited until they should return. Harry was in Mr. Burrowes's arms, and Willie was held by a three-quarter-grown Krooman. When the party returned, Mr. Kistler was introduced to each one before showing him his baby, and I said it was a shame to keep him waiting. Some one cried, "Let us see if he will know his own boy!" He looked first at Harry, who was quite near him, then said, "Let me see the other." After a look at Willie and a second at Harry, he stepped back, smiling, and said, "I cannot tell." That made us all laugh, and I called out, "Take the one with the black eyes;" another, "Take the biggest boy." . . . He ought to have known his own child, if he was accustomed to looking in the glass, for the youngster had his father's large, dark eyes. Mrs. Kistler has dark hair and eyes, too, but I thought he had half a notion to take Willie; perhaps because he was with a native, and he supposed that Mr. Burrowes was carrying his own boy. It was a trying position, I should judge; but he went through it very well. . . .

Now, I think I have kept you about as long in the path as we were from Kroo town up to the house. Mr. and Mrs. James met us very kindly, and both praised the baby, who would go to any one without seeming to know the difference between white and black. I do not suppose he does, either. They did not speak of any difference of color, as that is a subject I rarely heard mentioned in Liberia.... Anna, the little girl at Mrs. James's, was an orphan, having lost both her parents shortly after coming out to Liberia. She was almost white, and had soft pretty hair that curled as loosely as many white persons'. When we went ashore we would go first to Mr. James's.... When we went out, Anna often went along to carry the baby, and she was stopped every day by some one who called her to the door to get a look at the child....

Thursday, August 25.—We are anchored off Cape Coast this morning. We may be at Corisco in three weeks, but we were almost a week—over six days—in coming the four hundred miles from Cape Palmas here. We go next to Accra, then Fernando Po, then Corisco.

Mrs. Thompson is sea-sick so much that I have but little time to write. I keep Willie at night, dress and undress him, make his food, and feed him. Mrs. Preston occasionally washes him in the morning, because she likes to do it. If it were not for her I would get but little writing done, and she has sewed more for Willie than I have. When I get out some article to alter or cut out, or sew on, and have it well commenced, she will say, "Let me finish that, and you get something else ready."

On arrival at Monrovia the young colored woman, who had come with Mrs. Nassau from America under engagement to Corisco, left her service; but a faithful substitute was found in the person of a Liberian colonist, Mrs. Thompson.

Meanwhile in Corisco the coming of the "Greyhound" was anxiously expected, though Mrs. Nassau's presence on board was not known; the list of passengers and the announcement of the vessel's intended sailing having been forwarded while yet the question of obtaining passage was in abeyance. So it was startling when the mail came on September 1, and Mrs. McQueen opened for me the mail-bag, while I was in the confusion of some house repairs, and handed a letter from Mrs. Nassau written, on August 16, at Cape Palmas. There was some consternation, too; for vessels had been known to come in ten days from the cape; and, what if the new missionary company should come next day and find our house all in confusion! The instant determination to stay up all night and put the house in order was found unnecessary on reading the letter and finding that the vessel, instead of coming directly to Corisco, was to go up into the Bight of Benin, and therefore could not reach Corisco until the last of the month. Yet thenceforth daily the horizon was scanned to see the approach of anything like a ship. And when, towards the close of the month, Consul May and

Rev. I. M. Preston came from Gaboon with the expectation of finding Mrs. Preston already at Corisco, we felt that interests were concentrating on the little island and that joy was imminent.

By six o'clock, sunrise of Sabbath morning, September 25, Mrs. McQueen's early eye discovered a vessel at anchor dressed out in flags that meant joy; and the intensity of that joy for the half-frantic school-children was that Mrs. Nassau was there. There was anxious looking in that bright tropic Sabbath morning light to see whether the ship's two boats were being lowered, as it was assumed that the ship's company would be coming ashore to church. And there was hesitation, on the high standard of Sabbath observance that we had set the natives, whether the apparently unnecessary act of getting out our own boat simply for the gratification of a welcome would not be misunderstood, and be afterward cast up to the church-session by Sabbath transgressors. Missionary lives that preach by a consistency to principle more than by utterances of truths often have to make sacrifices of feeling uncalled for in Christian lands. While thus hesitating, some natives said, "Surely, you will send off a boat. We have eyes, and can see differences."

The boat was launched and Consul May and Mr. Preston went off to the ship, while I arranged for the usual morning services at Evangasimba,—

Mr. Paull having gone to his usual duty of a preaching service on the other side of the island,—and Mrs. McQueen dressed the girls for church.

The timely arrival of our mission boat at the ship's side gave all its company an opportunity to land. What a goodly company it was! What a happy Sabbath day! Restful after the separations of fourteen months, and after the life on shipboard wearying in its kindest phase.

The Evangasimba first bell for church was ringing as the three boats landed each its quartette of foreign faces: Mrs. Nassau and babe and nurse; Mr. and Mrs. De Heer; Mr. and Mrs. Preston; Mrs. Clemens, Consul May, Captain and Mrs. Yates, and a Rev. Mr. Heigart from Liberia on his way to America. Glad welcomes,—introductions,—hearts whose joy words did not express, and so lips were dumb,—faces, the occupancy of whose features was disputed by happy smiles and as happy tears. And all around a surging crowd of natives whose hands sought in their rude welcome each disengaged white hand. And so the company was escorted to Mrs. Mackey's on the top of the hill, and had a little respite from the native crowd, until the second bell rang for service in the bamboo church. The grateful thanks of that day made its low, unadorned walls as lovely to the Great Giver and Receiver as was ever any earthly Beth-el.

After church the people rather broke in on us, at the Maluku house, to see the baby, whom, while distant and "unseen," they had named *Ayŏnwŏ*. He was only the fourth white baby they had seen on the island; and they crowded the church, a week later on communion Sabbath, to see his baptism by Rev. George Paull.

So general had been the opinion that residence in Africa was necessarily fatal to infant life, that but few of our missionaries had attempted a test of the question, and had either separated from their children or retired from our work. To make my experiment successful I had, in anticipation of my babe's coming, gathered three goats. One of them had kidded about a week before the ship came, so that he had food ready. I had a confidence that God would not let the winds bring the ship to Corisco before "Annunciata" had borne her kid. So when I went to the enclosure every day and saw no kid, I knew no ship would come that day. And when little Esongi came breathless to announce a kid, with eyes that spake almost as plainly as the lips that, stumbling over the English name, said, "*Anunnisiata a jandi meyana*," the promise was near. And just when the kid could spare part of its dam's milk the babe came for his share. And we said, Jehovah-jireh.

Dr. Loomis had put a goat on board at New York, that was very useful across the ocean, until after passing Cape Palmas, when, in its search for fresh provisions, it got hold of some precious lily bulbs of Mrs. Clemens and choked itself.

MRS. NASSAU TO MISS J. W. BAIRD.

CORISCO, W. A., Oct. 14, 1864.

Your kind letter was received in America some eight or nine months ago, and my reasons for not answering more promptly ought to and shall be given. A long illness, a baby that keeps up almost perpetual motion, preparations for and a journey to Africa accompanied by said baby. And now, thanks to a kind Father's care, I am back again in my Corisco home; and though my strength is not much to boast of, I trust I shall be able to fulfill that which is allotted.

The "Greyhound" anchored off Corisco on a Sabbath morning, and we came ashore in time for church; but the children were not on the beach to welcome us, as they would have been another day. I was very glad to see my little girls again, and still more pleased with their improvement during my absence. They are delighted with the baby, and say they must not be angry with him for anything, as he is "the child of our mother." That is the term for *our* brother or sister; for the men here have so many wives that a "father's child" may only be a half-brother or sister.

Jennie Baird is the one I call on when the nurse is busy, and I want a child to take Willie for a short time. She is now one of the older girls; but that does not prove her to be very large, as almost all are small,—none are over twelve. Jennie is about eleven (or under); very quiet, gentle, and useful; intelligent for her age, but too modest to make much of a show. She is not in the habit of making smart speeches, or performing any unusual labors that might help to fill up a letter and make it interesting, but she is growing up to be a great dependence. Yesterday, when I asked what word I should send you from her, she could only think of "*Mbolo*," their usual salutation; but, when one of the others suggested that she should ask for a present, she indignantly refused.

Last Saturday, when we were all very busy getting some changes made, and trying to bring some order out of the confusion, Jennie took a great deal of care of Willie, and put him to sleep twice. My nurse, Mrs. Thompson, of Monrovia, was very bad with "a misery in her back," and unable to do anything; so it was necessity more than choice that left the baby with one of the children so much. . . .

The Corisco band was again large enough for companionship. The vacancy at Alongo filled by Mr. and Mrs. De Heer. Mrs. Clemens, a member of the Maluku household, and sharing equally with Mrs. McQueen in the instruction and care of the girls. And the Spanish Padres Garcia and Torre, with whom we occasionally exchanged visits, added two to the white faces to be met on island paths.

The admirable arrangement of dividing the work of the girl's school among three ladies made the assistance, or even presence, of a male missionary almost unnecessary. No one felt tied as in a tread-mill. If there was sickness, there were kind interchanges of aid; if all were well, some one or other of the ladies had time for village visitations among the women. And I being thus relieved almost entirely from care of the school, there was time for translations and other writing and teaching.

In such companionship each aroused the other from the depression which isolation induces, and which strips of the energy necessary to move out of a narrow routine into healthful change or even exercise.

Excursions for health and exercise were made. The gratification of the school-girls, who would weary of too long restraint, was always a primary object. Mrs. Nassau's cheerful spirit entered zealously into plans for the children who, though no longer under special instruction, were still under her care. In such excursions were mingled, with the pleasure for our pupils, the profit that natural sciences could afford our tastes by discovery of new specimens in the world of botany or conchology that lay so near us.

Sometimes the trip would be on a narrow, winding foot-path, with the Lagas pony " Charley," and hammocks on men's shoulders, to a little lake, Boldwĕ, two miles distant, in the centre of the island, that empties itself by two small streams into the sea. Every alternate year the natives in the cool-dry season, when the water was low, would erect a dam across the middle of the pond, and bail from one side into the other, catching what fish were left crowded into the bottom of the pool. The intervening year the almost exterminated fish were permitted to spawn again.

Sometimes the excursion was with horse and hammock and hand-cart, along the beach for four miles, passing Ugobi on the south end and across Lĕmbwĕ Creek around to the Elwĕ prairie, on the east side of the island. There every two weeks, after each "spring" tide, enormous quantities of shells, principally bivalves, were thrown up from the sea.

The eye was refreshed by the view towards the east: distant twelve miles northeast, the small trade-islands Elobi; fifteen miles due east, the country of a mainland tribe, Mbiko; distant eighteen miles southeast, the wide estuary of the mouth of the Munda River; and, dotting the bay to the south, several small islands.

Sometimes the excursion (chosen with reference rather to missionaries than to pupils) was to Alongo school, where the day was always a refreshing one for Mrs. Nassau, as, with her friend, Mrs. De Heer, she could look with longing eye north to the mainland beyond Cape St. John; or from Alongo promontory west on the wide sea, restful even when restless, and plan—and plan—and plan, even for plans that might never be accomplished, but which were pleasant to plan, just because they were plans. But the girls felt that the privilege of showing out their best dresses and of enjoying the pictures and amusing games their kind hosts provided, was somewhat marred by the consciousness that those same dresses were for exhibition, and not for romping.

Sometimes the excursion was to the islet Leva, one mile distant, southwest from the Evangasimba beach. One such "day at Leva" was noticeably happy, marked by the return from America of Rev. J. L. Mackey, on Wednesday, December 14. Not *any* day will suit for Leva. Of the *seasons*, the rainy was preferable, because of the ocean being warmer for the children in their diving. The *week* must be selected with reference to the state of the moon, and a spring tide; the *day* must be chosen to suit the ebb and flow, so that we could go there with the ebb, be at the island the six hours that its sand-banks were bare, and return with the flow, and have those intervening six hours occur about mid-day, for convenient going and returning to our households.

All the paraphernalia of a picnic were prepared, a reliable crew of men, a few boys for messengers, hatchet, axe, and cutlasses for clearing a path through dense, wet grass and thickets of the few acres on the top of the isle, dry fuel for kindling, a few boards for dry seats, and shawls and blankets for covering from sudden showers, umbrellas for the sun, the simplest of dress, a few pans, etc.

The Mission House was locked, and one man left on guard. What a motley company gathered on the beach!—missionaries, in not their finest clothes, and school-children, in positively their oldest and most ragged; the former prepared for wet, and the latter intending to seek it.

In the mission gig, the little "Draper," and its three oars, entered Mr. Paull, Mrs. Clemens, Mrs. McQueen, Mrs. Nassau and babe, and a few pupils. In a large Cape Lopez canoe, with four paddles, myself and twenty-two children.

Out between the reefs, and over the smooth sea, looking down into its shallows to see the sunlight shining on the ocean vegetation; miniature trees in the sea-weed, with apparent flowers and fruit of endless variety; fish darting from the shadows, or lying on the pebbly bottom, among the colored stones and shells.

Landed at the island, the girls dispersed along the reefs to dive for shell-fish, *konongo* (a certain conch gathered in great quantities); the boys whistled away with "Rover" to beat the thickets for iguanas or squirrels; Mrs. McQueen and Mrs. Clemens strolled on the long sand-bars for fresh shells; Mr. Paull started off in the "Draper" for a Spanish steamer, on which he suspected Mr. Mackey might be. With the cutlasses a path was opened to the top of the island, where Mrs. Nassau and a few of the little girls too small for company with the divers followed to an open space under a large tree, whose gnarled roots served as seats, where the cool breeze swept in from the sea, and where baby, safe from ants, could creep on the shawl spread out on the ground. At one side a bush spread its branches arbor-like, covered with white, star-like flowers, odorous as tuberoses.

Match, candle, pine-knots, and dead branches soon made two blazing fires, at one of which the children, pale and cold from their prolonged diving, could bring back their color, and put on the dry, extra dress they had brought, and where they could eat a portion of their fish with the cassava that had been brought as their lunch. At the other fire, when Mr. Paull returned with the news that he had just landed Mr. Mackey at Evangasimba, and when the ladies returned with their treasures of conchology, we had shell-fish, brought by the vanguard of the returning children, roasted in the fire on the shell and eaten with salt and fresh native Cayenne pepper-pods, plantains roasted in ashes, chicken browned on two primitive sticks before the fire, a fish just dripping from the sea and fried on an axe-helve, sandwiches, pine-apples, chocolate, and canned peaches (this last a gift from America, and kept for special occasions). Hardware had been forgotten, and so, having only two knives, three plates, one cup, one tumbler, one mug, one tin, the children were imitated, and fingers did duty.

When the risen tide bade return, a happy (some of the children a tired and all of them a dirty) company filed past Evangasimba, stopping to find the capping of the day's pleasure in the welcome of a missionary brother to his work, to which he had returned, though in health far from satisfactory.

The smallpox, coming from the upper coasts, had been raging on the entire West Coast during 1864. It reached the Gaboon, where there was no vaccine matter. Finally the French authorities obtained some from Calabar. When our mail-boatmen went to Gaboon, in November, Rev. Wm. Walker vaccinated them, and from them was obtained lymph for Corisco. All the school-children were required to be vaccinated; and daily, for more than two weeks, ten or fifteen villagers came voluntarily for the operation. No cases originated on the island; and the disease did not spread from the few that were brought there, for they were isolated by their people in huts in the forest near the sea, where food was carried them, and where they bathed themselves alternately in the cold ocean and in water heated in the kettle over the fire in their hut. They recovered.

MRS. NASSAU TO HER AUNT MISS M. A. LATTA.

Corisco, W. A., Dec. 16, 1864.

The people are here this morning, as they are every day, asking to be vaccinated, and Dr. Nassau is busy with them while I write. They say the smallpox is on the island; and I suppose it is,— on the other side, some four miles distant. It was at Fernando Po when we stopped there, in September; but I would not write you about it until we could have Willie vaccinated. The people have been dying over at one of the rivers, and at Gaboon, and it is only within the last month that vaccine matter has reached us. Willie was vaccinated a week ago, and his arm is a little sore; but it does not seem to trouble him. We thought, at first, it would not take. . . . He is getting along very nicely; and I want some shoes for him. . . . He is growing into those I bought for him, as large as they looked. . . . Mrs. Thompson says that Willie does not think our pantry-boy is neat enough, and so he goes to help him clean out the cupboard. . . . He still loves to be washed, if you don't try to take the dirt off his face. . . . Yesterday I put a chair on its side across the parlor door to keep him out of the reception-room with his clean frock. What do you think he did? Crept between the feet of the chair up towards the seat, then turned and got out between the rungs. He can get up off the floor and stand alone; but "he spreads out as if he were going to fly like a bird," as Mrs. Thompson says, and so he cannot stand long. . . .

Mainland work enlisted Mr. Paull's energy, as much as it did Mrs. Nassau's. He and the other member of the mainland committee made a journey to the mouth of the Bonita River on December 23, 1864, and spent all the next day, Saturday, in tramping along the beach on the north bank, and through the forest and over the prairie, looking for a site for a prospective station. The object of the journey was not explained to the curiously-eyeing natives; but they suspected it, especially as they saw the committee's eyes rest, with satisfaction, on the cove at Mbâdĕ Point. We called the spot "Benita," as that was the name which traders and natives gave the region bordering on the river. On returning to Corisco, Mr. Paull's urgency was assented to; and Mrs. Nassau's hopes were deferred by yielding a prior right which the Board's permission had given, and on January 4, 1865, Mr. Paull was appointed to Benita and the entire charge of its adjacent work. Mr. Clark's expected return to Corisco made this disposition of force possible; but the scarcity of money in the treasury, and of food in the storehouse, would have made it difficult for Mrs. Nassau, with her babe, to have gone to that work just at that time.

MRS. NASSAU TO MRS. REV. W. H. CLARK.

Corisco, West Africa,
Jan. 18, 1865.

It is a long, long time since I have written you anything, although I should have written you from the coast, if I had not thought Mrs. Clemens would give all needful information about all the babies. I ought to have remembered that none of them were hers; also, that she was probably not as much interested in the bringing of babies to Africa as I suppose you and I are.

I do not regret having brought Willie. . . . Are you bringing Walter and Anna? Oh, if you are, I hope they may both keep well. You will feel encouraged if you find Mr. Hoffman's children well at Cape Palmas, and hear that Willie has been (not well all the time) getting along very nicely.

Mr. Paull started this morning for the mainland,

but who goes next we cannot tell. On account of his new house, Mr. De Heer has permission before us now. . . . I am quite anxious to go, but it would seem too bad to leave Corisco when you and the children get back. Mr. Mackey is not at all strong, and everything stands as it is for the present, awaiting Mr. Clark's coming, and the pointings of Providence.

A second priest is on the island, but I have not seen him yet. The first has been very friendly, but either his friendliness or his tomatoes have given out.

Do not follow our example and borrow of the captain (any more than you can't help), hoping to get gold here to repay. If Mr. Clark gets stores they can be paid; but gold, for personal expenses, rates as in America. If Mr. Mackey has not written, the mission want all the rice and sugar Mr. Clark can buy; and indeed we are anxious to have some at less than it costs in America. White sugar is twenty-eight cents per pound, and the new rice thirteen cents. Butter nine dollars a keg. Ham twenty-six cents, and chickens very scarce. There is plenty of coffee on hand. Get cleaned rice if you can; and if you want to be sure, look at the whole batch and not at the sample. Mrs. Thompson says Cape Palmas would be the best place for cleaned rice, but it might be higher there than at some of the towns intermediate to Monrovia. . . .

Tell Mrs. Hoffman Willie is not fat, but full of mischief. The nurse pulled a young lizard out of his mouth one day,—the kitten having caught one for him and one for herself. . . .

MRS. NASSAU TO MISS M. E. NASSAU.

Corisco, West Africa,
Wed. night, Jan. 18, 1865.

To begin with,—I am certain I do not owe you a letter; but I do not see that that makes any difference if I have anything to say.

On questioning Willie's papa, after the completion of the first sentence, I find, what I might have suspected, that you get very little knowledge of baby through his letters. Isn't that too bad? "Well," he says "that everybody knows th—" (there! Hamill spoiled that letter) "all babies creep, and cut teeth, and begin to walk, and he doesn't know how to go into ecstasies over such things." Still he seems to think Willie is a tolerably fine child, and "has a very good head." . . . He has been sick; but is very patient and generally playful when awake. The few days that he was most troublesome he did not cry much, but always clung very close to me; and as Mrs. Thompson was sick, too, I had plenty to do. The silver lining of that cloud was that I found out how well I could get along even in a great emergency; neither do I forget who makes silver linings to all clouds. . . .

The Lord tried faith. Smallpox continued on the island in sporadic cases, interfering with our operations among the people. Famine came. Irregularity in the seasons made failure in the sequence of native gardens, so that in that land of fertility there actually was famine. The Lord gave us literally day by day the "daily" bread for the school-children,—each night finishing what was bought with greatest effort from the entire island; so that the number of pupils at the school had to be reduced by half. The time gained from the reduced school work was occupied by the ladies among the women in the villages. The costly price of our foreign food in the mission storehouse would have prevented its being used for the school-children unless actually to save life; and of that foreign food there was very little even for ourselves. Sickness came. Early in March, Mrs. Nassau had a severe fever, so that Willie had to be weaned, and there was no proper substitute to be found in the scanty mission supplies. Death came. Mr. Paull was stricken at Benita with malignant fever on Monday, April 24, came to Corisco on the 28th, and died on Sabbath morning, May 14. The arrival of Mr. and Mrs. Clark, with their little children Walter and Anna, and their Liberian nurse Louisa, and goodly supplies by the "Greyhound" on May 18, brought *relief* but no *help* for us. For he had at once to step into Mr. Mackey's work at Evangasimba; and the good food came too late for our infant's too-hardly-rationed frame, and we felt it necessary for him to go by the "Greyhound" in company of Mr. and Mrs. Mackey and Mrs. McQueen on their final return to America, on Saturday night, June 3.

MRS. NASSAU TO MISS M. E. NASSAU.

Corisco, W. A.,
Monday night, June 19, 1865.

This is my last letter for this mail, excepting a note to Gaboon; and I am not sure that note will be written, for to-morrow is washing-day; and I am sleepy.

Mrs. Clemens is boarding with her sister at Evangasimba, and I have charge of girls out of school hours and in the evening. I have changed the girls' washing-day to Tuesday, and the water is all brought the night before, which makes far less noise and confusion than we had formerly. With Mrs. Thompson's assistance about the house my duties are far from arduous. Hamill and I eat our meals alone together for the first time since our marriage. It would be more pleasant if we could have baby Willie to make a third at meal-time; but we get along without him better than you might suppose. To be sure we miss him every day and almost every hour of the day, but there is enough to do to keep hands and often thoughts engaged; and then we know we acted as God's providence seemed to direct.

My little Benga children are a comfort to me, although they cannot take up much of the vacant space in my heart. I always try to think cheerfully of our absent little one, and I parted from him on the beach the evening his father took him on board without a tear-drop. Mrs. Thompson went on board too, but I brought my colored family back to the house to get their supper. Hamill had the key in his pocket, and I was wondering what we should do for the girls' *mevândâ*, when one of them came to tell me that there was some in the boys' house, which they had been sent out to buy for the next day. "How providential," I thought, and I told them to take it, thinking what was in the house would do as well for the next day—Sabbath. The providence did not appear quite so striking when Hamill came back, and found that I had given to the girls the food which the boys had been all afternoon hunting for themselves—their Sabbath supply. The girls were to have had plantains for supper; but it did not make any difference, for we had plantains enough to feed the boys and girls the next day. The boys did not care, for they prefer plantains.

A few hours after all had gone off to the ship,

our mail came from Gaboon. I found from my letters that Uncle William would probably go South the coming winter; and Hamill does not want Willie down there. So the next question is, Will Aunt Lizzie take the boy? . . . I would be glad to have my little bird find so pleasant a home. . . . Poor Mr. Paull! or rather, poor those who remain behind! We did depend on him so much to carry forward the work on the mainland; and now he is gone. Hamill will ask permission, at the next mission-meeting, to go to Benita; and it is barely possible we may get off in August. . . . I am anxious to go, and yet I have never been more pleasantly situated on Corisco. . . .

MRS. NASSAU TO HER SISTER-IN-LAW, MISS I. A. NASSAU.

Corisco, West Africa,
Tues., June 20, 1865.

You are so good in writing us every month, and giving us so many items of interest, that I am sorry to see an envelope go without a line to you. If baby were here, however, the probabilities are that I would scarcely get a letter of tolerable length written to my aunts.

It is washing morning, and I am seated with my writing on a small platform under the house, while at the same time I am directing the children about under-garments, and dresses, soap and water, etc.

... The fruits, spices, and extracts, all came in fine order, and we opened two jars of the whole peaches the day before the ship left, when all the missionaries and ship's company dined here. . . .

MRS. NASSAU TO THE MISSES M. AND M. A. LATTA.

CORISCO, WEST AFRICA,
Mond., July 17, 1865.

... Perhaps the "Greyhound" may have a long voyage; in which case we cannot hear from the little traveler until the 1st of November.

I wonder where you all are during this warm weather of July, and where you expect the winter to find you?

We have had the coldest weather I ever felt on Corisco since the beginning of this dry season, and have had a fire almost every day this month. Sometimes morning and evening, and occasionally a fire kept up throughout the day. I put on last week the nice, warm, long-sleeved flannels sent out two years ago. They are a great comfort now, although during the heat of the rainy season I sometimes wondered why I had ordered such warm ones. I have not cut an inch off the sleeves. But the sun has come out so brightly this afternoon that I feel fully warm enough.

The dark wrapper that was fitted and nearly finished in Philadelphia was completed for me by

Mrs. McQueen before she left. I wear it to church almost every Sabbath, and find it very convenient to slip on when any stranger calls unexpectedly. I suppose it must make me look very youthful, for one of the old captains reported at Elobi that Mrs. Nassau was about twenty, and Mrs. De Heer about nineteen or twenty. I was advising a young sprig of a fellow to go back to England, and said his parents ought to keep him there, that he was too young for Africa. He thought himself as old as I was. And that I contradicted by a statement of my years, when he told me what Captain H—— had said. Mrs. De Heer and I both agreed that they were poor judges of ages at Elobi, and that the young chap was wanting in his upper story. But all the rest had the same opinion of him. . . . Mrs. Ogden wrote that she hoped to be in Corisco before the end of the year, and it is possible she may be coming on the "Thomas Pope;" but we have heard nothing that is certain. I do hope she will come.

My health is very good, but Mrs. Clemens is not strong, or at least she is far from well. Still, even when well, I am not much stronger than Mrs. Clemens partly sick, and if it were not for Mrs. Thompson I could not get along as easily as I do. I have all the care of the children out of school and on the Sabbath, and have not whipped one since Mrs. Clemens left. I spanked one yesterday for begging a very little girl to divide her plantain with her,—the one I spanked is a great beggar,—but I fear I hurt my hand as much as the part to which it was applied.

We have two new children—little bits of things. The smallest has taken a great fancy to me, but thinks she is not able to love her mother too. She will soon get over that, and be as fond of town as any of them. Mrs. Clemens comes up once a day for three hours; four afternoons she teaches sewing, one morning and one afternoon she teaches school. . . .

Tuesday afternoon, July 18.— . . . Another new scholar came to-day, and she makes the sixteenth on the premises; two are in town sick, who will be returned as soon as they are well. The new arrival seems to be about eight or nine,—a very respectable age to commence her training.

Several months ago Mrs. Clemens brought from Magani town a little girl that used to live with her at Alongo; and when she was expecting to go to Evangasimba, she promised the child, Esongi, that she should go, too. When Mr. and Mrs. Clark came they were so opposed to having girls, that Mrs. Clemens took with her only Maria, a child Mr. Clemens had redeemed from being put to death as a witch. Esongi was quite troublesome after Mrs. Clemens left, until she found she was certainly to remain with us; and from that time she was as pleasant as any of them. When she went to town in vacation she did not return at the proper time; and after a couple of weeks had passed Dr. Nassau went to see her father. He said the child should come back,—he did not want her in town, —and when we got her again we must keep her all the time. She came that evening, Saturday, and was reproved in the presence of the others for not coming back. (She had told the other children, when vacation came, that she meant to stay in town, because "Mamma Clemens had left her here.") Monday morning Esongi ran away, and told in town that she had been "whipped" here. Hamill sent word to her father to keep his child or return her, just as he pleased; but, if she came back, she must come that very day. The mother brought her in the afternoon, with a curious story for excuse : " White people and Benga people are different. If a person living at one place goes to another place to take something belonging to her, Benga people call it 'going to get something,' but white people call it 'running away.'" . . . I do not believe she will give any more trouble, now that she sees her father is on our side. She is really a nice child.

Now that Willie is away, you see I must write about my colored children. . . .

MRS. NASSAU TO MISS M. E. NASSAU.

Corisco, W. A.,
July 18, 1865, Tuesday night.

Our school is increasing; and this is wash-day; so, to-night I am tired, for it seemed to me that the children had more trouble than usual in getting the dirt out of their garments. . . . Hamill and I sent invitations to a young missionary couple, who are visiting at Gaboon, to come up to Corisco in the mail-boat; but we cannot get answers until the boat returns with them or their regrets. The room which Mrs. Clemens occupied we have now for a spare-room, but its only furniture is a bedstead and mattress, and a large pine wardrobe containing the children's clothes. We have not been able to get mats yet, and shall take up the carpet from our room, to put it down temporarily. A semi-circular board can be screwed up for a washstand, and curtained around, and a bureau from the dining-room, where we have two. Mr. and Mrs. Edgerley are Scotch missionaries from Calabar, both in delicate health. Mrs. Walker says they are charming.

The dresses of the Lawrenceville box have not all been given out. It is very rarely, if ever, that the children have any rips to mend in them; but, of course, they will wear out in time. The little plain-bordered gingham dresses for small children are the prettiest-fitting, to my eye; but the colors of the pink gingham are the most admired. . . . I am writing on the supposition that Willie is to be with you; still, everything is uncertain. It is a month and a half since he left, and it will be two or three months before we can hear; but time passes quickly in Africa. . . .

MRS. NASSAU TO THE REV. W. W. LATTA.

Corisco, W. A., July 18, 1865.

It is decided that we do not go to the mainland for the present, but Dr. Nassau hopes that we may get off in the "middle dries," next January. If more help arrives by that time, I suppose we may, but a slight fever of Mr. De Heer, and a dangerous one of Mr. Clark, seemed to prove that the mission could not do without my husband's presence just now. It was a great disappointment to us both, for as our own health is pretty good now, we wanted to make a beginning before the rains should commence.

Have you heard anything of Mrs. Thompson's husband yet? It would be a satisfaction even to hear that he is dead, as she has had no letters for four years. I think, too, she has some notion of marrying on her return to Monrovia, as she has had several offers. I suppose there is scarcely another woman in Liberia who would not have been married before this if in her circumstances. The legislature of that Republic divorced several whose husbands were in America, and who they knew were living, after a very short separation. Divorces have been very frequent there; but I hear that more stringent laws have been made lately. One physician in Monrovia courted the wife of another man while his own wife, a lovely Christian, was on her sick-bed. When his wife died, he supplied the other woman with money to procure a divorce from her husband, and in a week after the divorce was granted they were married. She was a member of the Presbyterian church, but they had the grace to turn her out. . . . Dr. Loomis sent by the "Greyhound" some Roman candles, fire-crackers, and torpedoes, and Fourth of July night we had a grand (?) display of fire-works. The people had never seen anything of the kind before, and were considerably astonished, as well as some frightened. The torpedoes gave about as much amusement as anything. We made some fire-balls here, and, although they went out every few seconds, the boys would run and pitch them, screaming with delight. . . .

MRS. NASSAU TO MISS J. W. BAIRD.

CORISCO, W. A., Aug. 18, 1865.

We have no Jennie Baird in school of whom to write to you, for the second has followed—or has been made to follow—in the footsteps of her predecessor, and is at present the little wife of a polygamist. And the next pretty child we may select to bear a name, respected by us all, might turn out just the same for aught that we can tell.

Jennie did not want to go, and Mrs. Clemens told the man that the child could not love him.

He answered, "She would love him now as a father, and after she became a woman she would love him as a husband." (I hope none of your young friends marry with the expectation of learning to love their husbands after marriage.) Now I know you will be disappointed, and the young ladies, too,—so are we,—for the child was one of the nicest in the school; had not a single prominent fault I can recall. If we change our plan, and take an ugly, stupid one, it might be just the same; for a one-eyed, dull scholar, who lately left us, we understand, was engaged to a man with several wives. Some persons think the girls' school a very unpromising field of labor; but I suppose their tuition is included in the great command as much as any.

Although I like this school very much, there is one station to which Dr. Nassau and I are very anxious to be sent, that is Bonita, the place occupied by Mr. Paull. But we must stay on Corisco until other help comes, and we hear of none to join us.

Was not Mr. Paull's death a great shock to you

all? It was a heavy stroke to all our little band, for he seemed to be doing so useful a work and doing it so nobly. We felt it *must* not be, that God surely would not take him; but He who chastens knows best for us all, and He chastens in love. We cannot always see that, and yet in our hearts as Christians we believe it. He was my husband's dearest friend in the mission-field.

Your letter came while Mr. Paull lay ill, and I felt as though I wanted to answer it immediately; but we were busy then, and were expecting every week the ship that would take three of our number to America, and with them our dear little boy....

Can you not try to persuade some of your student friends that it is their duty to come to Africa? I believe some gentlemen hesitate because they think the climate so fatal to ladies; but the ladies themselves have courage enough.... My little Willie had occasional fevers, but his severest illness was caused by convulsions in teething.... Please do not give up our Corisco girls yet, and may God bless your labors of love.

MRS. NASSAU TO MISS M. E. NASSAU.

CORISCO, W. A., Sept. 18, 1865.

I have a letter ready for sister Lizzie, of Warsaw, and I am sure after reading it she will not be so much afraid of writing to missionaries as she professed herself in a letter received a couple of months ago. . . . We intend giving our children two weeks' vacation instead of one, and the vacation begins next week. If we get permission to go to Benita, the girls will not be back again, except a few of the larger ones, to help us get things in order preparatory to starting. Indeed, though, I do not see much use in clearing up floors for the rats to scamper over.

Mrs. Clemens thinks herself unable to take charge of this station alone. She went to Gaboon last week in company with Mr. and Mrs. Bushnell, who had been visiting on Corisco. I trust she may return with improved health, for she was looking very badly, and has a troublesome cough. The cold was taken just before leaving America, and has never been cured. In her absence I attend to all her duties, so far as relates to the girls' school. She has only the sewing now, and teaches two half-days in the week. I get along a great deal better than I expected; but she cut out most of the work before she left. I have told the children they should not go to their homes until all the sewing is done, so they are working very industriously. . . . And kiss for me my baby boy.

The next three weeks were busy, crowded weeks. The school-children were given their vacation the next Monday, September 25, and were not recalled for another session. It proved to be the beginning of the final abandonment of the school. On the 26th, Mrs. Nassau accompanied me on a business boat-trip to Elobi Islands, taking that opportunity of saying good-by to them on what was her first visit there, and returned on the 27th. The 28th was occupied by a good-by visit to her friend Mrs. De Heer, at Alongo. Then came the gathering of native church members on Friday the 29th, for the preparatory services, and the communion Sabbath, October 1. And after the annual meeting, on Wednesday, October 4, there were two weeks of packing, that kept us from grieving too much over the destruction of a home that had been intensely happy, and at times intensely sad, and which we would have rejoiced to have seen saved from the ruin that our going brought on it.

The last acts of putting to rights and under lock and key were done at a weary hour of ten at night of October 16, 1865, at the close of a weary day of farewells. The children, weeping to part with a teacher to whom they had fondly clung, had scattered to their heathen homes; and the Maluku school was closed.

"Content, nay glad, to toil and climb, though oftentimes oppressed,
 Since she was in the path that led to victory and rest."

CHAPTER XII.

PIONEERING.

1865, 1866. Bonita.

"When late at night my rest I take,
When early in the morn I wake,
Halting or on my way;
In hours of weakness or in bonds,
When vexed with fears my heart desponds,
His promise is my stay."

WHILE awaiting the annual Mission-meeting of October, 1865, to obtain formal permission to assume Mr. Paull's work at the Bonita River, final assent to which had been given by the other two members of the mission in September, preparations were being quietly made for "the journey to Kombe." But about it,—until information could publicly be given to the Corisco natives,—instead of much talking there was a good deal of writing and thinking.

Mrs. Nassau thus thinking, and writing to America on September 18, said,—

"This is gardening-time, but Hamill is not doing anything towards the raising of vegetables at Maluku this year. All our thoughts and plans go forward to Bonita; and to-night Hamill planted some orange-seeds in little boxes to take up with us. Instead of taking the seeds out as usual, he cut the orange into four or five pieces, and buried all beneath the earth.

"We will not have much of a garden on the mainland the first year, as there will not be much time to attend to it. I am promised, though, an occasional monkey-steak; and, when I have tasted one, will send you word whether they are as palatable as report says. Mr. Preston, I believe, has eaten them; and, once, a still stronger dish. He and another missionary were dining with a native chief, and, being very hungry, partook largely of some kind of 'fish,' but the chief could not tell its English name. The meat was so mixed up with some other article that it was impossible to distinguish any parts; but, after the meal was over, their host took out the two visitors and pointed to some tadpoles in a pond, as the *fish* they had partaken of.

" Mr. and Mrs. Preston know something of what privations are in missionary life. They once lived for two weeks on parched corn, she told us on the 'Greyhound.' Mr. De Heer said, 'That was noble, Mrs. Preston.' But she laughingly replied, 'There isn't anything noble in it, Mr. De Heer; we couldn't get anything else, or we wouldn't have done it.'

" Leopards, elephants, and deer are plentiful on

the mainland,—at all events, not scarce. One of our young men frightened Mrs. Thompson by telling her the leopards walked around in flocks, like sheep. I told her that I didn't believe it; but, as Hamill reminded me that 'flocks' of sheep here usually numbered but three or four, I suppose it is very possible. The Gaboon missionaries never go out of the house after dark without a light; and we shall have to use the same precaution,—that is all.

"For my part, I stand more in dread of centipedes than of leopards; and white ants will probably give us more trouble than either."

Mrs. Nassau's journey to her new and mainland home was made on October 17, across Corisco Bay, seventeen miles north to Cape St. John, and thence thirty-six miles farther, following the line of the coast, to the Bonita River. Mr. Paull's house stood on a bluff of almost pure sand, on the north side of the river, just at its mouth, the Point Mbâdĕ of the bluff having a beautiful cove of the river on one side, a few hundred feet from the front of the house, and the ocean in the rear a few hundred yards. On the arc of the cove were native villages, Upwanjo; near by, northward, Haia; two miles farther, Paka, the seat of "King" Mango; and five miles, Meduma. Two and a half miles southward, across the river, at Mbini Point, was the trading-house of a young English clerk, an agent,

MBÁDE POINT, BONITA RIVER.

or "factor," and, therefore, it is called a "factory." Four miles across, on the coast, toward the southwest, were two other factories, an English and a Spanish. These three foreigners, with one living twenty-three miles north at Bata, were our nearest white neighbors short of Corisco, distant fifty-two miles.

After a week of confusion in her first entrance to her new home, Mrs. Nassau, writing on Monday, October 23, describes to her uncle and aunts her journey thither:—

"I closed my last letter to you a week ago to-day; and the next morning, Tuesday, October 17, we started for the Bonita.

"We had packed up all our last things after breakfast, Monday morning, and took the rest of our meals at Evangasimba, sleeping there the last night of our stay on Corisco. It was a great comfort to me that Anna Clark was better before we left; her fever seemed very persistent, but finally yielded to quinine. She is a dear little baby, and was growing so nicely before her teeth brought on such a severe fever; of course, Africa made it worse than it would otherwise have been.

"Our first moving up here comprised only such a part of our household goods as could be brought in one large surf-boat, the 'Manji.' Dr. Nassau and I, with Mrs. Thompson and two children, Julia and Mary Ann, with four oarsmen, came in the small sail-boat, the 'Charlotte Draper.' It was named for a colored woman in Baltimore, who donated the funds for its purchase; and I think it was a present to Mr. Mackey. It is a very useful little boat, but not fitted for sea-voyages, except in pleasant weather. We chose to come in the small boat, fearing the wind might fail, and knowing the 'Manji' would be difficult to row.

"We had a good many odds and ends with us, and not much spare room. The large boat contained a half-barrel of flour, a corn-mill, a small stove, a box with folding-chairs (wedding presents from Lawrenceville), and our clothing stowed around the chairs. There was also a box containing Mrs. Thompson's bedding and clothing; a chest with our bed-clothing, pillows, kerosene lamp, and patent iron; a chest of tools, in which was stowed three pieces of stove-pipe. In the litttle boat was Dr. Nassau's single mattress, for us to sleep on up here; a roll of oil-cloth from the storehouse; and a tub containing a bakeoven, spider, and several pots. I cannot enumerate all the small things in either boat; but our crockery, cooking-stove, and rice had to be left behind. The largest chest of all I forgot,—containing cloth, knives, pipes, tumblers, soap, beads, shirts, hats, etc., for our trade with the natives. Our 'trade' means buying of food and building materials, and paying workmen employed by the mission. Dr. Nassau has also the out-stations under his charge, and the Scripture-readers come to him for their monthly pay.

"We left Corisco between 9 A.M. and 10 A.M. with a fair wind, but we soon lost part of it and made rather slow progress all day. Part of the afternoon and evening the men were obliged to row, and we congratulated ourselves that we were not in the big boat, thinking it would stop after night at some of the towns along shore. We were in sight of land all the way. No one was much seasick, except Mrs. Thompson; and Hamill and I tried several times to eat of the supplies Mrs. Clark and Mrs. De Heer had provided, but the food did not go down well.

"We reached our new home about 3 o'clock Wednesday morning, and, although we were out some eighteen hours in the rainy season, there had not rain enough fallen to wet us. The big boat was here several hours before us, their large sail having caught the wind better than ours. A very few of the natives met us on the beach, and we were carried on shore and climbed up a short, steep path to the house.

"Day-dawn was creeping in through all the crevices of our bamboo house when we threw ourselves on a hastily-made bed to try and rest our weary limbs. First, we had partaken of a little food, and Dr. Nassau had offered up a prayer of thanksgiving to the God who had brought us in safety to our new home on the mainland. Mr. Paull's bedstead was in the study, on which we slept." . . .

BONITA MISSION-HOUSE, Oct. 18, 1865.

```
                              N.
    ┌─────────────┬─────────────┬─────────────┐
    │             │   PANTRY,   │             │
    │             │   12 x 7.   │             │
    │ BED-ROOM,   │             │ BED-ROOM,   │
    │  12x12.     │             │  12 x 15.   │
    │             │             │             │
W.  ├─────────────┴─────────────┴─────────────┤  E.
    │             │                           │
    │             │                           │
    │ STUDY,      │     IKENGA, 12 x 22.      │
    │  12 x 12.   │                           │
    │             │                           │
    └─────────────┴───────────────────────────┘
                              S.
```

In Mr. Paull's house, as entered that night, the study was the only completed room. The Ikenga was floored and enclosed, but not entirely doored. The floors, partitions, doors, and windows of the other half were yet to be made.

The voices of the natives crowding about the front door awoke us early. After prayers and the buying of provisions, dried corn, cassava, and plantains, a young lad, Ijabi (who had been Mr.

Paull's table-boy, and afterwards had gone to Corisco to Alongo school, but had left there sick), presented himself, and, without ceremony of engagement, asked what he should cook for breakfast. Other lads, and one girl, Kove, who had been in Corisco schools, were at once at home with us, useful in their knowledge of our ways, and helpful as pioneers to the hearts of their people. Crowds of people coming and saluting us as guests of the tribe. Compacts of friendship, from the women to Mrs. Nassau, and from the men to myself, by the "dash" (present) of a chicken, or plantain bunch, or string of fish. Meat was in plenty, and plantains rotted for abundance.

That same Wednesday in the afternoon I began flooring a bed-room with some thirty pine boards that had been sent from Corisco a week before we came, and the work was pressed every day till completion. The "Manji" was sent back to Corisco, and the "Draper" retained for mainland service. On Thursday the 19th, Maclachlan, the young English trader from Mbini, called to welcome us. On Friday evening a catechumen inquiry class was organized, that since has never failed to meet weekly, nor at any time has had less than three members. And Mrs. Nassau commenced an evening school for adults and children, whom she taught while sitting sewing in the Ikenga with Mrs. Thompson; this continued for weeks, until the completion and arrangement of the house gave time and place for school in daylight.

On Saturday, 21st, the old King Mango and other chief men came, with their duplicate copy of Mr. Paull's formal deed of the mission grounds, as sign of the compact between them and myself as his successor, to arrange according to custom a schedule of prices and wages. Naturally, their cupidity made an effort to advance on what had been current prices, taking advantage of my supposed ignorance as a stranger. But the young men frowned down the attempt, and Mr. Paull's list of prices being produced, it was accepted by them, and they dispersed harmoniously.

On Sabbath morning, 22d, the house was densely crowded. On Tuesday, 24th, came another mission-boat, the "Dispatch," from Mr. Clark, with welcome additions of food and furniture.

MRS. NASSAU TO MRS. REV. W. H. CLARK.

BONITA, Oct. 20, 1865.

This is Friday afternoon, and I have just come from town, where I went to see two of my friends and to pay them for their "dashes" and plantains. Another plantain came this afternoon, and Dr. Nassau has had a chicken and fish "dashed" him.

This morning Mrs. Thompson, Kove, and my two girls washed up the soiled clothes, and I cooked dinner with Ijabi's assistance. In the first place, my assistant killed the chicken, and I opened it. He took out the insides, and I washed, stuffed it, and put it in a pan to go in the Dutch oven. I also had hominy ground; but, first of all, made custard. Just as we commenced our dinner, some one brought a bowl full of tomatoes; so I pared them, and put them on to stew. When the dinner was nearly done, a man brought some potatoes to sell, and I must run in the house to get the pay. Well, we got everything cooked, —myself into the bargain,—excepting the chicken. I firmly believe it was an old, tough hen; or else Ijabi and I kept piling the fire and chips around the oven so fast that the outside browned and the tips of the legs burned crisp before the inside got done through. The next time I shall know better.

Yesterday I sent out cook for stones, according to Mrs. Thompson's advice, and we three made a fireplace. I intend to make a shovel out of an old tin can to-day or to-morrow. I used one long iron spoon for stirring pots, lifting lids, and putting coals around. Once or twice I had to take a chip and scrape the ashes out of it; but that didn't hurt. The only springs near us have red water, and the clear water is half a mile off. We have got along with very little clear water thus far; I hope to have more. Our dishes are very few; but it saves washing. Several of the young men are spelling nicely, and one of them will read very soon.

October 21.—Mr. Maclachlan called day before yesterday, and I think we shall find him a pleasant neighbor. The Spaniard has not been over yet. The bread you gave us was very good, and I was very glad I found a place for the last loaf. It was quite a surprise to find a piece of beef already broiled in the tin pail. I'll send your pail back some time; but we can't spare it just yet. We sleep and eat in the study, and keep the most of our goods in there. A nice large cupboard stands in the Ikenga, left by Mr. Paull. Mrs. Thompson sleeps in the Ikenga, and the children, too. The view from here is beautiful; and you must come up and bring the children just as soon as you can after we get fixed.

I do not think we shall suffer from the heat, although we have not had a fire made in the house before this afternoon.

We expect a boat to-night, and hope to hear that Anna is almost well. The rains commenced here before the women had made their gardens, and I do not know when we shall have fresh corn.

Tuesday, October 24.—We have just finished supper, which consisted of stewed mangoes, Indian corn-meal cakes, and shark in *jomba*. The shark was not done; so we sent it back to the fire for our breakfast. It was the first that our fisherman has brought, and, to my sorrow, I saw him this afternoon making shark-hooks in town. I do not admire that kind of fish. We had another kind of fish for dinner 'that was "a dash." It tasted strong, and looked like the flesh of coarse beef. We have not bought any chickens yet, but have had four given us. It is such a trouble to remember and return to all the donors, that it would be easier to buy. The boat came a little before daylight, and we were very glad to get the things and to hear that you are all well. Several of the things you sent we had down on our next order.

. . . . Children do not seem to be a very plentiful kind of commodity in these parts, and girls are very scarce indeed. Perhaps they have gone off to marry in other places. Plantains are more plenty than anything else, unless it is corn. I was very glad to see the can of butter,—scarcely knew what to use it on first. . . .

Mrs. Thompson baked Louisa a palm-oil cake on Friday, thinking the boat would be here that night; but it is all gone but a little piece. She has been trying some Kombe medicine for her toothache this afternoon, and the pain ceased for the present. Mrs. T. sleeps on a door which rests on two boxes. Good-by, and much love to all. I felt a little feverish yesterday, but am pretty well to-day. There is plenty to do, but not such trying work as in a girls' school. . . .

MRS. NASSAU TO HER UNCLE AND AUNTS.

Thursday, October 26.

This morning I received an invitation from one of my town friends to take dinner with her, and about noon some one came to call me, saying the food was ready. I went in fear and trembling, for I did not feel well; and, knowing a shark had been killed by her people a few days before, I expected to be feasted on dried shark and green plantains. My fears were not prophetic, for she had prepared a nice, fresh fish, cooked with a native dish called *ngândâ*. The ngândâ is made from seeds that look just like pumpkin seeds, and, after being shelled, either with the teeth or a knife (opened, I should say), the kernel is rubbed into a paste. The fish and paste are then mixed together with salt and plenty of Cayenne pepper; and, being tied up in plantain leaves, it is baked by the fire. We had yams and ripe plantains as vegetables, and a small pitcher and little blue tumbler served my friend and me to drink from. I appropriated the pitcher, leaving her the glass. When we went to the table, the fish was already on our plates. A colored table-cover served as a cloth, and we had knives and forks. A dinner-plate with some wet salt was also on the table. I ate heartily. Everything looked clean and tasted very nicely.

Hamill expected to go to Meduma this afternoon, a place five miles north of us, but the young man he wanted to place there as Scripture-reader was not quite ready.

Mrs. Thompson's fears of the leopards were all revived this morning by the sight of leopard-tracks in the soft sand around the house. Makendĕngĕ tells her the leopards will "love the fat on her very much indeed." Makendĕngĕ is Dr. Nassau's interpreter—a great friend of Mrs. Thompson, and a favorite with us all. He was with us several months before we left Corisco, and it seems several of the young men about here have been asking him whether Mrs. Thompson intends to marry again. He told them they must not ask so many questions about her or he would tell Dr. and Mrs. Nassau; that Mrs. T. would not have any of them; she would not marry in this part of the country, and if she did, it would be to no one but himself.

Yesterday afternoon Hamill and I went across the river to return a call from Mr. Maclachlan, the young trader whose factory is nearly opposite us. (He had come to church on Sabbath, and afterwards, to my dismay, my husband invited him to stay to dinner. I did not feel inhospitable, but we had scarcely dishes enough to set the table for ourselves, and, as it was, the gravy had to come on in a tin cup.) He gave us a cup of tea, some nice little crackers, and fried ham, before we came back. Learning that our supply of rice had not come from Corisco, he gave us a basin of rice and the same of barley. Basins of all sizes and colors are a great article of trade here, used by the people for holding their food, not for washing the face and hands. While we were sitting there, he brought out a small jar of mince-meat and asked me if I could tell him the use of it. He had been using it cold on his bread, but did not care very much for it that way. I told him he'd better let me bring it home and have a pie made for him; to which he willingly assented. The pie is to be baked on Saturday, and he will take it home after church. As I had no butter or lard, I asked for a piece of pork to get some shortening for the crust, and he sent his boy for *two* pieces of pork. We bought out of his factory a large bake-oven; our bread will not keep us busy all the morning now.

I had taken over with me a large pan of biscuit and a pitcher of palm-butter. So we both gain by being near neighbors. "Palm-butter" is like thick gravy, and is eaten on bread or any kind of vegetable, but principally on rice. The oil skimmed off the top is used for any kind of frying, and used to the taste it does very well. We put a little in our biscuits, and on baked chicken.

Before leaving Corisco, arrangements had been

made with a certain captain, an Elobi trader, to follow us to Benita with the remainder of our furniture, utensils, etc. His failure to do so necessitated the use of the little gig "Draper" for heavy sea-service on monthly trips to Corisco. Mr. Clark's boat also coming monthly in forwarding the mail, we for several months had communication every two weeks with Corisco, which, with the press of building, night-school teaching, visiting, and learning to adapt the Benga language to the Kombe dialect, quite took off the edge of the sense of isolation.

MRS. NASSAU TO MRS. REV. W. H. CLARK.

BONITA, Nov. 3d, 1865.

We have been looking for the boat since yesterday morning, and now we cannot tell what to think. . . . We did not expect our letters *much* until last night or this morning, and having our mail to get ready for the same boat prevents our feeling quite so impatient. . . . I have been a little feverish one or two days this week, but nothing of any account. . . . The weather has not been very cold, and we have not had much rain in the daytime.

Mbâtâ had a place on his leg lanced by a native last Friday, and Dr. Nassau says an artery must have been cut, for he came near bleeding to death. Kove is living at his town much against her will, and they do not get along very well together. She charges him with unkindness, and he says Kove is not faithful to him.

My friend Ndomi says when his child is born he wants his wife and the baby to come here and live all the time. He is a good fisherman, but not very successful in the hunt. The first day he went out he shot at a monkey, and it ran away; the second day he shot at something else and burst his brother's gun. After breaking the gun he picked up a turtle and brought us. I cooked it yesterday, but never having cooked a turtle before, and having no receipt-book with me, it was not a very fine dish. I have eaten turtle once or twice in America, and it was quite tender, but this old lady was about as tough as you could wish to taste. Mrs. Thompson did not know any more than I did about it.

MRS. NASSAU TO THE MISSES M. AND M. A. LATTA.

Mond. morn., Nov. 5, '65.

At two o'clock yesterday (Sabbath) morning we were wakened by the arrival of our mail, which brought letters from you and Kate, and my baby's picture. It is very like him, and just as good a treasure as could have come by mail. We went to bed again about four, and I slept a little, but it was hard work. Hamill did not sleep at all.

It was very kind of you to go to all that trouble about the fruits. We shall enjoy them highly when they come, and there will be enough to share with some of our less fortunate friends.

No letters came from Lawrenceville, but we hear through Mrs. Mackey that Sister Bella is not coming. She had not sufficient notice. Captain Yates asserted positively, when he said good-by last June, that he would not be back in Africa; he was sick of the trade here. Mrs. Yates laughed and said we would see them both back in six months; and it will not be over seven months, if they have a quick passage. . . . There are some pretty shells north of us, but no variety; none near us. A man walked six miles last week to sell a half-hatful of shells. Some came from three miles down the coast on the other side of the river. . . . We are getting along nicely here. I wish you could pay us a visit. Come out on one voyage of the vessel and stay until it returns on another trip. . . . I know Sister Bella feels badly that she cannot come. I will send you some of those little red Guinea-peas in the box.

MRS. NASSAU TO MRS. REV. W. H. CLARK.

Monday.

Here is a half-sheet additional. I am very much troubled since hearing of your illness, and I want you please to send up for me if you should ever be very sick and Mrs. Clemens not be there or not able to take care of you. I am sorry to hear that she is no better; if she can only help at Evangasimba, she ought not to attempt anything else.

We had good news from Willie. I send Kate's letter for you to read, but cannot spare the picture. . . . We have been paring mangoes this morning, and will put up this afternoon. . . . What can I do for you in this out-of-the-way place?

MRS. NASSAU TO THE SAME.

Bonita, W. A.,
Wed'y morn., Nov. 15, '65.

Our men are getting ready for a start, and we hope they may reach you some time to-morrow. They go for goods and mango-plums, and I hope the bats have left enough on some of the trees at your place or Alongo. . . . If Mrs. Clemens does not finish up all your sewing in about a fortnight after she comes back, I wish you could send me some to do. I cannot do it as neatly as your sister, but I will do it pretty well.

The Kroomen who brought over Mr. Maclachlan's letters told Mrs. Thompson there were two American ships at Fernando Po. The news comes in rather a roundabout way, and it would be too soon for the "Greyhound.". . .

We are sending a private order for some self-sealing cans that were ordered once on the general order. Will you send me besides some pickle-jars if you have more than you want, and ask Mr. Clark for some large corks from the study? . . . Some of those I put up are spoiling. I had no wax, and sealed them with stewed sugar, thinking it might make molasses-candy, but it did not get quite stiff enough. There ought to be a little resin stewed with the wax. . . . It is too bad that we have to trouble you or rather your husband so much. If Captain H——'s boat had come that next week, as we expected, you would have been saved some trouble. . . . We expect to get in our bed-room next Saturday. The men do not hurt themselves by working fast, but they make a nice wall. . . . Njâku begins to cook for us to-day. His predecessor was dirty, and had no sense for cooking.

Our new kitchen will soon be done, and then we will relieve ourselves of the host of visitors who go there to get a coal or get a drink. The boys' room being next our present kitchen, and two of them sleeping in the same room in which we cook, makes it impossible to keep people away altogether.

Dr. Nassau drove two posts in the ground and put an iron bar through the top for us to hang our pots on. Mambo wanted to know what they would do for their cooking when we took away the bar. A thing he never saw before, I reckon. I speak of Mambo, from Hanje, who lives here.

MRS. NASSAU TO MISS M. E. NASSAU.

Bonita, W. A.,
Tues., Dec. 5, 1865.

This is the first time I have had the luxury of writing on a table since we came to Bonita. A few times I took my paper over to a big chest, and sat on one of the board seats laid on blocks for the people; but usually I wrote on an atlas on my knee. To-day my head aches, and we carried the pantry-table in by way of luxury. We only boast two tables in the house, the one at which I am writing,—which is also our dining-table,—and another very small one that stands in one corner of the pantry, and holds various articles that can find no place in our one cupboard. The fewer our possessions the less the care and trouble.

About two weeks ago we moved into our bedroom, and I was very thankful to get out of such a confused and crowded corner as we occupied in the study. The *melângâ* (native rope used for tying on the bamboo) was all kept under our bedstead, and it was impossible to move the bedstead two inches in any direction; of course all sweeping under it was out of the question. In going behind to make the bed I had to step up on several bunches of melângâ, which made the process of bed-making very uncomfortable.

We are also occupying a new kitchen; and the great luxury of a stove arrived this morning. The stove in question is a small "parlor cooking-stove," brought out by Mrs. McQueen ten years ago, to be used in the house at Ugobi,—more for warmth than for cooking. Mrs. Ogden bought it when Mrs. McQueen went to America the second time, but supposed it was broken, and never had it removed to their new station. Mrs. Ogden afterwards made it a present to me. So when Ugobi was taken to pieces the stove was removed to our Maluku station. This morning it arrived in the mail-boat, and we propose to put it up in our kitchen, thinking it will do to cook common meals by.

The little stove we have in our reception-room; and it is a great comfort. The large cooking-stove, bought at WILLIAMS's, in Philadelphia, we left at Corisco.

Our first boy-cook received a kind dismissal two or three weeks ago, and we have one in his place who knows rather more, but does not love cooking. For my part I do not admire cooking over a fire-place, especially a fire-place without a chimney, where half the smoke goes out of the nearest window, and the rest goes up to the roof or in your eyes. Our first cook told Mrs. Thompson one day that he knew how to cook, but that she and I came into the kitchen and gave so many orders, and said, "Hurry, hurry," so very often, that it made him trouble. You see, he was not strong and quite slow, also averse to cleaning up any of his pots and kettles after one meal until time to begin cooking for the next. He was busy all day, never done, and never got his kitchen cleaned up; so no wonder the poor boy was discouraged. . . .

This morning we were awakened at three o'clock by a chicken squalling, and Hamill sprang to the door,—I suppose with visions of snakes floating through his brain. A snake that kills chickens had been destroyed in our kitchen only a few days before, and I thought another of the same kind was around. The disturber was only our cook seizing a chicken which I had told him to catch the evening before for our dinner to-day. We did not thank him for neglecting his business and waking us up at such an unreasonable hour, for we were both very tired. In less than two hours we were wakened again by men's voices in the yard, and soon found the mail-boat had arrived from Corisco. Hamill was so sleepy he did not get up until the men knocked at the front door; and after the things were brought in he came back to bed. The first thing after getting up was morning prayers, and then we only had time to look at some of the Corisco notes before breakfast. We always keep our Lawrenceville letter until both can sit down quietly to read it; but I am never the one who is to be waited for. This morning after breakfast Hamill was obliged to go out and start some of the men at their work, and then some other interruptions came; so it seemed a long time to me. I had read my uncle's letter through, and learned that Willie was safe in Aunt Lizzie's hands, and Mrs. Mackey's letter told me of the crib in which he slept. . . . I trust we may be spared to see him in a couple of years. Hamill's health is much better than when I returned from America; the annoyances connected with the girls' school seemed to keep him listless and feverish. . . . The last dose of blue-mass he took was the week we left Corisco; and I hope he will not have to take it soon again. We occasionally speak of going to America at some future time; Hamill thinks in two years or less, but does not want to leave until this station can be supplied with one or two families.

MRS. NASSAU TO MRS. REV. W. H. CLARK.

Bonita, W. A.,
Wed'y, Dec. 6, 1865.

We are so poor in this neighborhood that we cannot afford thick paper even for African notes;

so I have fallen back on this tinted for use about home.

For once, my husband has written "a news" letter, and I do not know that there is much left for me to say. We are moving along as usual, and hope to be moving down your way the first of the new year.

I send a few shells to be divided among yourselves and the Alongo friends. The long, dark ones came from Meduma, five miles to the north of us.

A few Sabbaths ago a young man arrived from some distance up the coast,—Etiyani's town,—wishing a book and instruction. As we have no boarding-school I referred him to Alongo; but he returned the next morning to his people. I think it likely he may yet find his way to Corisco. He brought some shells and three bad eggs to sell, but I believe he did not know the eggs were spoiled. He seems to place great value on books and instruction; but did not know, until I informed him, that Sabbath was not the day for selling eggs.

Ejuse has been down several times with shells. I send of a kind that Mrs. McQueen said are very rare, and they are seldom found on Corisco. . . . I had fever last Sabbath a week (the only day any one has been kept in bed since we came); took cold by getting my skirts damp on the beach. I only changed my dress when I came home, and paid for my carelessness by some fever with bad back-ache, and pains in my limbs. I tell you about the pain because of the cure. The first thing that relieved me was a large bunch of *mahepo* leaves heated in the bake-oven, wrapped in a thin cloth, and laid to my back. It was a delightful sensation, and I advise you to try it if you get any pains or aches. . . .

By the direction of Presbytery, a church was organized at Benita on December 11, 1865, and the first communion was celebrated on December 31. As I had to go to Corisco headquarters regularly on the first week of each January, April, July, and October, and Mrs. Nassau wishing to revisit her Corisco friends after the three months of almost utter deprivation of civilization, it was decided to close the house and go with the entire household for an absence of two weeks, covering the Corisco communion-season and mission-meetings.

Mr. Clark had sent up the " Manji" for us. The very last hour of 1865 was occupied in writing, at the request of a large number of the people, not only Christian but heathen, an urgent protest to young Maclachlan, begging him not to carry out his expressed intention of starting a rum-shop on the mission side of the river.

In the " Manji," accompanied by the " Draper,"

the journey was commenced, immediately after the hours of Sabbath, in the earliest morning of the New Year, January 1, 1866, and an unusually good wind brought us to Corisco before daylight of the morning of the 2d. Mrs. Nassau busied herself packing boxes of curiosities to send to America by the already-expected " Greyhound."

Sabbath, 7th, was Communion at Evangasimba. On the 8th, I had to go to Gaboon to have extracted teeth that had been aching at frequent intervals for weeks.

On Wednesday, the 10th, Mrs. Nassau, wearied with her packing, went on a visit to Alongo, and there was seized in the evening with a malignant chill. Mr. Clark prescribed for her, and sent a boat for me on Thursday morning, which met me at the mouth of the Gaboon, returning on Friday, the 12th.

Mr. Clark's remedies had been blest, and the fever was gone, but the prostration was very great. For Mrs. Nassau to return to Benita in that state was impossible. So my Kombe crew were sent back to Benita to their homes, and to let the people know the cause of our delay; and I awaited Mrs. Nassau's convalescence. Even when that was assured, it was decided to be prudent for her to remain at Corisco until the arrival of more nourishing supplies by the anxiously-expected " Greyhound" (which did not come until a month after), while I, with Mrs. Thompson, returned to Benita, on February 7.

There had always been kindly intercourse between us and the Spanish Jesuit priests, and a sending of favors and assistance in sickness. In our visits the conversation was solely in Benga. During Mrs. Nassau's illness, Padre Garcia wrote to Alongo, accompanying a watermelon and other fruits, a Benga note, of which the following is a literal translation:

"MISSION OF ST. IGNATIUS, Jan'y 13, 1866.

"MY FRIEND MR. NASSAU,—I have known with sorrow that your wife is very sick these days there at Alongo. I feel sorrow, my friend, for the sickness of Mrs. Nassau; but Our Father God can give her strength, and you, too, for enduring the Cross which the Son of God has sent you. Over there is so far, and I have many duties these days; but if there is a thing you can wish with me, I am yours. Padre Torre salutes ye. Salute also with all my heart your wife, and those of the station.

"Your friend,
"F. X. GARCIA."

MRS. NASSAU TO THE MISSES M. AND M. A. LATTA.

CORISCO, WEST AFRICA, Feb'y 17, 1866,
Saturday morn., Evangasimba.

It will be two weeks next Tuesday since Dr. Nassau returned to our home on the mainland, leaving me in the care of Corisco friends. I had expected to accompany him; but, going up to Alongo to make a farewell visit, I took such a violent cold in my face and teeth that I was unfit for the journey. Hamill thought, also, that as the "Greyhound" was still delayed, I would fare rather better in the way of supplies at Corisco than at Bonita. Being sick several days with the toothache, took away much of the strength I had gained after my attack of fever.

It is thought best by all that I should go to Gaboon, on the arrival of the "Greyhound," and spend several weeks there, to recruit still further. Hamill comes down to mission-meeting the last of March, and I return with him the next week.

Mrs. Thompson also returned to Bonita, and Julia remained with me. . . . We have all been out of butter since September, except an occasional present of a few pounds from some ship or trader. We have had no salt meat for some length of time, but got along quite comfortably with canned meat and chickens; but it is certainly providential that now that canned meats are exhausted, the fowls are brought in two or three at a time. Fresh fish are usually obtained without difficulty; but a fish diet is not considered the most wholesome. Flour is just about done, and we have been on short allowance for several months. I do not write this to worry you, but to let you see how very timely will be the arrival of our supplies, and to show how much we will enjoy the good things that are coming.

Mr. Garcia sent Mrs. Clark this week a hindquarter of fresh pork. She sent a piece to Mrs. De Heer, with whom I was staying at the time, and we did enjoy it very much. It was the first time I had tasted fresh pork in Africa. We had, with the pork, yams, sweet potatoes, plantains, and green corn,—the last a great rarity this season.

After Dr. Nassau went to Bonita, Mr. Maclachlan offered him some of the supplies he had lately received; so he sent the boat across for a little flour and butter. Besides the flour and butter, he received tea, pickles, desiccated milk, and something else I could not make out. Hamill sent down part of the flour and butter; and we hope, before it is done, to see the "Greyhound" anchor off Corisco. I have been gaining strength slowly, but feel much stronger and better to-day than I have since my illness. The weather has been unusually warm for Corisco, or, I think, I should have improved faster.

MRS. NASSAU TO MISS M. E. NASSAU.

CORISCO, W. A., Feb. 19, '66,
Mon. morn., Evangasimba.

. . . . I have been improving more rapidly in the last few days, and, if the "Greyhound" does not come very soon, I would rather go to Bonita than Gaboon. Every one else thinks it would be folly for me to think of returning before Hamill comes down the last of March; so I suppose I go to Gaboon. . . . I am feeling better than I have since the first of December, but am too weak to occupy myself with much sewing, or even much reading, so that the time passes slowly. I read awhile, and my eyes get tired; I try to sew, and my hands get tired; I try to think, and my head soon wearies. Still, I am gaining, and thankful for so much strength.

MRS. NASSAU TO THE MISSES M. AND M. A. LATTA.

Tues. morn., Feb'y 20.

This is my birthday, and I would be glad to have it celebrated by the arrival of the "Greyhound;" but doubtless patience must have its perfect work. . . . When Mr. De Heer came from America, the Board sent out the lumber for a house to be put up at his station Ugobi. As there were several changes, and Ugobi will not be again occupied by a white man, it has been decided to put up the house at Bonita. So now we have weekly communication with our station, as the boat comes every week for timber, boards, etc. I had not supposed at all we should have a frame house at Bonita for some time, and I was perfectly satisfied with our bamboo residence. After all the materials are transported, Hamill says it will not take long to put up the building. It is intended to be only one story, which is much nicer in Africa, I think. I have a box of shells to send you by the "Greyhound." . . . Hamill was in Gaboon, and I was not at all well when I packed your box. I did not think then that the weariness was a symptom of coming fever. . . . The house at Maluku is still vacant; the girls' school still scattered. Some of the trees that Hamill and I planted and watched over with so much care are just beginning to bear fruit. At Bonita we have commenced again the planting and watching of trees. I wonder who will eat the fruit! Hamill writes that my finest Avogado pear-tree is dead; but I knew it was dying when I left. Perhaps you think, as I did once, that everything grows very fast here; but it requires much care, watering and enriching, to make an orange-, bread-fruit, or pear-tree bear in three years,—that, I believe, is the shortest time. With ordinary care, those trees will bear in about five years. The soil on the mainland is mostly much better than on Corisco, but the mission premises at Bonita are principally sand (the people had too much sense to sell their good ground); but there are some places on it not so very poor. Mr. Paull chose for health and looks, and not in reference to agriculture. . . .

MRS. NASSAU TO HER HUSBAND.

CORISCO, Feb'y 23, 1866.

What do you think? I got up this morning a few minutes after eight, in order to attend to the sending of the Bonita boat. Mr. Clark is sick in bed, and has been since Wednesday night; so it is fortunate there is not much of an order. I counted the boards as Esaka took them down, and measured the floor-boards—13 feet. Among the long boards you will see one shorter and narrower, which I did not measure, but supposed from the size it was one of the floor-boards. Mr. Clark said it was likely, and you will find it among the others, twenty in all, including the short one. . . . I came from Alongo last Friday, and found the butter you sent me. It was a surprise, and has been a great treat. Food is getting very scarce, but I am stronger, and my appetite better; so I get along pretty well. . . . I amuse myself a little with Hebrew, and yesterday pressed some small pieces of sea-weed that I shall send to Sister Bella for her photograph-album —if they are pretty. . . . Ilanga and Etiyani came down on Wednesday for supplies, saying they dare not go to Bonita on account of the tribal war. Mr. Clark gives them each two dollars apiece, as they seem in such extremity, and you will please send them instructions for the future. I told Mr. Clark I knew you intended visiting Aje soon after your return, and you would probably see them yourself about it. They said they they had no means of sending you even a note.

MRS. NASSAU TO THE SAME.

Corisco, W. A., Feb. 28, 1866.
Wed'y night, Evangasimba.

... I have been reading a little hydropathy this week, and it certainly recommends itself more to my common sense (if I have the article) than anything I have seen on homœopathy. I was not persuaded into the subject, but took up the book when I got tired of the Hebrew.

Do you know this is our baby's birthday? I wonder whether he has been out in the snow to get rosy cheeks and freeze his fingers! Mrs. Walker wrote to Mrs. De Heer that she thought I ought to go on the "Greyhound" to America. ... If that *sloth* will only get from its last limb to Corisco some time this week or next, I think I ought to visit Gaboon to show them all how much strength I have gained in the last ten days. ... I take some exercise, but am not able to walk much without getting tired. Yesterday I walked several times around the front yard here, and to-day had four or five ticks taken off me, as a punishment for venturing on a grass-plot, I suppose.

Friday morn., Mar. 2.—The "Greyhound" has come!

MRS. NASSAU TO MISS M. E. NASSAU.

BARAKA, GABOON, W. A., Mar. 14, '66.

In coming to Gaboon on the "Greyhound" I believe I have reached the farthest point of my journeyings at present. By the last day of this month I hope to be in the mail-boat and on my way to Corisco, where Hamill and I are hoping to meet after a two months' separation. . . . Mrs. Clemens pressed a great deal of sea-weed; and the week before leaving Corisco I tried some small pieces. My eyes would not allow of my doing very much, but I thought you might like a few for photograph-albums — divide as you choose. You see it is on foreign paper, but it is all the unruled we had. The first sea-weed I ever saw pressed was so beautifully done that I never felt much like attempting it. . . . It would be prettier on stiff paper. . . . Last Saturday Mr. and Mrs. Walker, Mrs. Captain Yates and I went to visit the Roman Catholic cathedral, about three miles distant. It is the handsomest building I have seen in Africa, and the thick stone walls are different from anything else near us. I ought to except the cathedral at Fernando Po; it is larger, but I was not inside. The walls of the one we visited are pure white inside, and the windows have unpainted glass. There were a number of pictures, but hung so high I could not see them well; they were not very beautiful, I judged. The floor was a rough mosaic of red, blue, and brown. The holy water had a dirty-looking sediment at the bottom, and some very small animals wriggled around as if they delighted in so holy a bath. . . .

MRS. NASSAU TO MISS M. E. NASSAU.

GABOON, W. C. A., Mar. 24, '66.
Saturday morn.

. . . Yet I cannot help longing for a sight of the baby face, and wish that I might hear once more the sound of his baby voice. Do not teach him, as he grows older, to long too much for his papa and mamma so far away. If we come to him, he will learn to love us; and if not——. It is sad for a child from earliest years to feel the shadow of a great loss. I ask that for my baby's sake. I want his childhood to be a happy one. . . . I suppose we will leave Corisco on Thursday, April 5, for Bonita, and I shall be very glad to be at home once more. . . . You see we cannot help having some kind of plans even in Africa, and I write of these things that you may see how nearly they may be fulfilled, or how different all things may prove from our present expectations.

Mrs. Preston talks of accompanying me to Corisco for a change; but she dreads long boat-rides so much, I fear it will end in talk. It is not the going *to* Corisco, but the two days she must spend in the *return*, sleeping ashore at a native town. We can go from here in about nine hours. Well, I have a hundred miles of boating to be accomplished between this and Bonita, and dread nothing but the sea-sickness. . . .

Mrs. Nassau, in restored health, was escorted to Corisco by our Gaboon friend, Rev. Wm. Walker, on April 4, and on the afternoon of the 6th, with an ample supply of provisions, we started for Benita, arriving there at sunrise of the 7th. Then such happy days! opening boxes of delicacies, and peeping into letters and refreshing books, stowed away in unexpected corners of the boxes of presents, that in sudden abundance had come from Glasgow, and Lawrenceville, and Waynesburg, and Philadelphia. Some of the boxes had been wet in landing from the "Greyhound," and in the month's delay to open until both Mrs. Nassau and I could be present at the joyful act, some of the contents had spoiled.

Early in May a comfortable trip that united the pleasure of a picnic with the work of an itineration was taken sixteen miles up the river to Sĕnje, for the locating of two young men as Scripture-readers. Mrs. Nassau accompanied, and its exhilaration completed her convalescence from another fever that had threatened just two weeks before.

For three months materials had been collecting from the forest for foundation-posts, and sills, and sleepers of the Benita frame house. Its erection was begun just after the return from Sěnje; it was built connecting with the west end of Mr. Paull's bamboo house, gable to gable, with a board platform covering the ten feet space between the two. Our former Benga friends sometimes visited us in the frequently-coming boats that carried boards, etc. A member of Mr. Clark's household, Ijawe, one of Mrs. Nassau's Maluku pupils, was with us a few weeks, for medication.

MRS. NASSAU TO MRS. REV. W. H. CLARK.

BONITA, May 5, 1866.
Sat'y night.

The beginning of this week I thought my eyesight was going after yours, but the trip up the river seems to have strengthened my eyes somewhat,—perhaps by increasing my strength.

My fever came near being malignant, I think; but I could not decide on any special cause excepting the *climate*, and that has to bear so much blame, a small fever additional will not hurt it. . . . I send some cans that came from America, hoping you will enjoy them. All the dried fruit in both boxes was spoiled, also a variety of other things. A box of corn-starch came safely, and a tin case containing chocolate. There was a good portion of emptiness in the largest box, and a fine supply of Sunday-school papers.

We spent one night up the river, and I enjoyed the trip very much. I was afraid, if I did not go this time, it might be several years—if I live so long—before I should get beyond the mouth.

Is there anything I can do for you? . . . Do not feel troubled about me. I will take quinine pretty regularly, and have commenced the iodide of iron, besides an irregular practice of water-cure. Dr. Nassau let me put on all the water I wanted during my fever. He just laughs at me when I am packed; but I have only tried that a few times, as Mrs. T. does not do it very nicely.

The trade in India rubber (obtained from a *vine*) and red dyewoods increased at the Bonita River, stimulated by the wants of the Atlantic cable, and new factories were set up at Sipolu on the south side of the river. Among others, came a native, Mpongwĕ Sunĕ. Rum circulated most freely, and there were frequent altercations; one of which resulted almost fatally to our young friend Maclachlan, by gun-shot wounds.

The natives acted very promptly and justly. They burned the village of his assailant, who, when he fled for sanctuary to the neighboring Molenzyi tribe, was denied by them that usual right, and sent back to Mr. M. for punishment. He declined to be jailer or judge. In the long delay of appeal to H. B. M. Government, Mr. M., exasperated, forgot his respect for authority; and when the British consul finally appeared native enthusiasm had cooled, the matter had been smoothed over, and nothing was done, much to the loss of the prestige of white power.

MRS. NASSAU TO MRS. REV. W. H. CLARK.

BONITA, W. C. A., June 5, '66.

... Poor Mr. Maclachlan is not much trouble, but I fear he will be a long time getting strong, unless his appetite improves.

I have been pretty well, but I am nearly tired out with the work of the week so far.

Last Sabbath evening, at the close of rather a late monthly concert, one of our men came rushing in with the exclamation, "Mr. Maclachlan is killed!" A Krooman then brought a note from Sunĕ stating that Mr. M. had been shot, and asking that Dr. Nassau would come over immediately. The men had been waiting nearly an hour for church to close!

Five men quickly put the boat in the river, and Dr. N. started with instruments and bandages, etc., saying he would bring the wounded man over here if he could.

After crossing to the factory (Mr. M.'s) he

learned that the affray had taken place at Mr. Morrison's, some two miles below.

It seems that Mr. Maclachlan, with several white men from a vessel on its way to Gaboon, were spending part of the Sabbath afternoon at Mr. Morrison's. A native attempted to enter the factory through a window, and Mr. Maclachlan said, "Come in through the door." The man refused, and the Kroomen were ordered to put him out. He resisted, and Mr. Maclachlan (I think) told the Kroomen to take his spear away. In drawing it through his hand the flesh was torn, and the man went to his town in a rage. His uncle and other relatives came back soon after and fired his gun, and wounded the cooper of Mr. Watkin's vessel in the hand. Mr. W. started towards the town with two spears in his hand to investigate; and Mr. Maclachlan and a Mr. ——, just out from England, walked after Mr. W. to try to dissuade him from attempting to interfere with angry natives. As Mr. M. turned to go back to his own factory, and they were walking along the beach arm in arm, Mr. M. heard a report and felt something like pebbles striking him, and said, "I must be shot!" They turned back to the house, and the pain soon became severe. Three slugs entered his back, the upper one near the shoulder being the most painful; and that shot we fear is a piece of brass rod. He was willing to have the pieces cut out, but did not seem able to bear the operation when Dr. Nassau commenced yesterday morning.

No other cause of offense is known of, and the natives generally side with Mr. Maclachlan.

Dr. Nassau got home with his patient about one o'clock Monday morning, and we put him in our room, as the only one that would do. Dr. Nassau and I are in the study again, with the floor so crowded that it is difficult to move in any direction, and nothing that can be moved out.

Mr. M. has also three flesh-wounds in his arms.

To add to our perplexities, we have a new cook who is just learning; and Julia has been sick for a week. Ijawe has been a great help since Julia took sick; but I am sorry that she leaves,—on her own account as much as ours.

Our late cook and Julia quarreled, and we would not sustain the former's rights as a *man ;* and so he proposed to go to town. No one objected, and the gentleman is now out of employ; but we are all good friends. Our new cook is slow, but tries to learn, and is very reliable. He is named Jumba, or Njumba, a member of our inquiry class.
. . . Ask Ijawe about craw-fish, or shrimps (*meha*). She can clean them, and Louisa can cook them; and I think you will like to eat them. They are caught on Corisco, but I never knew they were eaten until a few weeks ago. Fry them in butter, lard, or palm-oil. Powdered cracker and egg make

them go farther. I wish we had more corn to send. Dr. N. told the people last night to bring corn this morning.

Mrs. Nassau and her Corisco friends, both white and native, were sending by each monthly mail-boat friendly messages and little gifts of food. There is a great variety of fish at both Corisco Bay and the Bonita River, but the large fish rather predominated in the waters of the latter. At Corisco was caught, in enormous quantities, a small fish (*nyĕngĕlĕ*) two inches long. The favorite mode of cooking them (and indeed all meat) was to tie them up in plantain-leaves, with a little water, salt, Cayenne pepper-pods, and bruised oily nuts (*ndika*); and this bundle (called *jomba*) was then heated on hot coals.

In our itinerations, investigations in the huts of the natives often revealed new articles of food, which sometimes were tasty, and thence added in constant use to our own tables.

MRS. NASSAU TO MRS. REV. W. H. CLARK.

BENITA, June 27, '66.
Wednesday night.

Please to send me a *jomba* of *nyĕngĕlĕ*, if they are in season. Isesĕ will put me up one, I think; just a little *ndika* in it. I have been wanting ever since we came up here, but they do not grow in these parts. . . . Mr. Maclachlan has gone to his house, but comes over to breakfast, and has his wounds dressed.

My washerwomen are quite irregular since garden-making time has come round, but promise to do better soon.

I am very well, and get too tired only on Monday and Tuesday. . . . I wish I had corn for you; but what comes is generally too old the day we buy it, and would not be soft enough to send on a three days' journey. Indeed, we have none now, and it comes but seldom. . . .

> "Thou, solemn ocean, rollest to the strand,
> Laden with prayers from many a far-off land,
> *   *   *   *   *
> Through all thy myriad tones that never cease
> We hear of death and love, the Cross and Peace;
> New churches bright with hope and glad with psalms
> And martyrs' palms."

CHAPTER XIII.

LITTLE PAULL.

1866, 1867. Benita.

> "And on his angel brow
> I see it written, 'Thou shalt see me *there!*'"

A SUNBEAM, that came to lighten the only shadow in the Benita home,— to answer Faith's prayer,— to show to brutal heathen hearts the beauty and dignity of a perfect Christian family,— and then flitted to the mountain-tops, to lead thought and eye and hope up and beyond.

He came to waiting lips that had asked the benison of his presence. Thus had a mother mused: "Buying for the baby always saddens me, especially anything that it will not need for a few months. It seems as though I felt too sure of the little life. Oh, I hope it will live! My little one! my blessed child! Even if it should not, it is pleasant thinking, talking of, and preparing for it beforehand. Long before I went to Bonita, in my regular Bible-readings, I would stop at an occasional verse that seemed to hold for me the promise of another little life that might shed some happiness on ours. I know there is a great deal said about its being wrong to have children in Africa. I do not know,—I tried to find something in the Bible,—I prayed for teaching, but perhaps my wishes misled; but I could find only in God's Word that children were a blessing. After Willie went away, I longed so for the baby voice, the baby hands and feet, that I asked of our tender Heavenly Father to send me another little baby, if it was His holy will. I think, I trust I always prayed, 'If in accordance with Thy will.' This is why I seemed to see the promise, because I had prayed. Oh, it is so sweet to say in my heart, '*My* baby,' when there is neither father nor mother, sister or brother, that I can call my own!"

And so when, a gift from God, he came where everything spoke of sainted George Paull,—George Paull's Station,—under George Paull's roof,—in the only room George Paull had completed, no other name was thought of but " Paull;" it was a baptism itself.

Down the swift current of the Bonita, as of other rivers on the coast, are swept floating islands of interlaced rushes, tangled vines, and water-lilies that, clinging to some projecting log from the marshy bank, had gathered the sand and mud of successive freshets, and gave a precarious footing for the Pandanus, whose wiry roots bound all in one compact mass. Then some flood had torn that mass away, and the Pandanus still waving its long bayonet-like leaves, convolvuli still climbing and blooming, and birds still nesting trustfully, the floating island glided past native eyes down the stream, out over the bar, and on toward the horizon of broad ocean. What beyond? Native superstition said that at the bottom of the "Great Sea" was White-man's Land; that thither their own departed found their happy future, exchanging a dusky skin for a white one; that there, white man's magic skill at will created the beads and cloth and endless wealth that came from that unknown land in ships, in whose masts and rigging and sails were recognized the transformed trees and vines and leaves of those floating islands.

When, on the 12th of July, 1866, a few, with hushed step and bated breath, came to look on little new-born Paull,—the only white child most of the community had seen, and the first-born in that region,—they said, "Now our hopes are dead. Dying, we had hoped to become like you. But, verily, ye are born as we."

The babe's simple presence had done more to dissipate a superstition, than had oft-repeated assertion and instruction from older lips.

The frame house, whose erection as an addition to Mr. Paull's bamboo had been, under unskilled, native hands, going on for two months, though roofed and enclosed and floored, had no complete room for little Paull's reception. So we were back again in the crowded study, until a room could be completed.

Before he was a month old his mother bravely accepted the necessity of being alone for a few days while I went to Hanje and Aje on an out-station inspection that circumstances made imperative at that time.

Prudent forethought had provided a goat for any emergency requiring fresh milk; but one night a leopard broke through the shed where the animal was tied, and, gnawing off her neck behind the rope, carried away the body. . . .

MRS. NASSAU TO MISS I. A. NASSAU.

BONITA, W. A., Aug. 13, 1866.

Hamill and the mail both leave this evening, and Paull and I, Mrs. Thompson and the children will be left to ourselves for a few days. Not much time to get lonesome, you will think, with such a company as that.

I suppose Paull's father has told you about his goodness and sweetness, as he seems to think him the dearest little baby that ever was. . . . When Paull was only three days old, Mrs. T. was taken sick, and the fourth day, I sat up in bed to wash and dress him, his father handing me the things. I have washed him ever since, but Mrs. T. was able to give me some assistance after a few days. If Paull had not been such a good baby, I do not know how we could have got along. He had colic occasionally while we remained in the bamboo house, as it was next to impossible to keep out the cold draughts of air. With a fire burning day and night in my room, it was very rarely that I felt the heat uncomfortable. Although the dry season, we had rain every day but one until Paull was two weeks old. . . . He looks well, and has rosy cheeks.

The missionary company on Corisco being reduced in August by the final return of Mrs. Clemens to America, at the usual quarterly journey in September Mrs. Nassau accompanied on a trying and (by theft, storm, and loss of anchor) disastrous voyage to Corisco, where she remained to assist her friend, Mrs. Clark; and I returned to Benita to see to the embarkation for Liberia of Mrs. Thompson, whose term of contract had expired. And then a sickness of Paull recalling me to Corisco, the Benita house was closed for several weeks.

MRS. NASSAU TO MISS I. A. NASSAU.

CORISCO, W. A., Oct. 20, 1866.
Evangasimba, Sat. night.

The care of Paull, who does not fancy the children, a little sewing, a little feverishness, and the few letters I felt obliged to write before commencing yours, have not left me as much time as I could wish. . . . It would do you good to see him, such a fat, hearty little fellow as he is. . . .

Monday morning.—The first day that we spent ashore on our journey down was quite a trying one for Paull and me. The first house into which we entered was soon filled by natives anxious to see the white baby, and quite a discussion ensued, principally in regard to matters previous to his birth. Some of our boatmen informed the Bapuku people that white people did not talk much of such things, and accordingly no questions were asked me.

The women were very much pleased to see that Paull derived his nourishment in the same manner as their babies, and they exclaimed several times, "A woman like unto us!" "A woman as ourselves!"

The house was very close, and when Paull went to sleep I asked for another place where he might sleep undisturbed by the bad air or noise of talking. There were three other houses in the village, and a young man unlocked one for us, which was probably owned by the absent headman. Just as I prepared to lay him down, the "driver" ants were discovered all around, and that would not do. The third house was occupied by a woman cooking, so we were conducted to a fourth. In it was a fire, and a sick woman on a bed near by; so I carried the baby back to the first place, where he managed to sleep a few minutes. It seemed too warm to stay in the house, and too sunny to stay outside; but the "headman," who soon came in from "the bush," hung up a large boat-sail, which made an agreeable shelter while we could have it to ourselves. Hamill must have had a pleasanter time, looking for the missing anchor, than I had in doing nothing,—that is, if you call it nothing to amuse a baby that will not sleep. Paull would not stay with either of the two little girls in our company, and while I played with him several women gathered round to ask questions.

One woman asked whether scalding water was poured over me when my child was born, and seemed rather surprised to learn we had not that custom. The young mothers would think it a wise omission, for they sometimes find the water too hot, and are *quite* instead of *nearly* scalded.

MRS. NASSAU TO MISS M. E. NASSAU.

CORISCO, W. A., Nov. 21, 1866.

Master George Paull is well and thriving; and his father and mother are,—at least the former,— but it will be a pleasure to get back to our home and work at Bonita. I enjoy visiting Mrs. Clark, because I can be so perfectly at home.

Mrs. Thompson left last month, and I know I shall miss her, for she was very faithful in all her allotted work. I shall now have the privilege of doing my own scolding, instead of checking her for dealing reproofs on all sides with a very unsparing tongue. When any great accident occurred through the cook's carelessness, I usually turned to her first with an admonition to be quiet; whereupon she always declared that she had not intended to say a word.

Early in December, after the birth of Willie Clark, as we were about to return to the Bonita, a half-grown heifer was obtained from Gaboon, and taken in the boat with us. On " Wana" were laid our hopes for Paull's safety. Not that he was sick then, or in need; but we remembered our Willie's starvation, and were making provision for emergency. There were no domestic cattle at either Corisco or Benita,—though wild oxen are common on the mainland,—but at the Gaboon mission, and with the French, there were a few cows brought from five hundred miles south, at St. Paul de Loanda, descendants of the stock probably imported a hundred years ago by the Portuguese.

MRS. NASSAU TO MISS M. E. NASSAU.

BONITA, January, 1867.

My bread ought to be made out, and my baby is ready to be washed, but here are a few lines for you. I have not much time these days. My three half-grown girls require a person to keep them in work and out of mischief, and I am the only person to watch them, and help the cook, etc.

Mrs. Clark and her baby are well, and our little Paull grows nicely. . . . Paull is losing his rosy cheeks. I put him in short clothes on Saturday; he was six months old then.

A very dangerous dysentery that seized Mrs. Nassau in the early part of February, 1867, required Paull to be kept away from her. This, which would be an affliction to almost any child, was providentially relieved for him by a remarkable forgetfulness of her. During four days he did not see her; ate other food,—panada, or rice-starch, or corn-starch,—and did not cry much, except when my unskillful arms gave him his morning and evening washing and dressing. When the violence of his mother's disease was past, and we thought to save for him his natural nourishment, he did not know her, and would not, until forced, take it.

The compulsion was not well. Himself was

seized with the same disease, and it was the beginning of a weary path that led to a bitter end. Cut off finally from his natural nourishment, he refused, or ate without being satisfied, the only artificial foods we happened to have at Benita. There were desiccated milk and canned milk in the mission storehouse, fifty miles away. To get it I could have walked that far along the beach, but the last seventeen miles lay across the bay. Tribal feuds between the Kombe, Bapuku, and Benga had become so intense that the mail-boat ceased to come; and my Kombe people, though kind enough and profuse enough in expressions of pity, were too cowardly to have even their cupidity aroused by tempting wages and offered rewards for a crew to go to Corisco for the milk that lay there in abundance, while little Paull was crying for hunger, or sickening on improper food. Of the usual numbers of goats there was none, though messengers were sent repeatedly throughout the region in search. Leopards had swept them away.

One day early in March two Christians were sent across the river, to the Mbini factor, a colored trader, Mr. Brew. He almost always had goats for fresh meat, and would give me, if he had any. I did not send to the other English factor, Mr. Sutherland, as I knew he was, just then, in as great personal want as we. They returned with word that Mr. Brew had none, but that he had tried to get one (that had recently kidded) from a native living near him, and that the native refused. The highest current price for such a goat was five dollars. The messengers were sent back on the spot to the native to offer him fifty dollars for the use of the milk, if not for the purchase of the animal. They returned, their eyes flashing indignation, as they brought the spiteful reply that he would neither loan nor sell to me.

There came thoughts of Judson, manacled, carrying his babe from hut to hut, begging Burmese breasts.

Mrs. Nassau heard of a sheep, in the adjoining village, belonging to a native Christian woman, whose husband was also a Christian, which had recently had two lambs, and she sent for the husband. We asked him for the use of the milk; and, willing to give play to Christian kindness, if it existed, did not offer a price, though intimating that he should be rewarded. It was sickening! He did not respond. But, presently, quietly saying, "*Mbi ka yĕnĕtĕ*" (I will see), left the house. *Mbi ka yĕnĕtĕ* was ordinarily understood to be an evasion when one did not like flatly to say, "No."

Human resource had failed. "Oh, God! wilt not Thou help?"

Next morning a bleat was heard at the boat-landing, and presently Mr. Sutherland came to the door leading a large female goat, and asked its acceptance as a gift, saying that it had just the day before come to him for purchase, and, hearing of our necessity, he had hastened over with it.

"We thank Thee, O God, for what thou hast sent!" *Sent?* It shall be her name. And "Lomwĕngo" soon learned she had the privilege of the house, and, as petted mistress of the premises, ruled heavily whatever animals were afterward introduced.

The owner of the sheep brought her for use, during the interval of a week, until Lomwĕngo kidded, and would take no compensation, though his lambs suffered in depriving them for our lamb.

My return in April from the usual mission-meeting was signalized by a cheering visit from Mrs. De Heer to Mrs. Nassau; and the boat being laden with abundant provisions from the recently-arrived "Edith Rose,"—desiccated milk and boxes of delicacies from private friends in America,—health was strengthened by these gleams of friendship and reminders of affection; and we were flattered by the hope that little Paull would, in spite of that crown of suffering and the oncoming teeth, regain his rosy cheeks and plump legs. These comforts at Benita and Corisco, and the addition of missionary aid at Evangasimba,—Rev. S. and Mrs. Reutlinger, who had come in February, and who were trying to revive the Maluku school,—made the mission heart beat lighter.

New goats came in from distant tribes, and by

July, when a nurse—Mrs. Sneed—in Mrs. Thompson's place, arrived from Liberia, Mrs. Nassau had aid, and Paull more milk than he could use.

The dry season—usually, by its coolness, the most healthy for foreigners—was trying to us, and especially to our little one. The mortality among the natives was great. Springs and streams, that had not previously failed, dried, and we used water whose impurity was not fully appreciated until, recognizing, too late for little Paull, its aggravation of the disease which had never entirely left him, we abandoned entirely the Upwanjo dark springs, and even the Haič Creek across the prairie, and found at Bolondo, two miles up the river, a clear little forest rivulet, whence our water was ever after carried by canoe in kegs, or along the beach in jugs on men's shoulders.

MRS. NASSAU TO THE MISSES M. AND M. A. LATTA.

BONITA, W. A., July 27, '67.

Paull has a bad cold and four swollen gums, though I believe one of the teeth has come through. Still, you may know he is very fretful, and hangs on me. . . . The most important news to you is that we have a woman from Liberia to assist with the baby and house. It is Mrs. Sneed, whose daughter Charity you saw with Mrs. Ogden; and Charity goes to Mr. Clark.

MRS. NASSAU TO HER HUSBAND.

Oct., 1867.

Paull is nervous, and cries easily, but takes great delight in his rides. . . . I sent Mr. Sutherland a piece of the chicken-pie we had for dinner, and a bowl of beans, with a few plantains. He told Makĕndĕngĕ he was ready to dance for joy, as he had tasted nothing to-day until that fowl came. I sent Mr. Brew a little stewed kid and stewed mango, with my best biscuit, and one orange.

The little one was fading away, and growing more beautiful as he faded; for an infant he often evinced a strange love of beauty by stopping his bearer on a ramble and insisting on having a flower which older eyes had not detected; and in public worship showing his satisfaction with music. While too young to sit quietly during the reading or prayer, he would, as soon as the hymn began, toddle back to his mother, and laying his head bashfully, with a satisfied look, on her lap, lie so, crooning until the hymn was done. His most constant attendant was a young girl, Âkâ, to whom Mrs. Nassau was tenderly attached by the girl's exceptional care for, and interest in, the white baby.

MRS. NASSAU TO MISS M. E. NASSAU.

BENITA, W. A., Nov. 9, 1867.

Since the timely arrival of Mrs. Sneed I have had more time and more strength for writing than when dependent on a few careless children for help about the house and baby. . . . He cannot talk, but makes his wishes very plainly understood by grunts and finger-pointings. Whenever ready for sleep, he throws himself back and begins to fan himself by shaking the end of his night-gown or apron or whatever he catches first, meaning that the person holding him must continue the fanning. Several times lately Mrs. Sneed has been shaking the skirt of his dress while he was on my lap, and Paull would pull it out of her hand and give it to me to shake. If I try to fan him when he wants to eat or go out, he will gather up the skirt of his dress and hold it tight with one hand, and look or point towards the pantry, or out of doors.

MRS. NASSAU TO THE SAME.

BENITA, W. A., Dec. 11, 1867.

. . . We have two goats giving milk now, and three more that will be giving soon. He will touch nothing but milk, and sometimes a little tea. . . . One night Mrs. Sneed brought it in a mug instead of his little tin cup, and he would not give her the bottle until she had poured the milk into his tin cup, from which it is usually poured into the bottle.

Well that the inevitable is veiled! But how unthinkingly we tread near graves! Only two days before Paull's was to be made, in sending off the monthly mail-boat, on December 11, when he was seventeen months old, we wrote: "Paull has been having a long, hard time with his teeth. He is cutting the fourteenth, and they have made him very thin. I hope he may now have a respite from them, in which he may recover flesh and strength, for I have plenty of goat's milk to feed him on. Without it I do not think he would have borne the exhausting process thus long."

And on the 13th of December he died.

A few months later Mrs. Nassau wrote to Mrs. Preston, of Gaboon, who had finally returned to America in health so broken that she was not expected to recover:

"When you hear of the death of little Paull, you will feel sorry that you never held him in your arms; but when you meet my baby in Heaven, robed in a shining dress, all purified from earthly dross, there will be no room for such sorrow. I would have kept him if I could. It was hard to give up my gentle, loving baby; and yet I would not have kept him against my Father's will. As

Mr. Mackey said of Mr. Paull, 'God never makes mistakes.' We all thought Paull a smart baby, although at seventeen months he could not speak a word. When a year old he tried to walk, but never accomplished it alone. He had a remarkably quick eye and ear; and, though he did not know the meaning of words, he understood, from the look and tone, a great deal that was said to him. He took the bottle to the last, and would rarely touch anything but milk, excepting, when he saw Mrs. Sneed at the table, he always wanted to go and get a share of her tea. When he had finished his bottle, and wanted more, he always held on to the empty bottle until he saw Mrs. Sneed coming with his little tin, and then he would yield up his treasure to be refilled. If he fretted for milk at night when none was prepared, I had only to raise my voice and call, 'Mrs. Sneed!' and he would lie quiet until she came down, got the milk, and brought it to him.

"He was a very gentle, loving child; and the few times that he showed a disposition to disobey, and I spoke to him decidedly,—not at all severely, —he cried as though his heart would break. His disease was chronic diarrhœa, caused, as we now know, by the water we were in the habit of drinking until a few months before his death. We have our drinking-water brought now a distance of two miles; but I suppose the change was made too late for our baby. He was very thin, but had cut twelve teeth, and we hoped when the stomach- and eye-teeth were through that he would improve. The beginning of October he was very ill for ten days; but we considered him out of danger at the end of that time, and kept hoping, hoping for the best, even while we saw his flesh and strength did not come back. The day before he died I had him out on the beach to ride, and he enjoyed it much in his quiet way. That night I hoped he would sleep well, but he was very restless, so that Mrs. Sneed came down twice in the night to help me quiet him. In the morning early I gave him to Mrs. S., and tried to get another nap; but after awhile I heard Paull moaning strangely, and occasionally screaming out. I got up and took him, and he seemed sick at the stomach as well as in pain, and we tried some remedies to relieve him. In a little time I, having returned him to Mrs. S., went to dress. And then his father took him to hand to me, after I had dressed and we both had eaten something. Paull seemed a little easier, but a short time after I took him his mouth moved convulsively, and I began to fear my baby was dying. I didn't speak, only felt for his pulse; it was gone. In a few minutes his father asked, 'Is he dying?' and I answered very quietly, 'I should not be surprised.' Another gasp, and my baby's spirit went back to God the Giver.

"I dressed him myself for the last sleep, and his father made the little coffin. How sweetly he looked!

"We buried him in an open space not very far from the back of the house. The spot is enclosed on three sides by forest trees, but looking under the branches of one tree we can see from our door the little grave. I do not think it will disturb any future resident; the view can easily be cut off.

"What need to speak of my sorrow? The loneliness must cling to my heart, and yet I try to be glad for my precious child that was so soon taken to the Saviour's arms. He has found now there is something better even for him than mother's heart on which he loved to lie, or mother's face and voice for which he used to watch and listen when I left him for a little while."

MRS. NASSAU TO MRS. REV. W. H. CLARK.

BENITA, Dec. 31, 1867.

You have heard of our sorrow, and there is little more to add. As day by day goes by, I miss my baby-boy, but I know that he has gone to a better country; and I pray God to give me contentment. I am thankful to have had for seventeen months such a light and joy in our household. Shall I murmur that the Giver reclaims the gift?

I have always felt that mothers should not mourn

too deeply the little ones gone to glory, and I still feel the same. "It is well." May a kind Father spare your little flock.

It was the first grave at Benita. True, from the rear-door of the frame house "the little grave" could be seen. But he did not lie there. The frightful customs of a heathen land did not let even the little thin wearied limbs rest in peace.

When the entire funeral company had dispersed, on the evening of the 13th of December, 1867, two Christians returned to me secretly, and in suppressed voice said, "Doctor Nassau, never tell who warned you, but we warn you to watch the grave."

"Why?" They were reluctant to tell. My horrible suspicions insisted.

"It may be spoiled."

"Surely, none here would do so."

"No, not just here, nor to-day; but other people, and after awhile."

I kept their secret from every soul; and no native knows it to-day. Natives cannot keep a white man's secret. I would not burden Mrs. Nassau with what was so terrible, and determined at first, secretly and alone, to remove the precious remains to an unsuspected spot. But though I could practice on others the fiction of visiting the original grave, I dared not on Paull's mother, and, to obtain her permission for the removal, was compelled to make her sharer of the secret.

And the grave was watched nightly; but not by natives, not even the trustiest. In a spot accustomed to our feet in daily walks and recreations, and that therefore could be visited without exciting suspicion, I dug, after twilight some days later, a new grave. And there, in the moonless night, nor daring to bear a light, reckless of beast of prey, we two, with superhuman strength, disinterred and reinterred. No mound was made, and the fresh earth was disguised. Sacrilege might covet the original grave, visited daily for a tearful memory; thoughtless footsteps might press on the actual grave, visited as regularly in recreation; but our secret was safe with ourselves.

The two natives' secret was kept; and we bore the burden of our own. For years no fellow-missionary knew it. And no native knows it till to-day. Even the final removal to the present cemetery, open and by native hands, was accomplished as if from the *original* grave in which I, for the occasion, had replaced the remains. It mattered nothing to little Paull. He was at rest. But that there should have been necessity for it was almost crazing. That night compressed the weight and marks of years. Mrs. Nassau never referred to it until a year later, when the marbles came from America and were set up in the cemetery. Then she was satisfied, and her little Paull was *rested*.

It was pleasant then to sit on his real grave at the sunset hour in the cemetery so near the sea, and find in its ceaseless breakings on the Mbâdĕ rocks beyond, and in the long sigh of the light waves in the Upwanjo Cove, a response to our own spirits. And with those sea-murmurings there seemed to come a response, even out of the Past, in a little child's voice that was startling in its recognition. Was it little Paull that spoke? Or the sea? What were those waves saying?

"Gone!"

And the long sigh from the Cove echoed,—

"Home!"

Sighing, sighing; echoing and re-echoing in dying cadences,—

"*Gone*, home,—C-o-m-e, h-o-m-e!"

And she answered, "It is well."

CHAPTER XIV.

IN THE WILDERNESS.

1866-1869. Benita.

"In perils of robbers, in perils by mine own countrymen, in perils of the heathen, in perils among false brethren."

GIRLS AND TEACHING.

IN the varied works of a new station, Mrs. Nassau tried to induce the native girls and women to come for instruction.

She could have had a large boarding-school of boys. But, aside from the labor to herself, it was unnecessary to put the Church to the expense of finding food and clothing for them, as would be necessary in such a school, while they were so desirous of education as to be willing to come to a day-school at no expense to the mission. Boys from far distances made visits of an indefinite length in the adjacent villages among their relatives and connections of the most remote kind, and, with commendable regularity, came to an afternoon day-school. At noon or at night, or whenever the men were free from their own work

A FOREST VILLAGE.

of fishing or mission employ, Mrs. Nassau would lay aside anything else and hear their lessons.

But the women, burdened with the mass of work that falls to heathen woman's lot, if taught at all, had to be visited in their own smoky huts. And girls were not permitted to come to day-school. Unlike the boys, the hold of their parents, or of the men to whom they were betrothed, was too great, unless they were cut off from it by being constantly in our houses and entirely under our direction, as our own children. Some three or four were always thus held in the mission households, even when there was no formal school. The missionaries on Corisco preferred the Kombe girls, as, by the distance, there were few relatives there to interfere with them.

MRS. NASSAU TO MRS. REV. W. H. CLARK.

BONITA, W. C. A.,
Tues., Sept. 4, 1866.

. . . Dr. Nassau has spoken to Mambondo three times about his wife, and I tried to get her to come to speak to me in town; but you will probably not see that child this time. Makĕndĕngĕ reports that she is "thin *mĕtĕ*," and I report, from a side view, that she is not promising-looking; but flesh on the bones, and a skin washed off, and a dress over all would make a wonderful difference.

Dr. Nassau has just sent for a man in town who has two wives, and *may* be willing to spare the younger. She has not occupied the position of *wife*, and is one of the brightest-looking girls near here. Girls are very scarce. I know of no one whose husband has no other wife excepting those who are too old for you. I know that Mr. Clark used to object to taking one who was under the control of a polygamist; but what else can be done in the present distress? If you are not suited, she can come back with us,—that is, if Bĕngĕ lets her go. She is very bright-looking.

We have *Iliña*, a "little wife," whose husband lives across the river; but he has three grown-up ones. We intended to send her home during our visit to Corisco; but will bring her down, as I think she may be useful. She is one of the smartest little things you ever saw, and not afraid of work.

Poor Iliña became so elated by the freedom that lay in woman's lot, as presented in the life of the Christian family and school, that she unwisely made her polygamist a subject of ridicule, and declared she would never live with him. Even as an adult woman, she would have had (with only rarest exceptions) no power to carry out this threat. Still less had she as a child. The sad story of her short stay in the mission-house is told in a letter of Mrs. Nassau to a Philadelphia infant Sabbath-school:

"In my first letter I promised to write again and tell you of a little girl that used to live with us, and of whom I was very fond.

"What was her name? ILINA. What does that mean? It means spirit, or soul. Do you think it a pretty name for a pretty little girl? Was she pretty? Yes, and smart, too; but she was too fond of talking, and too fond of having her own way, which two things brought her into great trouble at last.

"'Spirit' was about eleven years old, and belonged to a man who had five or six other wives, of whom she was the youngest. Do you want to know how many wives the men have in this part of Africa? Just as many as they can get the money to pay for. As for the poor young men, who have no money or friends, they have to go without any wife, unless they can steal one.

"Well, Spirit's husband was a cross man when anything displeased him. He brought her here one day, and said that he wished us to keep her as our little girl until she grew up to be a young woman, and then he would come to get her. The little girl did not like the man who had bought her and taken her away from all her friends, and she was very glad to come and live at the missionary's house.

"She was very proud of having a dress to wear, instead of a little piece of cloth tied around her waist; and when Dr. Nassau gave her a box to keep her clothes in, her eyes danced, and her feet, too, because she felt so happy. She was neat. One day she lost an ear-ring; and the owner of the ear-ring said, if it was not found, she would take Ilina's dress. 'Do you want to kill me,' she answered, 'that you say you will take my dresses?' And then the two girls began to fight.

"Children here, like children in America, are often so foolish as to be afraid of the dark; but Ilina never seemed to fear anything, and would go wherever she was sent. One dark night a woman living with me said to her, 'Go to the spring, and get water for the pitcher.' She took up the pail and started out; but I called her back, for a leopard had been about a few nights before and taken our goat, and I did not want him to take one of my little girls, too. The woman had only spoken so as to see what the child would do.

"Two of our other girls are engaged to be married to Christian young men; and Ilina soon said she did not like to marry a man with other wives, and she intended to have a young husband. When her husband heard that Ilina spoke so of her marriage, he came over to get her, and went first to the kitchen door to tell her to light his pipe. She refused, as it was against our rule for the girls to light pipes for the men at the kitchen fire. Then he was angry, and caught hold of her wrist; but she pulled her hand away, and told him to let her alone. He went into the house, and told Dr. Nassau that he had come to get his girl; and, though we were very sorry on account of the child, we could do nothing to keep her. Ilina cried as though her heart would break, and, after they started down the hill to the beach, she tried to run back to the house. Then a man caught her and led her along, and she began to cry and scream for me. 'O mamma, mamma, come and take me! They will kill me! O mamma, come!' So she screamed, until they got her to the beach, where her husband, who was vexed at her cries, beat her and had her lifted into the boat; and I have never seen the poor child since. My heart ached for many a day when I thought of the bright little girl who had so often amused us with her cheerful talk and lively ways."

Another most interesting girl, tenderly attached to Mrs. Nassau and to little Paull, was Âkâ, the betrothed of Etiyani, an elder of the Benita church.

The mission at the Gaboon, having been established so much longer than ours at the Benita, had raised up some native assistants. One of these, a young woman, Opanda, was employed in Mrs Nassau's household in various capacities.

Fugitive slaves, also, slightly acquainted with some arts of the semi-civilization of the adjacent Portuguese islands of St. Thomas and Princess, in fleeing from those islands to reach their former homes in Angola, were often driven by wind and current on to Corisco and Bonita shores, and were re-enslaved, as waifs, by those of their own color.

Mrs. Nassau wrote to Mrs. Clark early in 1867:

"I was very glad to see Âkâ, but wanted you to keep her so long as was needful. You know what Maria and Julia are; so I need not enlarge on them. I would be glad to get rid of them as soon as they would be bettered by leaving me. Just now we cannot get girls on account of that fuss Ilina made,—but I want no more. Opanda helps with the sewing, and I have had one of the Portuguese slaves sewing a little."

The station at the mouth of the Bonita was regarded as only a stepping-stone to the interior. The location of the two young men at Sĕnje in May, 1866, had been a feeler; and we kept our own counsel, not speaking to the natives on the subject (lest their jealousy be aroused) until a proper time should come. Mrs. Nassau always watched the blue hills of the Sierra del Crystal up the river as we crossed its mouth, and would sigh,

"Oh! *can't* we go there?" She wrote in January, 1867, to Miss M. E. Nassau:

"We want to see you all, but we want still more to get up the river. I think no one now in the mission has such kind friends as ours, for we are never troubled by letters begging us to 'come home.' But you do not know how often we think and talk of you all."

Rev. S. and Mrs. Reutlinger, on January 19, arriving in the mission at Corisco, the hope was entertained that they would either relieve us, if failing health should compel a return to America, or assist in the up-river step, if health permitted our remaining.

MRS. NASSAU TO MISS M. E. NASSAU.

BONITA, W. A., March 7, '67.

. . . Hamill and I would love to be at some of those home-gatherings, but we feel it a privilege to be permitted to remain so long on the field. Some of our Christians are walking well, and some, alas! are trying to gain the crown without the burden of the cross. Have you not some such on your side of the water as well?

Hamill is not looking well, but would look better if his hair were not trimmed in such a prison-like style. I was his last barberess, and it hurts my feelings every time I look at it. To be sure, he insisted on having all the long locks cropped off short. . . . We look for Willie's photograph again next month. I took the disappointment this time very philosophically, seeing that I was not sick in bed. I was very sorry when my dear husband told me he had said anything on the subject, for all of you are always so good, kind, and thoughtful. I never blamed any one, but I may have said too often, "Oh! I want my baby's picture." . . . Would you like to know what kind of flour we have been using since the beginning of December? They always send good from New York, but a long voyage to Corisco, and some months' stay in a warm climate, is no improvement to our breadstuffs. This particular barrel was so hard that we had to cut the flour with a hatchet; and as to weevils and small worms, it was next to impossible to sift them out, our fine sieve being the worse for wear. Such hard flour is not common; it must have got damp on the way from Corisco.

The kerosene being almost done, we use it only for a night-lamp, and for common purposes burn palm-oil. Our lamps are two tea-cups, our wicks two sticks with a piece of old cloth wrapped around. That is the way of burning the crude oil as we buy it of the natives.

AUTHORITY.

On my journeys, either quarterly to Corisco, or monthly to the out-stations, Mrs. Nassau had to be left at Benita, almost the only white person for fifty miles about. The Corisco absences were never less than a week. Only her taste for and knowledge of medicine, rare good judgment in administering it, and tact in dealing with the natives at the station, could make me feel that she and the babe, and the station, were well and safe.

On such occasions a reliable native was always left under her direction, to assist her in the morning and evening public prayers, and all the station employees were charged with only one word, "to watch her lips," *i.e.*, to obey implicitly her orders, even if, unintentionally, they should happen to contravene any of mine. This was necessary, for the disrespect with which the female sex is regarded by the heathen extended in some indefinite ways even to the missionary ladies, and male missionaries had to bestow extra honor on them in order to have proper respect accorded them by the natives. The latter soon came to perceive that a disrespect to myself was more readily condoned than one to Mrs. Nassau, and they gave her a special deference, even beyond what her own force of character would have received.

She knew during my absence that the workmen were hers to dismiss temporarily if there was no work she wanted done, or to retain for anything that her fancy might prompt. Generally there was something completed as a surprise for my return. On one occasion, imagining that some large wild beans growing in the vicinity might be edible, she told an employee, Isanga, to go gather some. He hesitated, objecting that they "were not eaten." That phrase did not necessarily mean that a thing "was not edible," for we had discovered several edible wild fruits which the natives, in their fear of poison, had not been accustomed to eat. She repeated her direction to Isanga; he obeyed. Making a careful experiment that day, she ate more largely the next, and on my return had a bowlful ready, with an amusing account of the man's hesitation to obey. Without knowing that Mrs. Nassau had told me, he soon sought a private interview with me, and said,—

"Father Nassau, did you not bid me watch only Mrs. Nassau's lips?"

"I did."

"And did you not leave me here as one of her guards?"

"I did."

"And would you not blame me if any evil happened to her?"

"I most certainly would."

"Then please, I pray you, my father, speak to that wife of yours that she do not bid me bring her poison; for if I disobey her she will vex, and if, in obeying, the poison kill her, you will punish. What shall I do?"

He was assured that Mrs. Nassau's wisdom would direct her in her culinary experiments, and that his safest path lay in obedience.

MRS. NASSAU TO THE MISSES M. AND M. A. LATTA.

BENITA, W. A., July 27, '67.

Mr. Reutlinger came home with Dr. Nassau after the April mission-meeting, and spent ten days with us. He is very pleasant, and has common sense,—a very desirable quality in missionaries. He and all the rest of the Corisco missionaries are believers in homœopathy; but Mr. and Mrs. De Heer take regular medicine very often. I could have some faith in Mr. Reutlinger's homœopathy myself, as he has no faith in those little boxes of sugar pills that are sold to the people at large. . . . Last mail I sent you only the letters I had written the month before, and which failed to reach Corisco in time for the boat to Gaboon. However, that mail sent from Corisco did not reach Gaboon, as the men ran the boat very carelessly among the breakers at Cape Esterias, and the boat was broken to pieces.

Mr. Reutlinger is very anxious to come to the mainland, and the brethren on Corisco are anxious to keep him there; so for the present he remains.

I have sixteen young ducks, and another duck

setting; seventeen little chickens, and a hen just hatching to-day, besides another hen setting. The leopard killed for us an old duck and five little ones, leaving seven young ducks that are in charge of a hen and growing finely. Doctor Nassau has just had finished for me a duck-house into which the leopard cannot get, and we do not allow anything to sit out of doors. . . .

STARCH-MAKING.

To encourage an industry and perhaps develop an article of commerce, Mrs. Nassau joined with zest in showing the people how to make starch from cassava roots. With her happy faculty of throwing the light of play over work, the days selected for starch-making were turned into rustic picnics.

A day chosen in the Middle Dries, when, with a bright sun for drying the starch, there was still plenty of water in Haië Creek for making it, but no rain to give wet feet on a damp ground; an early breakfast; house locked; and a troop of men and children carrying tubs, benches, baskets of roots, equipments for a dinner, etc. Under the shade of a tree, by the creek across the prairie, on the edge of the forest, all hands were busy playing at work. Children washing the roots in the stream, others peeling them, men grating on enormous graters extemporised from tin cracker-boxes. Mrs. Nassau, with baby in his carriage, or under a rude tent of shawls, with a book, or intent on botany, or assisting Mrs. Thompson over a chicken and some sweet potatoes in the ashes of the most primitive of cooking-places. Then the nooning under the tropic forest by the gypsy-like camp. Then, in the afternoon, as the piles of pulp increased in the tubs, the squeezing of it by hand through thin cotton bags held over other tubs, a child standing by and slowly pouring water into the bag to carry the starch-grains through as others' hands pressed the fibrous pulp. Then, as this starch rapidly precipitated, clinging to the bottom of the tub, the supernatant dirty water was poured off, clean water added, the settled starch broken up and washed around, allowed to settle, and the water finally poured off at the close of the day. After which every body, with dabbled, spattered clothing and shrunken washerwoman's fingers, took up their burdens of tub or bench or basket, and trudged home to a hearty supper and the rest that comes gratefully to tired feet.

One such day's work supplied starch for all laundry purposes, and for tapioca puddings or other culinary uses.

BUSINESS.

Often, during my itinerations, boats would come from Corisco with supplies, or from trading factories on other business. Mrs. Nassau was able to direct the disposition of goods and the payment of wages, though it threw on her a care our ladies are not expected to have anything to do with.

While at Corisco quarterly-meeting in the first week of October, 1867, the Corisco boat was sent up to Benita, and it returned about the 16th with a note from Mrs. Nassau:

" . . . The day after you left, Mango and Njonga got up a big 'palaver' about the death of their son Molongwa. They accused Musanga of Bolondo; but his party being powerful, the palaver ended in nothing on Thursday. I believe they just waited until you got off. . . . Isanga and Mweli do very nicely, and I have had no trouble with any one. . . . Mr. Clark said to put the screws in paper and send them back; but I used a few to close the chests, not wishing to make new nail-holes, and the nails not filling the places of screws well. . . . The goods are all locked up in the new storeroom." . . .

Though living literally in the wilderness, the mission premises were a sanctuary, and in their limits was peace rarely transgressed by the natives even in times of excitement. It was like an oasis in the anarchy of the land. There was a never-ending succession of quarrels, troubles of various kinds and for various causes, theft, adultery, marriage, trade, witchcraft, murder, in the tribe itself and between the tribes around, so that communication was difficult and often impossible between Benita and Corisco. But on the Mbâdĕ grounds we could sing,—

> "Loud may the troubled ocean roar,
> In sacred peace our souls abide,"

and the natives, with few exceptions, were to us kind and, for heathen, even considerate, however much they fought among themselves. The little church, too, was growing in size and grace.

MRS. NASSAU TO MISS M. E. NASSAU.

BENITA, W. A., Dec. 11, 1867.

. . . There have been several applicants lately for admission to the catechumen class, and I have not seen so many at church and prayers since the first few months of our residence here, when many came out of curiosity.

A middle-aged man, Vilangwa, came to see Dr. Nassau some time ago, saying that he wished to be a Christian; he observed the Sabbath, had given up rum and tobacco, and intended to put away three of his four wives. He lives miles away and we have not seen him lately, but if he should succeed in abandoning polygamy it would be a great triumph of the Gospel. One or two men have heretofore put away one wife on becoming Christians, but one of the two has gone back into heathenism. (On pausing to think, there are several that have divorced one wife.)

One of our Scripture-readers, Etiyani, had two children as his betrothed wives before he united with the church. He gave the younger to some of his family, took the elder, Mabito, to Corisco, and put her in the girls' school until she was ready to be married. She died a few minutes after giving birth to her first child; and, as the child had only an old woman's milk and plantains, it died too. He went a few months after and got the younger, Âkâ, and she is now with us, waiting until she is old enough for him to take. She took a great deal of care of Paull when he was younger, but since he has been sick so much he will go to no one but Mrs. Sneed and myself, or sometimes to papa when papa finds time and strength to run off with him. . . . I have two boils under my left arm, which, as they are getting better, I would be willing to dispose of,—five dollars for the two.

Mr. Brew sent us a half-barrel of flour this week to bake part for him and eat part ourselves. It is the best flour we have had in the last six months, and our last half-barrel was very poor, with an unpleasant odor from the first. Of course the odor, worms, and weevils got no better as we neared the bottom, and the last I did not pretend to eat. Fortunately we had a tin of Graham flour which was good, and I subsisted on that in part.

As a recreation, Mrs. Nassau still continued the work of making native hymns, commenced years before at Corisco. In a letter to Mrs. Clark, of date February 3, 1868, at Benita, she says:

"Tell Mr. Clark that I have corrected some hymns, translated a few, and made about one and a-half original. I would like to look over the hymns with himself."

THE UKUKU FIGHT.

In April, 1868, after Mrs. Nassau's return from Corisco, where she had bid good-by to her dear friend, Mrs. Clark, who was returning finally to America, and had welcomed a new missionary, Miss I. A. Nassau, who, with Rev. J. and Mrs. Menaul, had just arrived at Corisco, and who accompanied us to Benita for a short visit before attempting the re-establishment of the Maluku girls' school, an event occurred which showed how we were yet in the wilderness, and how thin were the lines of the civilization we had been cultivating, and how near we were to savage power.

An extensive conspiracy, after the manner of a "strike," was made by a large portion of the community in the vicinity of the mission-house, who took advantage of some discontent about the prices paid for native provisions. This discontent, fomented by some young men, renegade

Christians, if I had been aware of it, could have been amicably settled by conference. Invoking the power of Ukuku, the same oracle that had once assailed the Corisco girls' school, they suddenly assembled on a certain Friday afternoon at the Mbâde house, offensively demanded their terms, and, without giving time for deliberation, threatened in failure of immediate assent, the issue of a law that (1) no more food should be sold me; (2) no native should work for me; nor (3) should I be permitted to drink from my own spring on the mission premises.

Such tyranny, to enforce compliance after the manner of civilized Trades-Unions, was often practiced on their own incorrigible offenders, but especially on foreign traders, even to the point of forbidding the lighting of a fire for cooking. The traders always conquered by bribes of rum.

Of course, compliance to threat was declined.

Heathen servants at once deserted the premises. Those who were Christians were saved the dilemma of a conflict with Ukuku or disobedience to myself, by my not ringing the work-bell. Cessation of work wrought no trouble; the men would miss their daily pay more than the mission would their lazy help. And their *labor* was their own, to render as they pleased. Failure of native provisions was not important; for before our foreign supply in the store-house could fail, the conspiracy would break of itself for greed of the mission's valuable articles. And their *vegetables* were their own, to sell as they pleased. Water-supply could have been obtained by the rains from the caves. But the *spring* was *ours*. To be *ordered* was galling. And Mrs. Nassau agreed with me that staying away from the spring would seem to be bowing to a power which we had always preached against, which was based on a lie, and which stood in the eyes of the African as an idol in other heathen countries.

The next (Saturday) morning she assented that a public demonstration against Ukuku law should be made by my taking a bucket of water from the spring. Though she knew that violation of its laws, by a native, were instant death, and that at Corisco threats against missionary lives had been made by it, she took bravely that morning's goodby.

The spring was several hundred yards from the house, through a winding jungle-path. A spy there, failing to dash the bucket from me, and foiled in his thrusts of a spear at my back, left the water to be carried in triumph to Mbâdĕ, while he ran off to raise a mob in the villages.

The unexpected demonstration made the younger heathen see that they had gone too far. They rallied with the Christians to the protection of the mission, warned me that the mob was coming in the afternoon, and applied for powder to assist in the defense.

While I was fastening the doors and windows of the bamboo house, Mrs. Nassau was doing the same in her frame house, and before I could join her the mob were firing on the premises. Rapid shots were exchanged by the two parties, during which, as I crossed the space between the two houses, Mrs. Nassau had the door of her house opened. She and Miss Nassau, with Mrs. Sneed and two native girls, were sitting on the floor in the second story, calm, and, though pale, self-possessed, their anxiety having been for me, as had mine been for them, lest the doors and windows had failed to be barred before the assailants came.

It was a short, angry, bloodless fight of less than twenty minutes, and Ukuku was defeated.

MRS. NASSAU TO MRS. REV. W. H. CLARK.

Benita, W. A., Aug. 28, 1868.

We were very glad to hear by the last mail of your safe arrival in America; also that Mr. Clark was "just in time to vote for re-union." You see, I have a hope that the cause of Missions (both Foreign and Domestic) may be in some way helped by the union; and as to the doctrines, if everybody is ready to acknowledge that we are all born sinners, I do not see that it makes any practical difference how we became so. . . . The captain of that Boston vessel had flour for sale, or we would have been badly off. We had been on rations for some weeks here, and much longer at Corisco. The Glasgow goods are lying at Fernando Po.

Our bull was shot by a "bushman," and we, recovering the carcass, feasted on fresh beef for a week. As the cow has always been troublesome, we expect to send her to Fernando Po for sale, and give up the attempt to raise cattle at Benita, depending on goats for our supply of milk. . . .

I wish I could have a good long letter from you about yourself and the children.

I suppose the fashion of gored skirts suited dresses that needed to be altered. I have remodeled several of mine that needed some kind of renovation. . . . The longer I live on mission-ground the less desirable it seems to me that ladies should be sent out alone,—but no matter about that.

Tell Walter and Anna we have a little monkey that gets on the cat's back to ride, but the cat does not want to be monkey's horse, and so it just sits down and will not move.

The isolation of the Benita life was relieved in October, 1868, by the transfer of Miss Nassau and Charity Sneed from Corisco to Kombe, and their residence for six months at the Mbâdĕ house, while their own was being built—for the sake of water-privileges—by the Bolondo rivulet, two miles distant, just within the mouth of the Bonita river.

THE FUGITIVE SLAVES.

Mrs. Nassau's self-possession in exciting circumstances appeared on two occasions connected with the history of two fugitive slaves. Her sympathy was ever with the oppressed, and masters sometimes bore with ill-suppressed vexation her distinctions in favor of their slaves.

Two Portuguese slaves, a man Louis and his wife Joan, fleeing from the adjacent island of Princess, fell on the Biafra coast more than seventy miles north of Benita, and ran many hair-breadth escapes, hiding by day, and at night gathering shell-fish on the beach and plantains from the gardens, which they cooked in their only utensil, a small iron pot, with fire from flint and steel. Thus they had wandered aimlessly down the coast, until one day in December, 1868, they were discovered by some young men of Haië village. Fleeing along the beach, they observed the mission boat-house, and, assuming that the owner of so much wealth was necessarily a white man, and preferring service with him rather than capture by their own color, came rushing up the hill into the *Ikenga* where Miss Nassau was surrounded by her afternoon school, and on their knees implored protection in the name of the Virgin Mary, of whom they had heard from the Portuguese.

The Haië pursuers quickly followed, armed with spear, guns, and cutlass, and dared to enter the room, where the excitement had put an end to lessons, but they respected the right of sanctuary and did no violence. Only, the workings of their faces and the glaring of their eyes were a study.

To withdraw the noise and confusion which would necessarily follow for several days, until my right as protector should be established, and to give quiet to Mrs. Nassau, I committed Louis and Joan to the temporary care of Isanga, a church member living in the adjacent village, Upwanjo.

For several days there was intense excitement. Haië people made demand for the fugitives on the ground of discovery, but not being able to say they had had actual possession, their claim failed. Then the fugitives being in Upwanjo was misconstrued by Haië as a secret gift to a family of which they were jealous; then an altercation between the two families in the street of Upwanjo; then Isanga's own weak heart, tempted by the black heart of his heathen elder brother Tyema, daring to face the church and community, and retain as slaves those who had been intrusted as boarders, and, after various subterfuges, refusing to give them up; then a most affecting meeting by the native church members to plead with their erring brother,; a secret embassy at night from the community to know (strange fatuity of native duplicity!) whether I really wanted the freedom of the fugitives, or whether I was not actually playing into Isanga's hands; then the escape of the fugitives at night by assistance of Haič slaves and connivance of one of my Mpongwe servants; Isanga's violent attack on my premises and servants; the assemblage of the elders of the village to condemn Upwanjo, to establish my right, and to receive the publication of the freedom of Louis and Joan, and their reception into my paid service.

During all the seven days occupied by these events, though their noise was partly removed from Mrs. Nassau's ears only by an actual closing of the bamboo house, and the transfer of prayer-meeting, school, and market, to a native house on another part of the premises, she kept her equanimity, and insisted on being constantly informed as to the progress of events,—though new-born Charley's presence had just been added to her care,—gave her advice and encouragement, and exulted in the Mpongwe's final solution of the difficulty.

Joan, as she had been a house-servant, was found useful in sewing. But Louis had been a field-hand, bore ill his prosperity, like all freedmen in Africa, became lazier and prouder than either slave or freeman, and finally, a year later, led us into serious difficulty.

THE ASSAULT.

There was a renegade Christian, who had himself been a fugitive slave, rescued at Corisco, by Mr. Clemens. After a long course of consummate hypocrisy, in which he succeeded in deceiving the mission, and was trusted as elder and Scripture-reader, his crimes began to be reported, and though he strenuously denied them as slanders, they were gradually proven against him, and one after another the members of the mission ceased to confide in him. Mrs. Nassau was one of the first to suspect, with her quick insight of character, long before I had dismissed him from mission service; and he was degraded and excommunicated for repeated adulteries. Unable to get work with us, and having by thefts exhausted all credit at the traders' houses, he employed his wife as a decoy to Louis, and, when the latter fell into the trap, set up an outcry as an injured husband, and one day, about July, 1869, made an attack on Louis's house on the Mbâdĕ premises, seizing all his goods, and threatening to take him as slave.

In my indignation at Louis for bringing himself into disgrace, I failed to see the duty of resenting his persecutor's outrage against my premises, and sat still in the *Ikenga* while a great hubbub was going on in the outhouses, a large crowd having collected there.

Several young men, in the lead of a young friend, Beduka, presently interfered and prevented Louis being enslaved, the latter consenting to pay from his wages a fine. To that agreement I was no party, as I declined to treat with the assailant or to have anything to do with him. But I did promise Beduka that until he should consider sufficient fine to have been paid, I would not assist Louis to run away.

Poor Joan had in the attack been fleeced of all her own hard earnings (even of clothing Mrs. Nassau had given her), except a duck, which she brought to Mrs. Nassau, and deposited under her protection in our house. The persecutor, emboldened by my neglect to interfere for Louis, came to the door of the room where Mrs. Nassau and I were sitting, and said daringly, "I am going through your house, to search for and take that duck!"

Insolence had gone too far for her outraged sense of justice, and, addressing him by name, she exclaimed, with Pauline indignation, "You slave of adultery, go out of this house!"

Drawing a butcher-knife, with a flourish, he said, "I'll kill you both to-day!" He escaped my grasp at the door, and left with his plunder.

A few weeks later, in August, when we were

going to Gaboon, Beduka was induced to say that the fine had been sufficient. Mrs. Nassau was intensely relieved when Joan and her husband were taken into the boat just as it pushed off from shore too late for interference, and were finally delivered to the protection of the French at Gaboon.

This passage of the fugitives to freedom cost me, on the return to Benita, a vast amount of vexation, and Beduka some money for our not having consulted with the prosecuting husband; and the matter was not finally settled until long after Mrs. Nassau was in her grave, when, in self-defense, I, for the first time in Africa's ten years, took up a weapon of offense, and my enemy narrowly escaped the cutlass that should have felled him when he lifted his knife two years before.

It is a good illustration of the lawlessness of that wilderness, that during the whole year, while Louis's betrayer was annoying us, there was no power to actually lay hands on and *stop* him, and he was too devoid of shame to be affected by the rebukes and objurgations of the community. Yet, in the doing of all the evil he did, he was almost alone, not more than half a dozen actively sympathizing with him in his violence.

THE LEOPARD FIEND.

Leopards were not numerous, but they were very daring, made more so by the immunity of punishment that was allowed them. A strange superstition said that on whoever should kill a leopard there would come an evil disease, curable only by ruinously expensive ceremonies of three weeks' duration, under the direction of Ukuku. So the natives allowed the greatest ravages, until their sheep, goats, and dogs were swept away, and were aroused to self-defense only when a human being became the victim of the daring beast. Its tracks about the Mbâdĕ house were very frequent, especially as we kept more domestic animals (particularly goats for their milk) than most natives.

With this superstition was united another, similar to that of the "wehr-wolf" of Germany, viz., a belief in the power of human metamorphosis into a leopard. A person so metamorphosed was called *Uvengwa*.

At one time an intense *uvengwa* excitement prevailed in the community; doors and shutters were violently rattled at dead of night, marks of leopards' claws scratched door-posts, their tracks lay on every path, women and children, in lonely places, saw their flitting forms, or, in the dark, were knocked down by their spring, or heard their growl in the thicket.

It was difficult to decide, in hearing these reports, whether it was a real leopard or only an *uvengwa*. To native fear they were practically the same. We were certain that the *uvengwa* was a thief disguised in a leopard-skin, as thefts were always heard of

UVENGWA.

about such times. Such events did not occur often, for few natives would dare, even for theft, to be out at night without a light. Even we, at any time, rarely went out after dark, without either a light or company.

On one of the quarterly visitations at Corisco, the uvengwa tried our Mbâdĕ house,—the only time that Mrs. Nassau was subjected to trial during any of my frequent absences. Perhaps part of her immunity lay in the fact that she was very watchful, and left open no door to temptation or theft. One night, steps of two persons were heard around the frame house and on the platform between the two houses, but nothing was missed next morning except a few ripe plantains, which the cook had laid near the pantry-door ready for breakfast.

The next night a very strange event occurred. Mrs. Nassau was asleep in her room, in one of the four rooms on the first floor, with a low light burning. The out-door of the room (as were all outer doors) was locked at night; another, an in-door, open, led into the dining-room, which itself again led into a third room, the sitting-room, from which a steep flight of stairs ascended to the attic where Miss Charity Sneed and two native girls were sleeping,—also with a light. Charity woke suddenly, and saw a man's face at the head of the stairs; when he saw he was perceived he jumped down the stairs and she after him. He had to go through the two doors of the sitting- and dining-rooms, making two short turns, and thence through Mrs. Nassau's room, who, awakened by the noise, saw him flit through the opened outside door. She had locked that door in the evening, and had laid the key on the bureau.

How had that door been opened? What was the burglar's object? Not violence to Mrs. Nassau, for, on his way up-stairs, he had evidently passed by her sleeping under the lamp-light. If theft,—why had he not taken the clothing that lay loose or was exposed in half-closed bureau-drawers, none of which was missed next day?

Mrs. Nassau made no revelation of what had occurred; but kept quiet, hoping to entrap the man the next night. She placed two trusty (but timid) natives one side of the house, with directions to come on call; herself and Charity stationing themselves at different doors inside. The feet came, hands fumbled at the door-knob, a key was tried in the hole outside, but was obstructed by its own key having been left in the lock inside, and the feet departed, the watcher within not having been able to make her signal heard to the two assistants on the other side of the house. They heard the retreating steps, but did not pursue them, through either timidity or an unreasoning obedience to the directions to "wait until called."

Some native evidently had a duplicate key. Of

two pair of tracks in the sand at that door next morning, one suited the very peculiar foot of a certain man, the constant companion of a well-known thief, and who was about the size, shape, and color of the one seen two nights before. On these facts and his furtive looks in daylight, and other circumstantial evidence, Mrs. Nassau wished at once to have him seized, and fix the charge on him by a sudden audacity that would not give him time to attempt denial. Her timorous assistants demurred to the circumstantial evidence, falling back on the native proverb, "*Mwibi ĵa bweyakwĕ na itambi.*" (A thief is not seized by a footprint.) And when I returned from Corisco, the favorable hour for action had passed.

The suspicion was not publicly mentioned, and the suspected one, who we were morally certain was guilty, whenever he came for work or sale, seemed to be conscious of the distrust, and for a long while absented himself from the vicinity.

Mr. and Mrs. Reutlinger were transferred to Benita in January, 1869. They came in February; and we felt quite as if the wilderness were blossoming.

ROMANCE OF MISSIONS.

About this time was probably penned the following characteristic writing, on a scrap of paper, in Mrs. Nassau's chirography, without name or date, which I find among her papers, and of which

I know nothing except that I remember reading with her in the *Presbyterian* the letter of Rev. Mr Johnson, of India, to which she refers:

"My husband and I have been particularly struck by the truthfulness of Mr. Johnson's letter, and its applicability to Africa as well as India. On one point I can give my own experience: After a residence of nearly nine years on the coast, and a continual looking for the 'pale missionary' in a swallow-tailed coat, who preaches all day to an open-mouthed and open-eyed audience, I confessed to my husband this morning that I had only met with one who suited my model of a missionary in appearance, and I did not find him under a tree either,—never saw him preaching except in a respectable bamboo house. My husband inquired whether he did not represent that solitary individual, but I had to say, 'No! you are not half so pale and "interesting" looking.'

"I wonder, by the way, where that missionary under the tree gets his washing and ironing done? I know the natives in this part of the world would not be equal to the task. I wish that my native employés were. If I only knew how myself, I might be able to teach others.

"The week before I first sailed as a missionary I rose up early in the morning and went down to the basement kitchen to learn how to wash, and took lessons in washing of my cousin's faithful servants. I rolled up my sleeves and went to work with such a will that I was too faint to be very hungry for my breakfast; but of what I learned I have not the most remote idea.

"I have learned some of the theory since,—not much of the practice; for some kind of washers can usually be had.

"I do not write this as an encouragement to those who are totally ignorant of the mysteries of the wash-tub to come without learning more than I did, but to show that if one is willing to put a hand to anything, it is not *necessary* to know everything."

During the building of the Bolondo house our household was, in the month of February, large, and the refreshment of society revived Mrs. Nassau very much. At no one time before were there so many civilized friends near us: Miss Nassau, awaiting the completion of the Bolondo house; Rev. S. and Mrs. Reutlinger, planning an advance up the river, and Rev. Wm. and Mrs. Walker, visiting from Gaboon, having come on invitation to baptize baby Charley.

MRS. NASSAU TO MRS. REV. W. H. CLARK.

BENITA, W. AF., Feb. 16, 1869.

. . . As for our present family, Mr. and Mrs. Reutlinger came last week, and sister Bella and

Charity will be with us for about a month yet. Waneta came with her "ma," and Julia was sent from Corisco in October. . . . Mrs. Sneed is a great comfort; but my cook, who is also a comfort, will soon leave; his relatives give him no peace. . . . Charley is a great fat baby, and has no sickness of any account. . . . He sleeps in the cradle,—the first of my babies who would condescend to do so. . . . We have plenty of goats' milk. Mrs. Reutlinger looks very well. Dr. Nassau is pretty well, but the building of the new station is hard on him; he goes in a canoe every morning and returns in the evening. I send him his dinner, and he is home one or two days in each week.

Sister Bella has scarcely any fever, but she does not look strong. My health is very good at present, but I cannot do as much as I have sometimes in the past. Perhaps I am well because I am lazy. Mr. Hugh McLachlan was here a couple of weeks ago, and said I looked as well as when he saw me on Corisco in 1860. . . . I thank you so much for Charlie's beautiful hat; it will fit him in a month or two, but I do not know where he will go to show it.

Mr. Reutlinger, while up the Bonita on an exploration of a practicable route across the ridges of the Sierra del Crystal, was seized with erysipelas, was carried by his attendants in a hammock more than two days' journey homeward, and, lingering, died in July. A journey to Gaboon was made in August for baby Charley's sake; and in October we were again alone at Mbâdĕ, for Mrs. Reutlinger removed to the Gaboon Mission to assist in Mrs. Walker's Baraka school.

MRS. NASSAU TO MRS. REV. W. H. CLARK.

BENITA, W. A., Nov. (?) 1869.
I guess December.

... Since I wrote you last I have been at Gaboon with Charlie on account of his health; went in search of good milk, as all our goats had some disease. We lost five or six in all, and as many kids; but most of the goats were eaten by our native friends, and so not counted as a dead loss, —I mean not by them.

Charlie gained rapidly at Gaboon, and is now a fine healthy child, teething without any difficulty, —at least none to speak of.

We were at Gaboon two months, and came home from there direct on Mr. McLachlan's schooner, bringing with us a cow and calf, and a boy to milk her, until some one here learned how. Dr. Nassau has decided to purchase the cow, as she is so little trouble, and sent the money for her last week. We keep her tied, changing her from place to place, and during the rains she gets along very well. She is fatter than when she came, and also gives more milk; but I suppose it will be more trouble to supply her with food in the Dries. We fed her some at first; but she seemed to care so little for some of the food that we gave it up for the present, and she does just as well. We get rather more than two quarts of milk per day, and Charlie does not take quite all. We take the upper three-fourths for him and add a little water. Sometimes he takes all the milk; and sometimes the cow gives nearly three quarts a day, and that is more than the youngster needs.

Dec. 15.—Mr. and Mrs. De Heer left Benita this morning (Tuesday), having been with us since last Thursday,—that is, Mrs. De Heer stayed with us while her husband went farther north to the Vunĕ tribe, looking for boys, I suppose, or else looking after "the regions beyond." I didn't inquire which.

We were at the dinner-table on Thursday when the children came running in, exclaiming, "Here comes a boat with a flag." I ran down to the beach bareheaded as soon as a lady was seen, and was delighted, of course. . . .

Mrs. Reutlinger is at Gaboon. . . . And Mrs. Walker's health was feeble; so she left us, hoping to return at some time. My heart ached for her.

> "Sowing their seed with an aching heart,
> Sowing their seed while the tear-drops start."

CHAPTER XV.

JOURNEYINGS OFT.

1866-1870. Benita.

"Sowing their seed by the wayside high,
Sowing their seed on the rocks to die,
Sowing their seed where the thorns will spoil,
Sowing their seed in the fertile soil."

Mrs. Nassau's life at Benita was interrupted by frequent returns to Corisco, caused, sometimes, by a desire to see another white female face, sometimes to help a fellow-missionary in emergency, sometimes as an effort to find relief from labor's exhaustion by changing its scene, or by breaking entirely away from it.

She also accompanied me on itinerations on the coast or up the rivers.

Religious exercises were always part of the objects of every journey; and sometimes the trip, though arduous, was, in spite of rain and sun and fatigue, by its variety, conducive to health.

UP THE BONITA.

One such pleasant journey occurred in May, 1866. Two young men, members of the Benita church, were to be located as Scripture-readers at Sĕnje, a point sixteen miles up the river, the first of a proposed series of inland stations. It was with hesitation that Mrs. Nassau was taken, as her health was feeble, and almost too weak to endure the fatigue of the boat. But her wishes went with mine so strongly in all plans for progress interior-ward, that her desire to accompany was assented to. She was made comfortable on a narrow mattress in the stern of the little row-boat.

The sun was hot when, with the two Scripture-readers, three Christian boatmen, and a household company, the "Draper" started with the tide. Progress with the sail being slow, as there is but little wind between 11 A.M. and 1 P.M., the oars were kept moving most of the time. The wide river, lined with mangroves, with their wonderfully-interlaced roots and shoots and props by the million, made a forest scene that never wearied.

About 1 P.M. a dense, heavy rain-cloud was met in its progress seaward; and, as there was no village ashore, nor, indeed, scarcely a bank (the mangrove swamp has no solid bank) at which to stop, we rowed on in the midst of the drenching torrents. Mrs. Nassau was saved by having her sit up, crouching under an umbrella, shawls and coats over her shoulders, and the mattress lying across her feet. When the shower had passed, and the

MANGROVE-TREES.

sun burst forth again, the boat was bailed, and everything dried rapidly in the hot air.

A stoppage was made under the over-arching shade of the mangroves at the mouth of a creek, for a picnic lunch from a little supply of bread, butter, and dried herring.

Then we went on past the Mapanga villages and the islands at Manjanga, and strange birds and trees and flowers, with the view in front of ascending ridges of hills and mountains, romantically varied with each turn of the river, and refreshing to the eye as was the cool, swiftly-flowing river-water to the hands that dabbled in it over the gunwale, or lifted it in draughts to thirsty lips.

Stopped at the town of Isambi,—a man whose self-importance made conciliation desirable, lest, by passing him unnoticed, jealousy might be excited, and our future journeys hindered. We did not alight from the boat, but invited him to accompany us, which he did, with one of his wives and her child.

About the middle of the journey mangroves ended, and the screw-pines (pandanus) took their place, and the river banks rose in bluffs.

By 5 P.M. Senje, on the river's right bank, was reached, and we climbed the precipitous clay bluff on which the village was perched, forty feet above the water. The river current was swift and full of foam from a series of cataracts and the Yovi falls, a mile farther up. Mrs. Nassau was the first white lady who had ever entered the river. She was a great curiosity to the people.

After the usual salutations, the customary chicken that is presented to white visitors being slow in coming, I suggested to the chief of the village that my wife was hungry, and presently a young hen was brought.

Darkness, that so quickly follows the equatorial six o'clock sunset, had come, and it was time for worship before the people should scatter to their several villages,—some on the other side of the river. Mrs. Nassau had wonderfully recovered strength by the journey,—so delighted was she with those refreshing river views,—and had superintended the preparation of the chicken, while I was assuring the crowd of curious natives that there were other reasons than trade for which a white man would come that far. Leaving one of the boatmen to watch the pot and keep another of water boiling, we commenced public worship.

It was solemn and impressive; gathered in the street (for no one hut could have held more than twenty people), with a native *vitwa* (gum) light, flaring and flickering as a torch, stuck in the ground on a bamboo splinter, the awed and curiously-watching dusky faces,—the fluttering leaves of the plantain-trees around the huts,—the stars above clear, and the southern cross uplifted,—the dense forest shades by the rushing river,—and the roaring of the falls, mingling with our hymns of praise.

Everything was in the native language. A hymn, *Bato babe hilakĕni* ("Sinners, behold the Lamb of God"); the reading of the story of the birth of Jesus; a prayer (from which the startled superstition of the women and children could scarce be prevented from running away); a talk on Sin and Salvation; another hymn, *O na tongo e jadi ti* ("There is a fountain filled with blood"), and then an open "conversation" by my young men for questions on the part of those who wanted information on practical points growing out of the conflict of God's commandments and their heathen customs.

Then, faint for supper, we told the people we wished to eat, and they politely left us alone. In the hut were fixed our own boat-chests, and some of our host's chests, as seats and table. The savory-smelling chicken was brought in and emptied from the iron pot into a soup-plate; chocolate was soon mixed with the boiling water; a can of tomatoes was warmed; and these, with herring, bread, butter, and native cassava and plantains, made a sumptuous repast. Mrs. Nassau seemed strong again.

When alone, on other journeys, sea-sickness made me too indifferent to attempt to cook, and natives did not know how undirected. So, until I had become used to native foods, I often returned faint for very hunger. But the presence and assistance of Mrs. Nassau furnished a meal as good as if in our own house; and we both enjoyed it exceedingly.

Native pandanus-leaf-matting spread on bamboo poles, and mixed with our shawls and mattress, which the afternoon sun had dried, made tolerably comfortable beds. The heavy night-rain on the low, thatched roof of bamboo-leaf was good music by which to sleep, after we had ceased to hear the drums of the natives at their dance, or the cries of wild beasts in the forest.

Breakfast next morning was supper repeated; and, after prayer, and finally committing the two young men to the people as their teachers, we started down the river about 8 A.M. Stopped to disembark our native friend and his wife and child. Farther down stopped at a small village to say a few words and pray. Half-way down, at one of the Manjanga villages, stopped again to hold meeting, and to lunch on our bread and herring.

Emerged at 5 P.M. at the mouth of the river, with much labor against wind and tide, and, being overtaken by another rain-storm, turned aside to the Mbini trading-factory, on the south side, and at 8 P.M. were across the river, at our Mbâdé home, where Mrs. Thompson had a warm supper waiting.

Despite the rain encountered on the journey, Mrs. Nassau's health improved by the exercise and by this opening of a way for the spread of "the Gospel on the mountains," her constant interest about which made her often long for "a little home back beyond the mountains."

TO CORISCO.

On the occasion of the quarterly meeting at Corisco, Mrs. Nassau accompanied me in September, 1866, on a journey of much peril and loss.

The surf-boat "Manji" had come up for us, and at 5 P.M. of a Tuesday it started with its crew of five men, two native passengers, besides Mrs. Nassau and Paull, and their attendants, Oponda and the two girls. The "Draper," as consort, with its crew of four men, and two passengers, soon got ahead.

We all became sea-sick at once, on the unusually rough bar; and against the wind. About 7 P.M., after having gone three or four miles, the rudder unshipped by the loss of one of its pins, and, though the wind was good, not daring to use sails, rudderless, we had a long, hard row back to the house for repairs.

Starting again at 10 P.M., we had successfully made eighteen miles by daylight of Wednesday, opposite Aje, and had overtaken the "Draper." As the sun became hot and painful towards noon,

Mrs. Nassau preferred going ashore and awaiting the coolness of night. So, eight miles farther on, at Ulâba, where were the Bapuku villages of two native friends, Eyavo and Ivaha, we went ashore, leaving the boats anchored in Eyavo's cove.

We had brought food for ourselves, Ivaha also produced the best he had, and showed Mrs. Nassau all attention, while I was occupied with the "Manji," for with the afternoon swell of the sea it had parted the anchor-rope. Splicing the rope, and tying to it heavy stones as a temporary drag, two hours were spent with fifteen men and boys in diving and sounding for the lost anchor. The search was abandoned in despair at sundown. But at 8 P.M., when the chests, etc., were carried to the beach to embark again, the boat-hook, in poling, suddenly struck the anchor, and it was recovered. A drizzling rain was falling, and the wind was so fierce that Mrs. Nassau, never anxious for herself, was fearful for the babe, and we returned to the village.

A final start was made at midnight with oars, the wind still contrary. It was slow work in the heavy and heavily-laden surf-boat. Land was hidden by the mists. To go ashore was impossible for the rocks and reefs of Italamanga and Ibunja islets. White lines of breakers, indicating sunken rocks, flashed with phosphorescence on every hand, and the men slowly, carefully rowed through the passages, not daring to use the more rapid motion of sail. Their strength gave out, anchor was cast, and we lay in the rain, "wishing," like Paul's company, "for the day." By the aid of a small thatch shelter in the stern, and by exposure of herself, Mrs. Nassau kept her babe dry.

About 4 A.M., of Thursday, the rope parted again; it was in vain to search for the anchor in the darkness, and to prevent drifting on rocks the men sprang to their oars, and aimlessly rowed until daylight showed a safe channel to the Benga villages on the St. Thomè Creek, near Cape St. John. The "Draper" was there awaiting, and all went ashore to dry.

Then was discovered that a chest containing all my clothing for the Corisco visit, and a casket in which were a set of dental instruments, heavy gold pen and pencil-case, and ten dollars in cash, was missing. In the confusion at the eight o'clock attempt at embarkation the night before at Ulâba, the chest had been left on the beach.

The "Draper" was sent back to recover the property, and returned in the evening with the empty chest and a part of the clothing. A Kombe man who had fled for crime to Corisco was staying in Eyavo's village at the time of our visit, and had found it on the beach; had broken it open with a hatchet (as the marks showed), and appropriated everything.

Leaving Mrs. Nassau, I took the "Draper" at once, at night, and in a drenching storm went back to Ulâba, called a "palaver," and obtained the rest of the clothing. The thief denied having anything else, although he returned the casket (which had evidently been knocked apart and then roughly tacked together again), saying that he found the pieces floating loose with the clothing in the tide. Going to sleep in our dripping clothes, the talk was renewed in the morning of Friday, but nothing more was gained. Eyavo said that I had been Ivaha's guest, and that therefore himself had no responsibility about the matter; although the loss had occurred on his beach and not at Ivaha's. Had it been the latter's, all would probably have been recovered. So thin are the walls of morality that make a native either a hospitable protector or an accomplice of theft.

Returning to St. Thomè, both boats started to get around Cape St. John for Corisco. The "Draper" succeeded against the wind in her teeth, but the "Manji" failed; and unwilling to lose, by a return to St. Thomè, even the slight advance of a mile, we put into a cove on the point. There the afternoon was passed sitting in the boat with a stone for anchor, waiting for a change, and hoping to get out at night.

It was becoming very painful for Mrs. Nassau, and doubts as to the duty of persisting on a path, every foot of which had been traversed with difficulty or loss, made us less certain of safety than when a course of duty was clear. Evening prayers were held in the boat, we slept, and at 9 P.M. started to get around the Cape toward Elobi Islands. But a fearful wind blew the boat out to sea, the slender mast bent too dangerously, and the order to turn back was given, an order which even the reckless natives willingly obeyed; and under a drenching rain which hid the land, we with difficulty found the way back to St. Thomè. We aroused the people, took possession of their fires, and spent the night in drying. Mrs. Nassau had borne it all bravely; while her clothing was dripping, not a drop of water was on baby's.

By the fifth day, Saturday, the supply of beads, etc., with which was purchased the boatmen's food along the way, was expended, and the villagers, whose hospitality we had so tried, were asked for a loan. To this they readily assented, except one woman. That was the only willful unkindness I remember Mrs. Nassau receiving either on that or any other journey. A very savory pile of freshly-cooked *mevândâ* was lying in the house, and our own provisions had been exhausted on the third day. I said to the woman of the house (they happened to have nothing, as they never provide beforehand or lay up, and the crew had cleared their scanty stores of the day before),—

"Get me something to eat, and I will repay you on my return."

"I have nothing."

"But here is a great pile of *mevândâ!*"

"It is not mine; it belongs to this stranger," pointing to a woman sitting in a corner, who had just come in from a distant village.

I said to the stranger, "Loan me an *uvândâ* for my wife, who is hungry, and I will send you anything from Corisco."

"*Diaka na nja!*" (Stay with hunger!) she said, spitefully.

It was a rare piece of cruelty in a people who are ordinarily so hospitable.

We started immediately, and did "stay hungry" until our arrival at Corisco after five o'clock that evening, in time for baby Paull's baptism the next day.

We were just an hundred hours from Benita! Once Mr. Paull had made the distance in less than twenty, so variable were the winds and seasons.

Journeys with ladies, whatever the season or wind, always took more time than others, when only men were in the boat. The thatched shelter built over the stern for the ladies' protection from sun or rain only partially accomplished that end, and was a great hindrance to progress by catching the wind unfairly. Rapid trips were often made without Mrs. Nassau, but invariably by my sitting unprotected with the crew.

A new whale-boat, larger than the "Manji," some twenty-six feet long, six feet beam, sharp at both ends for meeting waves either way, and capable of being either rowed or sailed, was sent to us at Benita by personal friends of mine in Lawrenceville, and of Mr. Paull's in Dunbar and other places. The money for it had been given in 1865, but transport from New York was not found until 1868. We called it the "Benita." It was more comfortable for travel than any other we had had. Mrs. Nassau went in it in February, 1868, to Corisco to assist Mr. and Mrs. Clark and their family in the preparations for their final departure for America on the 12th of the following March. On the following Tuesday, the 17th, their vacant places were taken by the arrival of Rev. J. and Mrs. Menaul and Miss I. A. Nassau. Mrs. Nassau, following Mrs. Clark to America with a letter dated Evangasimba, April 8, 1868, where she was awaiting the close of mission meetings for our return to Benita, says, "You left Gaboon on Monday, March 16th, and on Tuesday an American yacht, the 'Coquette,' came sailing in, bringing the new missionaries from Fernando Po. Of course we were surprised and delighted, and the excitement almost made Mrs. Reutlinger and myself sick. We were just getting ourselves rested from the week before, and Mrs. Reutlinger had not been well."

TO GABOON.

In August, 1869, another trying journey was necessitated by the rapidly-failing life of baby Charley. For eight months he had been uninterruptedly well and hearty. Then for two months he began to droop with chronic diarrhœa, the cause of which was not known until it was discovered that the goats on whose milk he depended were diseased. An epidemic carried them off; and, as it was prevalent among the goats of the community, it was determined to seek milk among the few cows kept by the mission at Gaboon. Our attempt to introduce cattle at Benita two years before had been a failure.

With the usual complement of boatmen, attendants, and passengers, amounting to fourteen souls, we started in the afternoon, and, running all night, landed next morning through a heavy surf at Aje, there to stretch limbs contracted in the boat, and to dry clothing wet by the spray.

On coming to start again in the afternoon, a heavy, drizzling mist hung around the shore, dampening clothing that had been barely dried by the natives' fires, and recalling the disastrous hundred hours' journey of two years before, when Mrs. Nassau had vowed that to take such another would, by its audacity, be putting ourselves out of

Divine protection. *That* had been for various good objects; *this* was for Charley's life. As she stood on the Aje beach, hesitating to enter the boat, and looked on the rough sea and blinding mists, she shrank. Then, as she looked on the weak baby in her arms, and saw that the only hope of his life lay in the milk eighty miles distant, she held up her hand in tearful appeal, calling Providence to witness that devotion to the life He had given demanded His protection on the dangerous path she dared to tread.

Heavy black clouds after nightfall, with gusts of wind that piled up waves preventing the use of either sail or oar, compelled stoppage at Ulâba. While the crew disembarked some baggage for the night, Mrs. Nassau sat with her native children on the beach, awaiting my return from a search for the winding path that led to Eyavo's town, which had been removed into the forest from its former proximity to the sea. The night was wild, —with black clouds, and waves tearing on the reef, and the flaring of the torches of the aroused villagers who had returned to the beach with me, and who gave every attention and assistance.

In the morning, starting early, we succeeded in passing Cape St. John, and, the wind being light and sea unusually smooth, went far out to sea, hoping to meet the afternoon breeze that would carry us to Corisco. That wind, utterly and most unusually, failed to come, and there was no alternative but a long, exhausting rowing. There were no waves, but it was rather trying to nerves to see whales, just then in season, on their sportive curves, making directly for the boat. One whisk of a tail would have destroyed us; they reconnoitred, and then dashed away on other tacks.

The night-wind brought us near Corisco late after dark. It was tantalizing on a certain tack to fetch only to Alongo Point, on the north end of the island. Friendly lights were gleaming from the mission-house on the steep promontory. We could almost have flung a stone ashore where Mrs. Nassau knew that her friend Mrs. De Heer would have been so glad to welcome our weary company. But we feared to land on that rocky, dangerous shore in the darkness of night,. and had to leave the warmth of that light, and toil on by sail and oar several hours, three miles farther, where, though waves were just as heavy, the entrance was safe and wide, and the beach clear of rocks.

But even then the landing was fearful. It was late,—near midnight. A native at *imâti* (night-fishing) was hunting crabs on the shore with his *mwanyo* (bamboo-torch), but the roar of the waters made our voices inaudible, as we called to him to summon aid from the Evangasimba mission-house. Our only expectation was to save ourselves; wreck

IN THE SURF.

seemed inevitable for the "Benita," for no number of hands would seem sufficient to ease the stroke when finally it must surge heavily-laden on the beach. The anchor was thrown out at the bow, and one man stood by the chain to let out a fathom or two as the boat rose to each wave, so as to ease the jerk on the anchor, that its hold in the loose sand might not be torn away, and then as the wave receded the extra fathoms were drawn in to keep the boat's stern from grating on the shallower depths near shore. A second man stood at the stern, and with the boat-hook as a pole kept the bow on to the waves, any one of which was enough to overturn it had they struck broadside. Two men swam ashore to arouse the mission-house. They were a painfully long while at that, and in a search in the villages for men to help. Mr. Menaul could obtain none; at that late hour, the inhospitable Bengas declined to leave their warm fires to help. So I bade the fifth man, a tall, stout Krooman, having girt his waist-cloth tightly, to fling himself into the sea and hold himself ready by the gunwale. Then, as the wave receded, he could just touch bottom; and in that instant, before another wave came, Mrs. Nassau laid herself in his arms, having Charley in her own, and the man waded ashore supporting her above his head on the palms of his hands, as one would a doll. Before Mrs. Sneed could be carried ashore, a wave swept the boat and filled it, so that the boxes of clothing, etc., were drenched.

Life being now safe, an unknown strength was given for the saving of the baggage, etc. Alone I lifted boxes and barrels that had taken three men to lift at Benita; handed them over the gunwale to the three men in the water, and they carried them ashore. When thus the entire cargo had been discharged, I swam ashore, the anchor was taken up, and on a favorable wave the boat was permitted to drive into our hands, and was successfully worked, after desperate efforts, toward the top of the beach, away from the violence of the surf.

The next (the fourth) day, Cape Esterias was reached.

On the following day, after tacking many miles away from shore, so that it was scarcely visible, we made one long tack ashore, and just rounded Point Clara, through boiling breakers that flung their white foam on each side and lifted the boat bodily as the practiced hand and eye of helmsman and pilot guided it through the intricacies of the bar and reef. And to crown the work with a smile, the sun came out beautifully as we glided into the smoother water of the Gaboon river.

Then, while resting in a cove during the noon-calm, the smoke of the French steamers could be seen, twelve miles distant, by their depot at the plateau. Going ashore in the cove, we refreshed ourselves at a forest rivulet, bought fresh fish of a passing fisherman, roasted them on an impromptu fire on the sands, made changes in toilet to be less unpresentable in the civilization of Gaboon, and with the first puff of the afternoon breeze sailed gayly up to the Baraka landing.

Calm in the danger of the breakers, Mrs. Nassau had yielded to no fear,—though danger was real,—nor had given way to helpless expostulations. Only, as a wave curled by and flung its spray in our faces, her eye sought the captain's to see in its look whether he was satisfied with the boat's course, and reading assurance, she too was satisfied. And when the "Benita" sped, bounding under the cleared sky and safe wind in the smooth river-water, and the children exulted in the animation and safety, she joined them heartily and gayly, as if "again a child."

TO BOLONDO BY CANOE.

Several months later, after the return to Benita, Mrs. Nassau had occasion to visit Miss Nassau at Bolondo. I was busy at the building of the church, and as the river was smooth, it was not imperative that I should accompany her. So, with four men, she went with Mrs. Sneed and Charley, in our large canoe, that was some twenty-five feet long, two feet wide, and eighteen inches deep, carrying along the Bolondo weekly supply of groceries, etc., station goods of nails, etc., intending to spend the day. In half an hour one of the men came breathlessly repeating, "*Bwalo bo wendi! Bwalo bo wendi!*" (the canoe is dead!) He was so excited as scarcely to be able to give a straight account. At last he reported that as they were paddling vigorously, sitting two and two on the thwarts, a cleat supporting a thwart had given way, and one end of the board striking the bottom with the force of the weight of the two men who were precipitated by its fall, had knocked a hole some sixteen inches long and two inches wide, through which the sea had rapidly entered.

Mrs. Nassau's own account afterward was as amusing as the native's had been distressing. His account was true, but she chose to look on a ridiculous side. One of the natives divested himself of his only clothing, his narrow loin-cloth, to furnish material wherewith to stop the leak, and then for decency sprang into the river and swam ashore. Good Mrs. Sneed held Charley above the in-rushing water, and sat helplessly praying. Mrs. Nassau sprang to the emergency, and while the three men paddled the canoe to the nearest point of the shore, she stuffed the cloth and her shawl into the break. One of the church-members, fishing near by, came to the rescue, transferred the company and the cargo to his own canoe, and carried them on to their Bolondo destination;

where, Mrs. Nassau, I am sure, at a proper point in the adventure, having worked so efficiently with her hands, did not fail to give a grateful heart's prayer of thanks.

TO SIPOLU BY HAMMOCK.

Besides the regular Wednesday evening prayer meeting at Mbâdĕ, the Benita church had two other week-day prayer meetings; one five miles north, at Meduma, on Tuesday (afterward transferred to Bolondo), and one three miles south, across the river, at Sipolu, on Friday. To the Sipolu meeting Mrs. Nassau sometimes accompanied me, the excursion occupying from early in the afternoon, allowing for a visit to the villages, to announce the meeting in the evening,—the services early after night-fall, and before the elephant-watchers had scattered to their various plantations, —a long chat on various topics of civilization, with those who remained in the villages, and a return about 9 P.M. The women were always delighted listeners to one of their own sex, and their hearts were promptly opened to her confiding manner. The little lamp set in the window of our house, a guide to the Mbâdĕ beach in some dark nights, often made us think of the more blessed Light we had been trying to spread, and she ever looked confidently to the day when the little rays, thus scattered, should grow larger than that little lamp's.

TO MEDUMA BY HAND-CART.

In a letter to her aunt Latta, May 13th, 1870, Mrs. Nassau speaks of a pleasant journey to Meduma, accompanied by Charley. She had brought with her from America, in 1864, a two-wheeled wagon, like a hand-cart. Drawn by two men and pushed by a third, it was used on the beach at Corisco in the Alongo visits, and at Benita in excursions to distant villages.

"I had him in town two days ago, and he wanted to hold a little baby so much that he walked up to its mother to take it. The baby was afraid, and clung to its mother screaming, and Charley caught hold of the baby with both hands and pulled away, screaming himself all the time,—partly with vexation that the child would not go to him and partly with fear. After a little while I told Julia to give him some boiled rice that we had taken with us, and when he had eaten a few mouthfuls, he filled one hand with rice, and got down from Julia's lap to go and give it to the little baby. Soon after, another woman came in with a little girl about Charley's age, and he walked across the room to make acquaintance. That baby stood on the floor, and the two little things put their arms around each other very sweetly.

"The town was five miles off; Charley and I rode in the wagon, and Dr. Nassau walked. I had never been there before, and I suppose Charley's visit will be talked of for years to come."

"In journeyings often, in perils of waters, . . . in perils in the sea."

CHAPTER XVI.

FADING AWAY.

1869-1870. Benita.

"In weariness and painfulness, in watchings often, in hunger and thirst, in fastings often."

WHILE awaiting response to the appeal for relief that would enable us to find needed rest and revive sinking life by furlough in America, Mrs. Nassau retained an animated interest not only in all mission concerns but also in the operations of the Church at home. The "Envelope System" of church collections, now so generally and efficiently used, was really proposed by her at the same time that it was being agitated by Rev. R. Strong and others in America.

Among her papers in her own handwriting are three specimen schedules of a ten-weeks' promise, entitled "One Cent Union, in aid of Foreign Missions." One is directed to a family in Waynesburg; a second, dated "June, 1869," is directed to her uncle; and on the third is the following memorandum: "Subscription from January 1 until March 10, 1869." (The plan included the names of all connected with the Benita household, but, as is evident from the blanks below, was never actually presented to all.)

	First week.	Second week.	Third week.	Fourth week.	Fifth week.	Sixth week.	Seventh week.	Eighth week.	Ninth week.	Tenth week.
R. H. Nassau............	1	1	1	1	1	1	1	1	1	1
Mrs. Nassau.............	1	1	1	1	1	1	1	1	1	1
Miss Nassau.............	1	10	1							
S. Reutlinger............										
Mrs. Reutlinger.........										
Mrs. Sneed..............										
Miss Ch. Sneed.........										
Ngombalendo...........										
Julia.....................										
Irongido.................										

Her completed plan she sent to her uncle, Rev. W. W. Latta, of Philadelphia, in February, with a request that he would have it printed at her expense and distributed throughout the churches so as to create some public interest on the subject. Without her knowledge the same thing was being accomplished in May, at General Assembly of that year. In August she received a reply from her uncle, while she was at Gaboon, and wrote me at Benita thus:

"A word more about that plan for penny subscriptions. I scarcely think it is needed in addition to the other previously before the churches;

but of that other I did not know when I wrote to uncle. As he did not hasten, I might have written to him to abandon my project, and the letter would have reached home in time. (It seems to me I did say something of that kind.) If it does good, I shall be glad; and if it fails, I trust I shall be more glad to see the other succeed. The principal thing for which I am sorry is that it will look like a supplement to, or substitute for, Mr. Strong's paper,—but that did not reach Africa until after I had written all directions to uncle."

As if in preparation for her own departure from earth, some of the ties that bound her here were being loosened by the deaths of two of her aunts, Mrs. Rev. W. W. Latta in February, 1869, and Miss Margaretta Latta, June, 1869.

At times, the affairs of the mission, through differences of opinion with regard to proper methods of prosecuting the work, were in a disturbed state, that wearied Mrs. Nassau's gentle spirit, and (while her love for the mission work never for a moment hesitated) made her long for more harmonious action. While at Gaboon, watching Charley's returning strength, she wrote in September, 1869,—

"Would it not be better for us to leave this mission and go elsewhere if our Board choose to send us? It may be we are not fitted for the work; it certainly seems to me better to work where there would not be so much friction. I urge nothing; I know not what is for the best,—perhaps it is wrong to write this. . . . Yet would it be right to leave Benita when the work seems to be prospering? I seem to be all in the dark, and I think that trouble was half the cause of my fever. Good-night. May God guide us. Act as you think best.

"*Sept.* 30. . . . How glad I would be to be away from all strife and turmoil and confusion; but I suppose that will not come to pass in this life."

In her sprightly way of writing, it was a common practice to write little notes for her babes, as if they had said the words thus put into their mouths. She wrote thus for Charley at Baraka, September 20, 1869:

"My dear Papa,—I eat and I sleep and I grow. Esambi gave me a little tusk from a little elephant to make some little napkin-rings. Mrs. Boardman gave me some dresses. Suna gave me a pigeon, and I think it is very pretty; but I would rather play with my mamma's shoe than all the toys and pigeons in Baraka. Sometimes I have a piece of plantain. If anybody tries to take a bite I put my fingers in their mouth to get the piece out. If anybody puts a finger in my mouth I can bite. Everybody says I look well. Good-by, papa. I rode on horseback with Captain Browne. I guess I'm a man."

After the transfer of Mrs. Reutlinger to Gaboon, in October, 1869, we were again alone at Mbâdĕ. Miss Nassau's failing health and departure in December, on a three months' furlough to visit the Scotch Presbyterian Mission at Calabar, required the closing of Bolondo. When I went on the quarterly journey to Corisco, in the last of December, Mrs. Nassau would have been entirely alone, as in the early days of the Benita pioneering, had it not been for the presence of a welcome visitor, a Christian gentleman, Captain W. R. Browne, trade-agent at Gaboon for the only American firm there, and the only trader who did not permit liquor to be used in his business with the natives.

MRS. NASSAU TO MISS M. A. LATTA.

Jan'y, 1870.

Dr. Nassau and Mrs. Sneed left for Corisco last Monday, and Charley and I are keeping house, with the native children for assistants, and Captain Browne still here as visitor. He is waiting for a vessel that he expected several days ago, and for all we can tell it may not be here for a week to come; so I am not altogether alone at night. Hamill will be home in a week, but Mrs. Sneed is to remain with Mrs. Menaul until after her confinement, so I may be without her valuable assistance for six weeks or more. It was our own proposal to have Mrs. Sneed go, as Mrs. Menaul's health is very poor, and they have no good help. I suppose they will go home via Ireland, as soon as Mrs. Menaul is able to travel, and then our mission will be sadly reduced. . . . Charley is the best baby I ever saw, and it would do your eyes good to see his arms and legs. He weighs twenty-six pounds, and is thirteen and a half months old, and has twelve teeth.

When I went into the pantry this morning, my boy-cook had the griddle on, and what do you think he was going to bake for cakes? Flour and water made up into a paste. I tried to explain, without hurting his feelings, that such cakes would be rather tough, and set his paste aside to add yeast for tea-biscuit. (I should have said "kitchen," as my kitchen and pantry are all in one, a room in the bamboo house.)

The schooner that took Sister Bella brought a box for Dr. Nassau, containing a rifle, and a magic-lantern for the Bolondo school. It had come by steamer from America, through England, of course. There were also some books for Sister Bella's school. Some one had sent her three cups of jelly pasted over with paper. The cups were not broken, but most of the jelly had soaked through the paper. . . . Five young men were baptized at our last communion, one restored, one suspended, and one received on certificate from Evangasimba church.

A young man who has just lost his wife applied to us to take his baby, who can creep. We consented, but the mother's friends may oppose the plan. I think the baby would be far better off with us, unless the father knows some one who has a babe, and who would share the milk with his child. They know very little about bringing up of children by hand, as they do not give goat's milk.

I must go make my biscuit now, and may not have time to write more before the captain goes; or if I have the time, I will probably be too tired. . . . And may the Lord spare us all to meet again on earth. Such meeting seems a long way off.

The babe referred to was not permitted by the superstitions of the heathen women to come under Mrs. Nassau's care, because she used cow's milk, and they would not permit "a human being to drink the milk of a beast." For that sole reason we had seen other babes allowed to die. Once, a few years before, so great had been the superstition even about "foreigner's milk," that objection was made by the women to a motherless native infant's sharing our little Paull's superabundant nourishment at the time he was only a few days old. Not till it was actually dying did the father dare to bring it clandestinely to Mrs. Nassau, and it died in her arms. In both cases, native superstition prevented her assuming a labor which her generosity—not to say humanity— prompted and would have performed.

The wished-for "meeting," that seemed "a long way off," became, by the decisions of the January (1870) mission-meeting, farther off—even hopeless. The announcements at that time of the intended American furloughs of Messrs. Menaul and De Heer, in respectively four and six months, and the transfer of the storehouse and mission headquarters from Corisco to Benita, left us the last family in the mission, and with the responsibility of the entire field on utterly-wearied hands.

Mrs. Nassau, on being informed of the arrangements that tied me to Benita, refused to leave me, and instantly wrote to America a long list of garments for a two years' supply to her wardrobe, both of us having permitted our stock of everything, even of clothing, to diminish to a minimum, in expectation of our post being relieved. She took up the burden of the accumulated work falling from others' hands, cheerfully and submissively, as had ever been her wont.

MRS. NASSAU TO MISS M. A. LATTA.

BENITA, Jan. 11, 1870.

Captain Browne goes this morning by way of Corisco, and I am afraid that my letters will not reach Fernando Po in time for this month's mail. The schooner he was expecting has not come, and he has concluded to wait no longer. It is just three weeks since he came. . . . Dr. Nassau came back last Friday night, bringing with him a young bull, two villainous-looking black pigs, and a female kitten,—cats being something I cannot abide about the house. You will say I am not like my mother; but it is so hard to keep the cats from the baby's milk, and they break more things in the pantry than the rats do, and trouble all the food more.

Will you or Katie please have me another set of under-clothing made? . . .

MRS. NASSAU TO THE SAME.

BENITA, W. A., Feb. 1, 1870.

Charley is asleep, after getting a bath, a dose of quinine,—a medicine he does not often have to take,—and a bottle of milk; and I hope he will sleep away a little feverishness that he has had since yesterday. He is cutting now his eye- and stomach-teeth, which Willie did not cut until after he went to Lawrenceville, and that dear little Paull never cut. . . I can scarcely realize that I have a little boy in Lawrenceville, who will be six years old the last of this month. And who can tell how much older he will be before I see him? or, shall I ever see him on earth? . . . We have heard but once from Sister Bella since she left, and she had then been a few days at Calabar, and she mentioned having had a kind reception.

Last evening we had biscuits from a new barrel of flour, and the taste reminded me very forcibly of the biscuits you used to make in dear old Chester Valley. I never made biscuit so near like them before, and it was quite a surprise to myself. While we sat at the table, Dr. Nassau and I had a long talk of the time when I was a little girl, and used to make long visits at my grandfather's. I told him of grandfather's rides to Charlestown,—of the biscuits he took for his Sabbath lunch,—the late getting home on winter evenings; and it seemed scarcely possible that nearly a quarter of a century lay between that past and the present. Yet at times I feel so old it might have been fifty years ago.

February 3.—We were surprised yesterday by the arrival of our mail, and I was glad to find you had not let the month go by without writing, as it is always a disappointment not to hear from you. I had also a letter from Mrs. Paull, with whom I have kept up an occasional correspondence since her son's death.

Your letter told of the kind present from Mrs. Lewis, and I wish you would send her my love and many thanks for her kind remembrance, and assure her I place a high value on anything which comes to tell me I am not forgotten in my dear uncle's former charge.

I am afraid I shall look too fine when that grenadine arrives; but perhaps Dr. Nassau and I will have to take a journey for our health to some more fashionable place than Benita.

About three years ago I thought it was time to stop sending orders home, as we would soon need to go ourselves; but, having outstayed our own expectations so long, I have no idea when we will go, and I rather expect to keep on writing for what I may want until we begin to pack our trunks for the voyage, or nearly up to that time. I do so long sometimes to see you and my uncle, but that is no reason for leaving my work while able to stay.

I was discouraged at the beginning of the year, when Dr. Nassau came home from mission-meeting and told me of the breaking up there was to be on Corisco in a few months; that Mr. Menaul expected to leave in a few months, and the storehouse (iron) and contents would be removed to Benita, which would be regarded hereafter as headquarters. I don't know what the Board in New York will say, as they have always clung to Corisco.

But I think want of faith is the very best way to bring about our fears; and so, while trembling a little, *I do feel a calmness* in the thought that the ark is the Lord's; and I do believe He will give needed strength. Oh, for more faith! And then, surely, we should "run and not be weary, walk and not faint." I fear my faith will not attain to the running without weariness; but I hope to "walk and faint not" through all the way the Lord has marked out for me. I should lose a great deal of comfort were I to lose my belief in predestination.

Mrs. De Heer is not at all well, but she has done nobly for the first time out. Mrs. Sneed is still at Corisco with Mrs. Menaul, who is in good health and spirits. Mr. Menaul is worn out and discouraged, and a letter has gone to America, begging our board to send speedy relief. . . . The news from other missions cannot but make us rejoice. The cheering accounts from India, China, and South America ought to rouse the most desponding, and make converts of all disbelievers in missionary work. . . .

Feb. 15.—Last Sabbath morning, as we were at the breakfast-table, one of the men came to say that he saw a boat which must be from Corisco, and it was near the beach. I felt *sure* there was bad news, and said so to Dr. Nassau, for the boat was probably manned by some of Mr. De Heer's mainland boys, and I knew they would not complete even a small part of their journey after daybreak of Sabbath, unless there was great necessity. My fears proved true. The boat had started Saturday evening, and brought a letter from Mr. Menaul, begging Dr. Nassau would go to him, as his wife was dangerously ill. The baby was nine days old, a little girl, and Mrs. Menaul was taken suddenly worse on Saturday afternoon. Dr. Nassau started back with the men about sunset, and hoped to get down some time on Monday, as this is a good season of the year for traveling. . . . If Mrs. Menaul should be taken, I have offered to take the little one while it stays in Africa.

MRS. NASSAU TO THE SAME.

BENITA, Feb. 21, 1870, Mond. morn.

. . . We are all well, and Charley as stout as any one could wish. . . . Sister Bella is still away.

Now for the sad news, for our mission has again been stricken, and just when we are so few. Mrs. Menaul went home to God last Thursday, Feb. 17th, leaving a little babe two weeks old. Dr. Nassau had been sent for, and reached Corisco the day before she died. She was brought to Benita for burial, and little Bessie is with me for the present. Her father expects to leave with her in May. Mrs. Sneed was a great comfort to them, and it is a great comfort to me that we proposed her going. We are waiting until some one arrives from America. We know of no one. I wish Mr. White, of uncle's former charge, would come out,—I suppose he is Rev. Wm. White now, and I think he ought to suit. Won't uncle ask him? . . . The storehouse and contents are expected next week, also the materials of the Maluku house, where I had the girls on Corisco. The mainland will hereafter be the centre of operations. . . . Please send two copies of "The Physical Life of Woman," by George H. Napheys, M.D. . . . That is the advertisement in Dr. Nassau's *Reporter*.

Mrs. Nassau's sympathy for Mr. Menaul and care for his babe (as her own Charley monopolized Mrs. Sneed), revived him from disheartenment, and—as my own time was taken up with superintending the building of the church, voluntarily begun by the people—he vigorously occupied himself with the re-erection of the iron storehouse.

On the back of a letter of his to Mr. Clark, dated March 22, 1870, is a postscript, in April, by Mrs. Nassau:—

"I just answer your husband's last kind note, and will say I would write oftener if I had the time and strength. Charley is getting on finely. Thanks for your Willie's picture. Bessie is well, and both babies live on the milk of one cow. We keep the cow tied. . . . Charity and Sister Bella are back; were gone three months on a visit to Calabar."

MRS. NASSAU TO MISS M. A. LATTA.

BENITA, W. A., May 9, 1870.

You ask in your last letter about boxes sent to the Mission House last June, and I can only say that we are hoping to see them next June, as a vessel is expected out then. There has been at least one vessel out since you forwarded the things to New York, but Mr. Cutter may not have known of its sailing until too late; or, if the boxes were sent by it, they never reached us. The "Edith Rose," with supplies for our mission, is due next month, and I suppose we shall receive a host of things by her that you have been expecting to hear of months ago. . . . Mr. Menaul and Bessie have been gone nearly three weeks. We were ready at that time for them to go, and expecting the schooner "Janette" daily, when, one morning, a little cutter anchored near the mouth of the river. Dr. Nassau sent off a canoe, and it soon returned bringing Mr. Smith, a white trader, who wished a tooth extracted. He was on his way to Fernando Po, but had no idea of calling here until daylight that morning, when he found himself opposite the Bonita River, and concluded to come and have his aching tooth out. Dr. Nassau had relieved him in a similar manner once before. He brought word that the "Janette" would not be along for three weeks, and Mr. Menaul immediately asked passage in his cutter, the "St. George," and he and Bessie went off that afternoon. God surely sent that poor man's toothache for my relief, as the care was becoming almost too much for me. A young man from here went to Fernando Po to help with the care of the baby that far, and he returned ten days later, saying that they had got along very well. A note from Mr. Menaul reported Bessie as well, and said they were being kindly entertained by Methodist missionaries from England.

The "St. George" was only a very large boat, but it had a kind of cabin, big enough for the baby and for one or two grown persons, in case of rain. They left here Thursday, and reached Fernando Po Sunday morning.

Since the revolution in Spain, Protestant missionaries have been allowed to come to Fernando Po, and two Primitive Methodists, with their wives and one child, came out recently. . . . We hear that Mr. and Mrs. Walker, of Gaboon, are going to America soon. I do not know, indeed, whether they will have strength to wait Mr. Bushnell's arrival. . . .

May 13.—Thank you for the seeds that came the last mail. I sent some to Bolondo the same day,—as Sister Bella has better ground than we have,—and the cucumbers were up several days ago; I think the tomatoes, too, but I am not sure. Dr. Nassau thinks he can make a rich place for me to plant some cucumbers. Please send another paper of cucumber-seed and one of egg-plant,—they will get here for the beginning of the rains.

Did I write that the medicine in bottles came safely? The pepsin was not as good as that which came in the silver paper,—moulded some; but Charley did not need it. . . .

Mr. and Mrs. Walker did not leave until a year later. They held on hoping, even as we, and, after the departure of Mr. and Mrs. De Heer, in June, those two Gaboon friends (besides the Benita trio) were the only missionaries in the field. The Gaboon Mission had not then been transferred from the A. B. C. F. M.; but the mutual loneliness of the two missions bridged over the narrow separating line in Africa before that line had been removed in America. Occasionally there came a gleam of hope of reinforcement that left the shadows darker when it failed. Such was the expectation of a medical missionary for whose coming from Missouri we had been encouraged to look. Expected supplies from America did not come; and, as our own storehouse was exhausted, we would have had to rely on native provisions, except for the occasional gifts of trading vessels.

MRS. NASSAU TO REV. W. W. LATTA.

BENITA, May 9, 1870.

We are very much cheered by the intelligence in the last mission-letter that a physician and his wife from the West would probably be added to our number shortly. Dr. Lowrie thinks the gentleman is an elder in the Church, and I suppose their coming is about a certainty. I hope they may be sent out by way of England just as soon as they are able to come, for we certainly feel the need of reinforcement.

Mr. Menaul will doubtless visit you; and, as he has a warm Irish heart and a high appreciation of the little I could do for him, you may be surprised with quite a eulogium on your niece's good qualities. I warn you in time to make due deductions. . . . He has great mechanical ingenuity, and helped me clean my sewing-machine more perfectly than it had been cleaned before in eleven years. Afterwards he complimented me by saying to Dr. Nassau, "I think that, next to myself, Mrs. Nassau has the most mechanical genius of any one in the mission;" and my husband was kind enough to reply that he did not doubt it. I guess I must resemble my uncle somewhat.

I was very glad to get your last letter, and I would write to you every mail whether I had a letter to answer or not; but I have not always energy for more than the letter to Aunt Mary Ann to let you all know that I am still in the land of the dying. . . . I believe I am complaining oftener than any one else, though not sick enough for bed. . . .

Because of tribal quarrels between the Kombe, at Bonita, the Benga, at Corisco, and Mpongwe, at Gaboon, we were dependent for the sending and reception of letters entirely on irregular transient trading-vessels. For this and other favors of the gentlemen of the trade we are greatly indebted. While their rum traffic and the dissolute lives of most of those connected with it distressed us in our work, their personal kindness to ourselves constantly merited our thanks. Especially was this true of the agents of a Glasgow firm, John Laughland & Co., and of Dr. R. B. N. Walker, agent of a Liverpool firm, Hatton & Cookson. Mrs. Nassau mentions, on May 13, 1870:

"I never met him until lately; but he is only too kind in all his offers. The last time he was here I was thinking of going to Gaboon with Bessie, and asked passage on his vessel. He replied that neither his captain nor accommodations were fit for a lady, but he would send a vessel for me next week that should stop and let me sleep at Corisco and take me on to Gaboon. Mr. Menaul's serious illness, however, decided him to go home immediately, so Bessie was not taken to Gaboon."

> "No! earth *has* angels, though their forms are moulded
> But of such clay as fashions all below;
> Though harps are wanted and bright pinions folded,
> We know them by the love-light on their brow!"

CHAPTER XVII.

THROUGH THE WATERS.

August 30–September 10, 1870. Benita.

"And at even my wife died."

WHEN tropic tornado storms are coming, all beings, even the lower animals, can see the definitely-outlined cloud gathering, and are warned by the lull and apparent peace. Yet the initial crash of wind, rain, thunder, and lightning startles, and, by its suddenness, finds them unprepared.

Our own eyes had seen the danger of a too-long continuance at the Benita post. And loving, anxious, friendly hearts had written, "Do not longer stay: come back to America and recruit." But those kind hearts—not knowing that we three stood, last of the mission, alone—had not intimated that there would be no dishonor in leaving our post. So we stood by the dismantled ship as engulfing waves curled around it.

Blind, so blind! Even yet we did not talk of death.

"Weary and so tired!" she would say on the lounge, even while planning for the future.

And still it was *her* hopeful spirit that encouraged; and *her* accustomed smile that aroused my own crippled feet to the weekly visit by canoe to the sister at Bolondo, or that rose to welcome that sister's return visit.

And we still planned for the future.

MRS. NASSAU TO MISS M. A. LATTA.

BENITA, Aug. 16, 1870.

Here is the middle of the month, and our mail not yet arrived; but we are hoping to see it as soon as that slow bird of passage, the "Love-Bird," arrives from Fernando Po. She was expected on the twelfth, but as she is always behind her time, no one expected her very much. I suppose you do not expect to hear regularly in these degenerate times. Benita is certainly very much in a corner.

We have a captain with us at present, who has come ashore to recruit, from a trading vessel lying at the mouth of the river. He is not sick in bed, but—what is about as bad—he has no appetite; and it is almost impossible to find anything he will eat. His vessel has come to buy red-wood; and they have given out "trust," which will stay *out* awhile, I fear, before they get it in in any shape. The sailors do not like the captain, and are glad to be rid of him for awhile; so I suppose he troubles me less than he does the crew.

How many more comforts we missionaries have than those who come out to trade on the coast! And yet there is not often any lack of young men ready to run the risk of dying alone, for a little money. Their salaries are not high either; and I doubt whether any of them save much,— that is of the clerks. Perhaps some of the agents make money; and the owners at home must make large profits sometimes, or there would not be so many houses engaged in the West African trade.

The cucumber-seed you sent grew nicely, and the vines bore well; but the dry season has nearly killed them. Sister Bella sent me a few tomatoes the other day; but I do not know whether they came from the seed you sent, or some she received at the same time from Lawrenceville,—I think the latter. When the rains come, I intend to try raising a few cucumbers by having good earth carried for the hills.

Mr. Walker sent Sister Bella a present of a little pig last month; so we are going to kill our big one soon, and let the little one grow. We are also expecting to eat our old turkey-gobbler next Thursday, as I had a present of a pair of turkeys from the vessel lying near us, and we have to keep the new gobbler shut up until the other is disposed of. You see we are not in danger of starving immediately, though we would like to know where our supplies of sugar and butter are.

Thus she cheerfully wrote and spoke, even while stinting herself to lengthen out the few necessaries that yet remained in the almost empty provision-room of the mission storehouse.

So I did not think strangely of her long lying on the lounge, as, hopeless of receiving anything from New York, I sat Tuesday, August 30, making out a large order for goods and supplies to Glasgow. Nor was it strange, after awhile, when she arose and had sat by me to watch my pen or suggest for the order the names of needed articles of ladies' wear, and food, and medicine (it was the last work she did for the mission), that she asked for some medicine for biliousness, and went to her room sick at stomach. It was not a new story. Nor, next morning, when I was called from marketing, to find her in a severe chill; it seemed only the usual intermittent.

Only after Thursday and Friday had gone by,—not constantly confined to the bed,—Saturday presented a gleam of the old sprightliness, as she dressed in the afternoon, and under an unusual appetite ate a hearty supper, and joked about "breeding a famine." A gleam that went out.

On the next day, Sabbath, September 4, the chill returned with more frightful power. The meaning of that congestive remittent was no longer mistakable.

Then those long, intense days,—Monday, Tuesday, Wednesday, Thursday,—minutes for years. No thought for work, or natives, or religious services, or even baby Charley. Every intense energy lay in that little room, and for the quiet, emotionless face and lustreless eyes, and lips parched, apathetic,—that longed for ice where ice had never been,—and saffroned skin that felt sirocco-touched even while the cold sea-breeze played on it. How each hour was watched, each symptom met, every possibility studied! How life's chances were weighed in that and this combination of plan and effort!

There was one little hope.

This vitality that has lasted a week, where strong men have sunk in three days, if transferred to different air may survive.

Shall she go to England? Can this house be closed and the premises left in care of a native? Can Sister Bella, until I return in three months, be left at Bolondo with her Liberian assistant? Shall Charley accompany or stay? Shall the journey be attempted to Fernando Po, one hundred and sixty miles north, with winds favorable, but over a rocky route, with which this tribe is not acquainted, and which includes the crossing, out of sight of land, of forty miles of a bay marked by treacherous currents? Or shall we go ninety miles south, to Gaboon, in the teeth of an opposing wind, but over a route I know, and at the end of which are missionary friends? Can a crew be obtained to go in the "Benita?" None! The ill will of a former Benga friend at Cape St. John, who imagines I have interfered with his trade prospects, has caused him, some weeks previous, to utter (about a missionary) the rare threat that he "will seize the 'Benita,' and any crew" I may send in it. But surely he would make no assault while an invalid lady is in the boat? I think not. I trust him. But none of the Kombe will trust him or venture themselves. But there is a little sloop-rigged cutter, the "Witch" (no longer, and not as fast, but stronger and wider than the "Benita"), owned by Hamilton, a colored Sierra Leone trader across the river, near Mbini.

Perhaps he will lend it! "Go and ask for it at

any price!" He has received kindness at her hands, and promptly assents to the use of the "Witch," offers his own Kombe crew and personal aid and presence, to the limits of the next tribe, the Bapuku, and there will obtain another crew who are not afraid of Benga or Mpongwe.

How those four days, intense to the watchers, passed wearily to the sick one! Dozing, but not refreshed by sleep; faint for food, but not tempted by even the variety that love's art could educe from paucity of resource; patient to swallow again and again medicines against which the stomach painfully rebelled; uncomplaining of what she had accepted as inevitable; submissive as if to God's will; pleased even when it was an effort to smile; enlivened, as—borne in a hammock slung from a bamboo pole on the shoulders of two affectionate natives, with most careful tread—she passed under the shadow of the church-roof, and asked "When will it be finished?" and "Where will I be then?" gentle, under all arrangements made without asking advice, which prostration had made her too emotionless to give; or consent to plans to which apathy had no objection. Even the purpose to go to Gaboon excited no inquiry as to details. Only thrice did the characteristic life gleam; when generosity spurred to an earnest charge for the future care of a faithful nurse—when friendship designated parting gifts to native friends; and, when mother-love overheard and vetoed our intention of leaving behind two-year-old baby Charley.

At last the repairs of the trading-boat were complete, and a Kombe crew obtained, who were to return with the crew of another (a small native) boat, which would accompany us to the rendezvous at Ajĕ.

Early on Friday, September 9, the baggage for the journey to England was stored in the "Witch." Besides ourselves and little Charley's nurse, Mrs. Sneed, the company consisted of our Sierra Leone friend, who took charge of the rudder, three of his Kombe crew to manage the sails, and two native Christians, young men of the Ŷunĕ tribe, who were willing to go with me as far as Gaboon, as cook and servant. For the journey thither, that time might not be lost by running ashore for food or water, we took water and fowls and fresh provisions for five days, fuel, and a box of sand for stove; a goat and canned milk for Charley; ropes, twine, and tools for possible damage.

At 5 A.M. the hammock was brought to Mrs. Nassau's bedroom, laid on her bed, and she lifted into it and gently carried down the descent to the water-side, and thence, these same bearers standing in a canoe, was paddled to a boat. She would have preferred our trim "Benita;" for the "Witch," used for purposes of trade, was rough and less cleanly. But its greater width furnished space in the middle, where a level flooring seven feet long and five feet wide was placed as a bed-frame in the bottom, over the swash of water that would persist in leaking. Over this, just high enough to sit crouchingly, was built a palm-thatch roof resting on the gunwales. This bed-frame was covered with an entire mattress, and was made comfortable with blankets and other covering, not against cold (for Mrs. Nassau constantly had said she was too warm), but to keep the bed soft.

Loose things were stowed away; and, as far as possible, provisions and other things offensive to invalid eye or nostril were placed to the leeward. And we started, leaving Sister Bella and Miss Sneed to close the premises, and take the keys to their own Bolondo house.

A slight drizzling rain, premonitory of the rainy season, alternated with sunshine, until the wind increased. It was the toilsome Monda (south wind) directly ahead, and against which there is no progress but by "tacking." How we tacked all that long weary day! counting each point of coast as we crept around them: Sipolu, three miles; Duba, six; Ndoti, eight; Hanje, ten; Ilĕndĕ, fifteen. Then night fell, and we ran in toward the breakers that line the mouth of Ajĕ creek. Only eighteen miles in fourteen hours!

We were too sea-sick to eat, except Mrs. Nassau,

who drank at intervals during the day a little toast-water or chicken-soup or wine. The only space for the fire was forward, and the wind drove the smoke aft. She could be saved the discomfort only by extinguishing the embers after each use of them for herself or Charley, whom the narrow limits of the boat—so unlike his daily wide range—made capricious for his frequently-warmed milk.

The native boat soon came alongside, and our Sierra Leone friend went ashore to obtain a Bapuku crew for Gaboon. The Ajĕ people had heard of my Benga friend's charge and threat; some of them assented to both, for Ajĕ had thought I had prejudiced traders against them also. He readily obtained one man, a Benga, an Evangasimba church-member, who was one of the first three I had baptized at Corisco, and who had been in Mrs. Nassau's service there. After hours of effort a second man, an Upuku, was obtained.

At 11 P.M. the wind had so increased in violence that we dared not take up anchor; and yet lying just at the creek's mouth we caught every rolling wave that broke on the surf inside. The uneasy jerking of the boat hour after hour prevented rest. Rain fell continuously but not heavily. The thatch over the middle of the boat protected Mrs. Nassau; but, it being open fore and aft for air, the bedding and extra clothing at the ends became damp. For the other three of us umbrellas were useless,—even Charley preferring the open air in Mrs. Sneed's wet arms to the close air by his mother, who, as we waited for that wind to subside, in intervals of incoherent moans called for him to come to her under the protection of the roof.

By 3 A.M. of Saturday the rain had beaten down the waves to something of quietness, and itself had ceased, and we began to put up sail. Our Sierra Leone friend had stayed by, waiting to see us fairly under way.

As he was about starting in the little native boat, with his two Kombe crews to Benita, it was proposed to Mrs. Nassau—as in the extremity of her weakness and in the face of the inevitable discomforts of the journey—to send with him baby Charley, restless for the shore, and fretting under the restrictions of a boat. The proposition had to be repeated very slowly and distinctly three times before her fading perceptions gathered its full force. Then she rose on one elbow, as if to seize this last one of her jewels, and said clearly and decidedly, " I am going to Gaboon, and Charley goes too."

We started immediately with a light, though still opposing, wind. When daylight came the sun shone bright and clear and hot, and dried clothing and whatever else was wet with night's rain. With constant tacking we were *moving* rapidly, but making very little real progress. The crew was small. My two Evuně men knew but little about the sea, but the Benga and the Upuku were skillful sailors, and they two held tiller and drew sheet with care and hearty interest to gain every point in the wind. The reluctance with which they had hired for the journey disappeared, as they looked with pity on the invalid at their feet, or with subdued voices calculated chances of turning cape after cape.

Her symptoms grew more distressing. Then again the pain would ease and she would fall into stupor, from which she would arouse to ask of the progress, and would awake almost to interest as on a landward tack she would want to know whether we had rounded the point of land or were driven back. How our eyes measured the distant shore, as she asked during the day, "Have we come to Itěmbwě?" "Have we passed Ulâba?" "Are we near Cape St. John?"

The only thought of all at the start was to keep on uninterruptedly to Gaboon; but as the day wore, the first utterance of her wish to stop at Elobi Islands in Corisco Bay—whither the sea-breeze would probably compel us—found a prompt response not only in the assent, but in the tired wish of all. She spoke with pleasure of the stopping, seemed interested in calculations of time of arrival there (which it was hoped might be by sunset), and we talked how she should go ashore to a certain trading-house, should be bathed, and should rest on the Sabbath.

When not crouching by her under the thatch roof, I was sitting just outside by and above her head where her face was at my feet, and when her lips moved could promptly creep down to her assistance. A shawl or piece of matting, hung at each open end of the roof, was let down or flung back according as sunlight and her wishes indicated.

The stiff sea-breeze dissipated the hope of reaching Elobi by sunset. Then we hoped for arrival there by 9 P.M., but she had ceased pleadingly to ask, "Are we almost there?" and either lay still or spoke wanderingly.

Late in the afternoon, when, refreshed by the cool wind, she lay awake and had eaten a little food, she asked for an opium pill to relieve some symptom; and at sunset, finding we were only just laboring around Cape St. John (only 18 miles from Ajĕ), and the hope of being at Elobi by 9 P.M. failed, she accepted the assurance that we would certainly be there in time to enjoy the rest on Sabbath.

"Yes! we'll rest on Sabbath."

She did not speak again.

The curtain that tropic night lets fall so quickly after the uniform six o'clock sunset found us, with great skill on the part of the crew, turned the

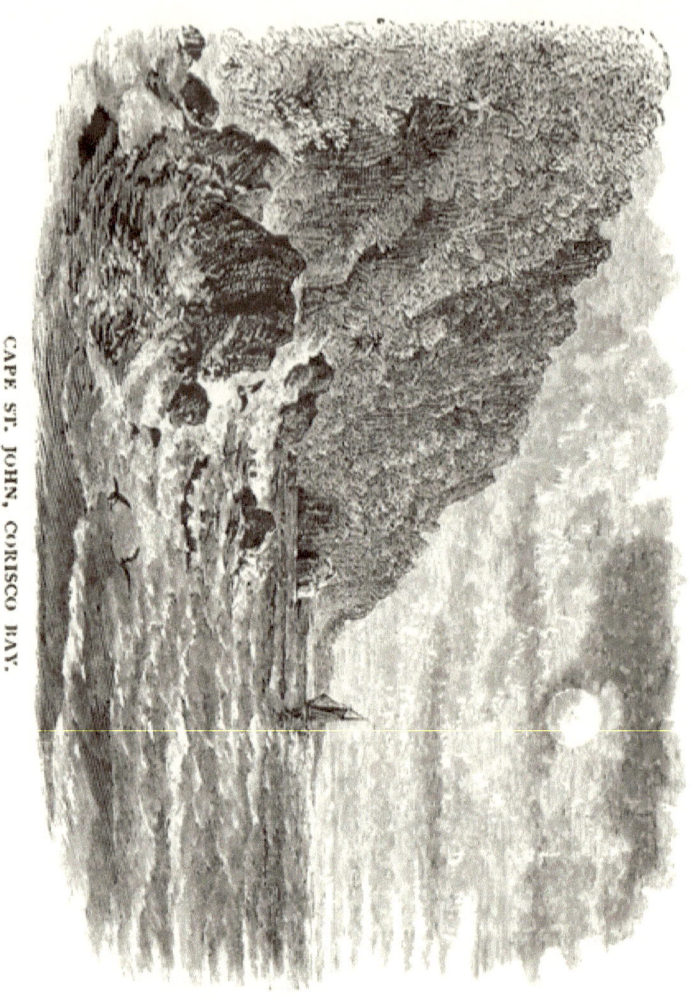

CAPE ST. JOHN, CORISCO BAY.

rocky southern point of Cape St. John, and the strong sea-breeze on our quarter fair for Elobi. The boat was gliding beautifully, and with apparent rapidity, through the water, but the strong current of the tide ebbing out of the bay prevented progress, as was marked by one after another of the trees on the near shore.

The night was clear and starlight. All so quiet! All except the man at the rudder and I were asleep. The two Vuně men on the thwarts forward, Charley on Mrs. Sneed's lap, in the stern one side of the steersman, and I on the gunwale on the other, could hear Mrs. Nassau if she should speak, but could not see her face in the sail's shadow.

The tide is ebbing swiftly and must soon turn, and we'll be at Elobi long before daylight. Is a life ebbing away under this thatch? Stoop and listen to her quiet breathing,—infant-like,—not stertorous as during the fitful day.

It must be as late as nine o'clock. All is clear and safe.

Will, that has not eaten or slept for forty hours, fails, and eyes sleep.

How long passed, I do not know. An hour? Perhaps two.

Suddenly starting awake, alarmed vigilance is relieved by the steersman's response that the boat is all right and bounding on the way to Elobi.

The tide has ebbed out, and, turning, is bearing us rapidly on its flow.

But of the life at my side: has it ebbed away?

As my hand seeks the forehead and wontedly smooths the temples, they are warm and pleasant. Her hands, fondled, are cold.

Startled? No; it's only the cold of the night air on the uncovered arms. Chafe the fingers to warmth.

They do not flinch even at an accidental twist!

Thrust a hand into her bosom. It is warm.

But, such silence!

Heart-throb, pulse, breath, there is none!

But drag out the mattress, with the energy of a last hope, into the fair moonlight! Waken these sleepers to assist in chafing hands and feet! Sprinkle briny sea-drops in her face! Pour stimulant through these lips! Vain, give o'er. The fastened teeth cannot swallow. Cold creeps over face and limbs.

And the little hope was dead.

The tide had ebbed; was out. It has turned; but it flows only in Eternity.

Close the eyes, they cannot see; close the lips, they cannot speak. Replace the mattress and its unconscious burden under the thatch.

"Turn the boat back to Benita!"

There is no watch to tell the hour, but the tide and the gibbous moon mounting toward the zenith, tell about eleven P.M. It will soon be the Sabbath.

All these now-electrified eyes had been asleep except the steersman's. Had she spoken?

Fatal hour! "Couldst thou not watch with me one hour?"

Perhaps she spoke. Possibly it was a word from her that aroused me. Sounds as slight had awakened the unquiet, broken rest in other boat journeys on the restless sea. Perhaps the rustling of a spirit's wing! Had she asked for help in vain, in breath too faint for sleeping ears? Was this last hour of martyr-life crowned with thorny pain?

Believe, rather, that she quietly slept away, without pain or motion. Posture, photographed on memory in that terrible light of events and the clear light of the moon, was marked, when smoothing her forehead on first awakening, as the same natural flexure of body and limbs,—the same quiet crossed hands on the breast, the same calm, painless face that had been breathing so peacefully when I looked for her wishes an hour before.

"Back to Benita!"

Nothing has a voice, nor a tear!

The crew sit silent and motionless, except to tighten a rope or trim the boat, as it slowly works back against the tide to Cape St. John.

Voiceless and tearless. Even the sea ripples only subduedly now that it hath wrought its ministry of pain.

The hours go slowly by. And the blessed ministry of sleep comes to all again, save to steersman, who must not, and to watcher, who cannot sleep.

All as silent as those who sleep the sleep of the pale sleeper at my feet.

> "Would we could sleep as they,
>   Stainless and so calm; at rest with Thee,
>   And only wake in immortality.
> Bear us with them away,
>   O Night!
> To that eternal, holier, happier height."

The moon sinks. It is past midnight. Sabbath. She has entered into its rest.

Voiceless and tearless. Nothing has a voice, save the waves that fling their white hands so madly on the remorseless cliffs of Cape St. John. Thou mayest

> "Break, break, break,
>   On thy cold, gray stones, O Sea,"

thou hast accomplished thy bitter service of tumultuous pain and agonizing weariness.

Pitiless Night! that can look so calmly and beautifully, where beauty meets no response, and calmness is not prayed for. Thy beauty and thy calmness, thy tumult and thy dread are alike bootless to the dead.

The morning light streaks the east, but the light, too, is pitiless. It gives back nothing. No promise, nor even tears. It gives not even Sabbath rest. She has already found the rest agony prayed for. Ere this

> " morn came dim and sad,
> And chill with early showers;
> Her quiet eyelids closed,—she had
> Another morn than ours."

Voiceless! Tearless! Even the sea, smoothly heaving, does not ripple against the prow. The fitful wind only flaps the sail. Are all the silent forms still sleeping? Will no one speak?

Pray for the ministry of tears; these eyes

> " must weep,
> Or else this heavy heart will break."

Thought becomes tangible,—as if it were an object of sense. Bodily organs and limbs and members have all become as one organ; and all senses one new sense,—the sense of flow,—that takes cognizance of all else as atoms in a stream of thought, flowing through that one organ. And being consists only in recognizing that sensation of flowing. So, these are not clouds in the sky,—there is no sky or cloud; they are only atoms with the many other atoms flowing through me. Are these forms men? and do they speak? or boat? or sail? or trees on the passing beach? or beach? or earth? or sea? They are not organized; they only float as atoms of thought; and, with space and time and everything else, plunge through this new organ with its new one sense. There is no hearing, seeing, feeling, smelling, tasting,—

† *Is* there *anything?*
O, Thou!—if Thou art, help me,—if I am.
God *is*. Brain would craze, away from that pivotal truth.

And this is baby Charley pulling at my hand; and the Upuku man is asking, shall he "stop at Ajě?" "No! I want your aid to Benita. Go on."

Yes, this *is* the boat! and the crew have been awake for a long time. And it *is* baby Charley! And this form, outlined through the white cover, was his mother,—and she had helped me bury baby Paull,—we two, alone, in secret, at night,— and we had sent away her first-born across the sea. All, with a thousand other truths come back; and organisms locate themselves naturally. But with pain.

> "And I hold within my hand
> Grains of the golden sand;
> How few! Yet how they creep
> Through my fingers to the deep.
> O God, can I not grasp
> Them in a tighter clasp?
> O God, can I not save
> One from the pitiless wave?"

A few miles beyond, the Benga, in his tribal fear of Kombe, thought it not safe for him to go farther, and he was permitted to disembark in a passing canoe near Hanjĕ.

About 1 P.M., in crossing the mouth of the Bonita, our approach was observed from Bolondo; and messengers, with Miss Sneed and the Mbâdĕ keys, were sent along the beach to meet us.

At Mbâdĕ a well-dressed company, just dispersing from the prayer-meeting held by natives, in place of the regular morning service, came down the bluff to the water-side, and, regardless of their best clothing, waded into the water to seize the gunwales as the keel grated on the beach. The quick instinct of the gathering crowd read our quiet faces, and there was not a word of the usual boisterous welcome,—nor a salutation,—only an electric whisper, *"A wendi"* (She is dead). They were very pitying and respectful.

I do not know to-day who they were; I believe some were Christians, some heathens,—some were my own employés, some townspeople. I saw hands lifting out Mrs. Sneed and Charley,—felt that the thatch was flung aside,—some one lifted me ashore, as many hands gently but firmly raised the entire bed-frame and preceded me up the hill and laid it at my feet, as I sat down on the step of the end door of the bedroom. The natives gathered round the covered form of their friend.

They were kindly unobtrusive, but wept for themselves.

Soon the keys came, the mattress was lifted into the room, and Miss Sneed gave the remains her last care, while I opened the carpenter shop. The natives had known how to make only oblong boxes. I had learned to make a coffin twice before. Two of my young men, with a taste for carpentering, had since learned from my hands, and were able, with the measures given them and outlines penciled, to make from the pine boards neat work without supervision.

The usual Sabbath-school was omitted. Many people came and went, or sat in respectful, tearful silence. A few manifested grief in their native way of wailing and wringing of hands, or hands laid on their heads, and moaning, "I-i-i-i, mama-o;" "Mama Nasâ-o-o;" "Paia-o-o;" "Jai-ĕ;" "Ngĕbĕ mĕtĕ;" "Bamâni, bamâni;" "Mbi wend'-o-o."

Some of the poor women took off their ornaments, and said, "Now we women are left alone!"

My elder and his wife came from Hanjĕ. He had seen the boat when the Benga was discharged in the morning.

Sister Bella had come and dressed my dead, and in the evening conducted family worship; and then we laid the remains in the white-muslin-lined coffin.

Twenty-four hours is a long time to delay a

burial in the torrid zone. Nearly thirty-six had elapsed when the funeral company gathered on Monday morning: our Sierra Leone friend,—the three white men from the ship and the trading-houses on the other side of the river,—all the prominent chiefs of the region,—educated young men,—heathen men and women, who had been recipients of Mrs. Nassau's gentle kindness,—representatives from more than twenty miles distant.

That electric whisper of the preceding day had flown!

While I had to see to the proper making of the grave in the difficulty of loose sand, other hands had surrounded Mrs. Nassau's head and breast with white tropic-flowers.

Standing outside the house, under the broad eaves, by the coffin, while the assemblage stood or sat around, I read the 90th Psalm, in English. Then was answered the question, "Why this waste?"—then a hymn, and a prayer. For natives' sakes these were in their own language. For their sakes, also, it was an occasion—even at a sacrifice of feeling—to enter or act a protest, more earnest than words, against their extreme superstitious fear of death. As but few of them had had an opportunity of seeing her face since the return, permission was then given.

And then, partly to the same end, baby Charley was shown the flowers by "dear mother's" face,—

his hands and lips placed on hers,—and " Good-by, mamma," said for him.

Then I drove the twelve nails to their places. Six young men, Christians,—special pupils, or faithful servants of Mrs. Nassau,—took up the coffin, most of them voluntarily, as I led the way down the arbored path, through the pine-apple garden, by the trellis of passion-vines, and up the knoll to the cemetery, a few hundred feet distant.

At the grave, the coffin was placed immediately; 1 Cor., xv: 51–58, and Rev., vii: 12–17 was read. After prayer, on my expressed wish, the entire company dispersed, while the bearers remained with me to complete a careful closing of the grave, suggested by distrust of heathen sacrilege.

Then custom required my presence in my accustomed seat in the public reception-room, to receive the parting salutations of the heads of families,—politeness forbidding them to go without that ceremony.

" When thou passest through the waters they shall not overflow thee."

CHAPTER XVIII.

CAIRN-STONES.

"Now, here, let us place the gray stones of the cairn."

"—— this marble tells the rest,
Where melancholy friendship bends and weeps."

In a savage land, where distress is apt to be made the occasion for oppression, there were often touching incidents that showed humanity when least expected. Some kindly demonstrations towards myself, connected with Mrs. Nassau's decease, I regarded as monumental contributions to her memory.

KINDNESS OF THE NATIVES.

On returning from boat journeys, it was the custom to give pay to those who assisted in unloading and carrying boxes, etc. I always indicated who of the crowd on the beach should be permitted to help.

When the "Witch" returned on that Sabbath, Sept. 11, 1870, I did not choose any; they put hands to service voluntarily, and none came on Monday to ask for his pittance. The boat was discharged without my presence, or even a direction, and I afterward found all the trunks and boxes placed properly on the porch, and whatever was wet spread out on the grass.

When I told the Sierra Leone trader, Hamilton, that I wished him, in settling my bill, to pay the Upuku his entire wages to Gaboon, as if the journey had actually been made, he said the man had told him "he did not care if he received nothing, 'for the pity of the death.'"

People, both at Kombe and Corisco, showed a delicacy of consideration and respectful sympathy of which I had not supposed the heathen capable. They seemed to transfer to me, for Mrs. Nassau's sake, a portion of the respect and affection her character had evoked.

The absurd charge and strange threat of my Cape St. John Benga friend, which had given so much difficulty in arranging Mrs. Nassau's last journey, had, from the first, determined me to go to his town, demand the cause of his enmity, and show my innocence. The Kombes feared so exceedingly that I could get no one to go with me; then Mrs. Nassau's sickness prevented, then my own serious illness a week after her burial made me fearful of exposure to the rains. On Sept. 28 I obtained a passage on a transient trading-schooner to Corisco to attend to the Evangasimba Communion service. There I obtained a boat and crew to bring me back to Kombe, telling them I intended to stop at Cape St. John and see my enemy. Scores of friendly Bengas came, expressing regret that their only remaining missionary should be slandered by one of their tribe, and begging me not to stop at Cape St. John, declaring that I would be subjected to violence. When I persisted, saying that it were better to suffer violence than to seem to admit a charge by shunning that village, four young men, without my knowledge, and making all arrangements without reference to myself, got another boat, and accompanied mine across the bay to the village as guard and advocates. My truth was so apparent that the enemy became again a friend.

While at Corisco at that time, a very old man, who was rarely out of his palm-wine,—one of whose daughters had been at Maluku school with us and was my favorite,—whose manner was rather unpleasant and imperious when he used, half drunk, to visit us and his child, and who did not seem to have taken much more notice of Mrs. Nassau than to ask her for little gifts, said to me, pointing upward, "And so she is gone! How she used to fondle Beyânâ!"

"Yes, she loved your child and all the children; she played with them, she walked with them, she——"

"Stop, stop! talk about other things! I must go and drink my palm-wine and forget the thoughts."

The old man was tottering on the edge of the grave, and obliviousness was his only peace.

On returning to Benita, numerous unobtrusive visits were received from the principal men. King Mango, an old gray-headed heathen, who lived two miles away, and who had made his ceremonious visit only ten days before, came and spoke thus, literally translated:

"I have not been to see you for a long time. To-day I had business at a village on the way; and, when it was done, I said, 'No, I will not go back; I will go and see him.' God took away my child, and I buried it, as you did yours, near the house, at the end of the garden. And I said, 'I will tear down my village and remove to another place.' But all the people came to me in mass, and advised me, and told me not to do so,—that God could lay his hand on me at any other place. And so I said, 'Let it pass,—I sit down.' And I come to you to-day, hearing that he had said he would go away from this country; and all your other friends will come to see you and to talk to you, each at his own proper time, saying, 'Let it pass.' Remain as you are; what has happened to you happens to all; attend to your usual work, and after awhile you will forget your pain and affliction."

I objected to his last verb.

"Not even after five years?"

"Affliction can be relieved, but not by forgetting."

I do not think he fully understood. Poor old man! Forgetting loved ones was the best relief his heathenism could afford for their absence. But he meant kindly. He was the only heathen who had attempted *direct* comfort.

THE COMING OF MR. GILLESPIE.

Rev. A. Bushnell, on furlough in America, was at Princeton, N. J., addressing the students of the theological seminary, in December, 1870, appealing for recruits for the Corisco Mission, and pointing that appeal by stating that the number in the field was reduced to Mr. and Mrs., and Miss Nassau. He had not yet heard that the number was still less. A student in the audience had just seen the announcement in the *Presbyterian* of December 17, and handed up the paper to Rev. Dr. Charles Hodge, who was presiding. At the close of the address, with voice scarcely controlled, and with all the sympathy of his great heart aroused, he read:

"Died, September 10, Mrs. Mary C. Nassau, wife of Rev. R. H. Nassau, M.D., of the Corisco Mission, West Africa. With this mission she has been connected for ten years, during which time she once visited America. For her chosen work she was admirably adapted both by nature and by grace, always calm in danger, patient in tribulation, generous in giving, correct in judgment, full of faith, and abounding in good works. How much the sable converts from heathen darkness and superstition felt their loss was seen as they surrounded her corpse and 'wept for themselves.' Last spring her failing health led her husband to arrange for her return by an opportunity offering in July. But when the time arrived, feeling better, she declined to leave, and it was concluded to wait for expected reinforcements to the mission. But August 31 she was attacked with the chill by which African fever is preceded. The medical means employed broke the disease, and it was hoped that with a change of climate she would recover. Dr. Nassau set sail with her for England; but on the following day unfavorable symptoms supervened, her exhausted frame sank as in peaceful slumber, and her spirit rose to Jesus from the Atlantic wave to receive a martyr's crown. Her precious remains were interred at Benita, in the ground which three years before was first consecrated as a cemetery by the burial of her beloved child."

The meeting was dismissed; some left in tears. Some went away to think and pray. The next morning a visitor was announced at the missionary's door, and said, "I heard your address and that obituary notice yesterday. I was going as a foreign missionary, and I decide to go to Africa to help Dr. Nassau."

It was Samuel L. Gillespie. He had heard the voice that came from my wife's grave, and was literally standing for the dead. After having served his country against the rebellion as captain of a company in an Ohio regiment of cavalry, and passing unscathed through more than fifty battles, he bravely flung himself into the breach, at the very front of the strife for the Master's kingdom, and in a position of danger from which others shrank.

THE PURCHASE OF THE ELFE.

From the beginning of the Mission, open, row, and sail boats,—the size of ship's gigs and surf boats,—had been the only mode of communication between distant points. In such an one died Mrs. Nassau. When the story reached New York the enlarged liberality of some friends of Missions was shocked, and they said to Messrs. Bushnell and De Heer,—

"Never let that happen again."

"It would not have happened if, at our wishes, better transport had been granted earlier."

"Is there no vessel you can purchase in the Gaboon?"

"Yes; a large schooner."

"Buy it at any cost."

"It is too large for our service."

"Then buy some yacht in England on your way back to Africa."

Mr. Gillespie spent two months in traveling and making addresses, and in collecting funds from the Sabbath-schools for the memorial "little ship" which was "to wait on" Jesus in the persons of His missionary servants.

In passing through Great Britain, the brethren visited the Clyde, but on a hasty survey, found nothing to suit, and passed on to Africa, hoping to find something on the way.

They arrived at Gaboon June 11, 1871. At that very time was in the river, lying at anchor and for sale, a yacht of forty tons burden, sloop-rigged, that had been built of best materials, and handsomely equipped by a German merchant in Hamburgh for the use of himself and family. The demands of wealth requiring something new, he had condemned it to the rude service of his West African trade-houses. In her hold were then lying billets of ebony and dye-wood, casks of caoutchouc, and tusks of ivory, and palm-kernels. The very spaciousness of the cabin unfitting her for large freights,—the cause of her exposure for sale by the trade-agent,—specially commended her to the Mission; and in five days she was ours for $2500.

We retained her appropriate German name,—

THE ELFE.

the "Elfe." Good fairy never helped distressed children more opportunely. God could have given us no white-winged angel more precious. Had she but come only a year before!

One month she still had to fulfill a contract in trade. Another month in refitting. And in August she made her first missionary trip. It was to Benita,—with a new missionary company. The captain, unacquainted with the river channel, anchored outside the bar, three miles from the Mbâdĕ dwelling, and the missionaries landed in a boat sent off for them. Immediately afterward, when I went off in a canoe to the yacht, the captain temporarily resigned the command, while with two native pilots, my church-members, we brought her, with strongly-flowing tide, and stiff sea-breeze astern, across the bar, and up the channel opposite Mbâdĕ. She was drawing seven feet. The shortest throw of the lead marked eleven feet. The surf was slight; and she seemed, as a thing of life, to join our exultation, as she sped across the bar into deeper water in the river's quiet anchorage.

A proud half-hour of command, to give the little vessel its first introduction to the eager, excited crowd of natives that lined the shores, and that especially surrounded the new missionaries at the landing-place. But a sad half-hour for memory. The opulence of that present time contrasted bitterly with the wants of the year past. That comfortable little vessel, safe in storm, protective against noon's fierce rays; the fresh and hopeful reinforcement, whose hands and hearts in strength and numbers would supplant weakness and isolation; the deck I trod in brief captaincy covered hundreds of dollars' worth of goods, provisions, and delicacies, long-before ordered, strangely delayed, just then freshly arrived; in the hold, the monument-stones for my wife's grave. Had this vessel, or these supplies, or that reinforcement been sent a year sooner, infancy and sickness would not have been rationed, and those stones need not have been carved.

Within two years of that day the "Elfe" has ended its own most useful life, and lies a wreck on the waters of the bay whence passed away her spirit to whose memory the yacht was a contribution and from whose grave it seemed to spring.

THE HINDOO GIRL AT DEHRA DOON.

A communication dated May 7, 1870, from Miss Agnes C. Ralston, Oakland Female Institute, came to Benita, inviting Mrs. Nassau, as an alumna, to attend the First Reunion of its Alumnæ Association on June 28, 1870. When it arrived Mrs. Nassau was already in Heaven. I replied to the invitation with a letter of thanks and a few lines to the missionary prayer-meeting of the Institute. In response came a letter in 1871, asking me to nominate some child in Africa, or to choose any other heathen country in which the Institute Missionary Society might nominate some child, for whose education they would provide, and who should bear, as a memorial, Mrs. Nassau's name.

I suggested either Rev. J. M. W. Farnham's school, in China, or the school at Dehra Doon, India, and that the name be *Mary Latta.*

Since arriving in America, has been handed me an extract from a notice in a Norristown (Pa.) paper, of the Alumnæ Association Reunion Meeting in June, 1872 : " The exercises of the morning were closed by the reading of an interesting letter from Miss Margaret A. Craig, missionary to India, addressed to the young ladies of Oakland, relating to a Hindoo girl who is being educated by them in the Mission-school at Dehra Doon. She has been named Mary Latta, in honor of a graduate of Oakland who laid down her life in the cause of missions in Western Africa."

The girl's name is Karo. Her teacher, Miss Craig, was an early acquaintance and a schoolmate of Mrs. Nassau.

Karo had been previously in the Lodiana Orphanage, but in March, 1872, was transferred to Dehra. She is described as "a very nice child, about fifteen years old, rather good-looking, of light complexion, with dark eyes and black hair; in her studies, rather smart," and willing, even anxious for the reception of the English name. Like her name-bearer, she was an entire orphan, and had only an elder brother, a soldier in the British East India army. She had recently become a Christian, and was soon to be married.

MRS. THOMSON'S WISH.

On my way to America, there was a day in Liverpool, England, January 16, 1872, when a small, social, Christian company was gathered at 99 Grove Street, and I remember how one of that company, Mrs. Dr. William Cooper Thomson, spoke her interest in the memory of Mrs. Nassau. Then turning to me, she said, "I wish you would write her life in memoir?" She startled me as if she had read thought. For it had been a daily thought held in utter silence since that earthly life had faded away. But an audacious thought. Could any one describe that life aright? Would not a husband be misjudged in the attempt?

Still, Mrs. Thomson's wish was the same, and was the last word she uttered as we parted on the steamer "City of New York" two days afterwards, to cross the Atlantic.

I promised. And I said to myself, "To this friend, whose lips have thus first given bridal to my modest thoughts, shall be the acknowledgment of whatever thanks may be due in the realization of a wish no less mine than hers."

She is herself in Heaven; she passed thither from Glasgow, on November 28, 1872. I cannot thank her now.

A COMMUNION SET.

Shortly after arriving in America, on the 2d of February, 1872, I saw in the *Presbyterian* of February 17, the following:

"WHO WANTS A COMMUNION SERVICE?

"The Session of the Fairview Presbyterian Church have resolved to present to some needy organization in our connection our old communion service. We are enabled to do this through the kindness and liberality of Misses Clara A. and Maggie V. McClure, who have presented to the church a very handsome and modern set. Any church in need of such a service is requested to correspond with the Rev. A. Nelson Hollifield, Norwood, Chester County, Pa."

And I responded:

"*I* want it for my church at Benita, West Africa, of the Presbytery of Corisco, Gaboon and Corisco Mission.

"I arrived in this country less than three weeks ago, compelled to seek strength and life here, after more than ten years of uninterrupted service in Africa.

"Our present communion service is an ordinary glass tumbler and iron-stone china plate and pitcher. I do not want anything very fine, for it would be inconsistent with our surroundings. But I told my brethren when I left that I would ask some church here that might be getting a new set to give us their old one.

"I have not been among the churches yet, of course; and so have not preferred my request. Your offer I take as providential.

"But I CLAIM the service. 'Norwood, Chester Co.' My angel wife, Mary Cloyd Latta—a rarely noble woman—has made the name of Chester Co. very dear to me. And you, of course, are familiar with the name of her grandfather, Rev. William Latta, D.D.

"Please do not give that service away, even if you already promised it, if you can with any propriety retract. I want to gather about her memory, and about the spot where she lies, anything tha' was connected with any place or region where she has lived." . . .

My application was one of twenty-three; but it being the first, and the circumstances being so interesting, the service of pitcher, two goblets, and two plates was awarded me. Afterward, in the month of August, on a visit to the Fairview church, Mr. Hollifield made an affecting presentation; and

J. M. M'Clure, M.D., replated the pieces, and engraved the following inscription on the pitcher:

>To
>The Presbyterian Church of
>Benita, West Africa,
>From
>The Fairview Presbyterian Church
>of Chester County, Pennsylvania,
>U. S. A.
>A Testimonial to the Memory
>of Mrs. Mary Cloyd (Latta) Nassau.

And the gift is already in use at Benita.

THE MRS. NASSAU SOCIETY.

Among the Treasurer's acknowledgments in *Woman's Work for Woman*, in the spring of 1872 there was a certain sum contributed by the "Mrs. Nassau Missionary Circle of the Pennsylvania Female College."

Who had given that name? That she was known in different parts of the country, I was aware. That she was loved was a synonym with her being known. That her memory should be honored was no surprise. But I wanted to know the circumstances and the special friend who had erected this monument for her. I wrote to the Rev. James Black, D.D., President of the College. But, before reply could come, was myself on a pilgrimage of respectful duty to the parents of my beloved friend George Paull, in Fayette Co., Pa.; and, being detained in Pittsburg, visited the Female College in East Liberty, and was there told the story of the organization of a missionary society among the pupils of the institution, and how, when a name was being adopted, George's aunt, Mrs. Black, remembering his and my wife's association and friendship in life, and their now sainted communion in Heaven, suggested hers.

HER BOYS' HOMES.

Mrs. Nassau's untroubled self-assurance on her dying bed, that her two boys would be "well cared for," was already fulfilled for the elder in his paternal grandparents' home, Lawrenceville, N. J., under the devoted love and untiring care of an aunt. To the younger, though several doors stood open with tender welcomes among his relatives, a touching series of providences led him, without human seeking, past those doors to a friend's empty home in Philadelphia, to give the joy of babyhood to an unsatisfied mother-love that had turned to him in Africa just when he was orphaned two years before, and to receive—as far as any human being could possibly compensate the loss—protection from the shadow of the loss of the love he could never remember.

THE PORTRAIT.

A photographic likeness of Mrs. Nassau, in the hands of her brother-in-law, Rev. J. E. Nassau, D.D., of Warsaw, N. Y., happened casually to come under the eye of a lady-artist, Miss Slade, of that place. The artist's eye was at once attracted and permission asked to paint the face. The photograph was an imperfect one, but with the aid of a lock of hair and the picture of character as presented in an obituary sketch, Miss Slade made a correct portrait.

She said that the expression of no features she had ever painted had so struck her, or had so grown on her at her easel. Though an utter stranger, she had taken up the work, attracted by the magnetism of a face, had continued it under her interest in the story of a heroic life, and completed it as an expression of her admiration of a character, and of her sympathy with missions. Of this portrait one of Mrs. Nassau's most intimate companions said, "It is Mary's face in repose; but not her radiant, happy expression, which no artist could catch, but which her friends all remember with so much pleasure."

THE BENGA HYMN-BOOK.

A collection of eighty-three hymns, translated in the native language, mostly by Rev. Messrs.

Clemens and Clark and Mrs. Nassau, was printed by her in 1864, bound with the "Benga Primer," a primary spelling- and reading-book compiled by herself and Rev. Messrs. Mackey and Clark.

After that date, she and Mr. Clark and his native interpreter continued to translate and compose hymns, and she corresponded with Mr. C. in revising them after his return to America in 1868.

The result of all this work appears in a handsome little volume of "Benga Hymns," issued October, 1873, by the Board of Foreign Missions. Of the two hundred hymns in that collection, one-fourth are by Mrs. Nassau. Her interest in a native hymnology had commenced the work of collection in 1862, her zeal had incited others to assist,—command of the language and correct taste (in spite of inability to sing) fitted her for a work which was to her as much a recreation as a task,—and this energy in supplying the want of a hymn-book did not fail even to the last year of her life.

The "Hymns" are a monument to her. They are sung in the mountain regions where she had hoped to live and labor, and will have their effect on native Christian life after the individuality of her and others' works has been lost in native memory. And the subjects selected for translation are a revelation of the workings of her religious thought. All those fifty hymns are confined

GRAVES OF MRS. NASSAU AND LITTLE PAULL, BENITA CEMETERY.

to "Hymns of Church Work," and "Hymns of Christian Experience."

> "—— but remember only
> Such as these have lived and died."

CHAPTER XIX.

CYPRESS LEAVES.

> "Sad cypress, vervain, yew, compose the wreath."
> "A crown for the brow of the early dead."

FLOWERS of affection, no less beautiful and more lasting than the ephemeral blossoms of the furred *Nyuwe-nyuwe*, of the yellow *Uhange*, or of the *Ilanda* with its green and purple leaves, that soon covered the white sand above her, came by every mail to lay their tribute on her grave. From relatives, from connections, from fellow-missionaries, all who, having so well known, had loved; from traders on the coast, who could not fail to honor one whom they respected, though her life was so constant a protest to their own; from native friends, and from strangers who had watched her ten years' work, or had heard of her lonely death.

From those many flowers, these few petals are here gathered.

FROM REV. WILLIAM WALKER.

GABOON, Oct. 17, 1870.

Yours, of Sept. 15th, was received Oct. 8th, just four weeks after your dear one had fallen asleep. I thank you for writing that first sentence, "My dear wife is dead." Your letter would have been just one prolonged agony, but for that. But my heart sinks when I think of those two weeks of alternate hope and fear, of agony for pains you could not alleviate. But I will not dwell on the terrible scene. . . . The sympathies of the blessed Saviour and the healing hand of time will cure a part of these sorrows of earth. . . .

Mrs. Reutlinger had been trembling a long time. The boys came in with the package about ten at night. Mrs. R. came across, and asked the news. I showed her the black border. She groaned deeply. Soon she asked, "What is it?" I showed her the first line of your letter, for I could not speak. She fell on her knees and wept and cried and prayed. Mrs. Walker was in bed. I would have waited till morning, but she had heard part. We did not sleep much that night. But I cannot go over these scenes. You know how we loved her. . . .

FROM MRS. REV. WILLIAM WALKER.

BARAKA, Oct. 13, 1870.

. . . Some of us had retired when the notes came, and all through that night's watches Mrs. Nassau's beautiful character was before me. So amiable, so gentle, so *un*selfish!

She was the truest, sweetest wife any man was ever blessed with. And what a patient, careful, judicious mother she was. And, oh, so loving and sympathizing as a friend! She stayed with you to help relieve your life of care and perplexities, when, perhaps, she ought to have gone to a healthier climate. You regret now, perhaps, that you did not insist or urge her more to go; but how could she go? And it was *so much* easier to decide to remain than to go. . . . Oh, that sad, touching scene! We think of it continually with mournful interest, and seem to see our sweet friend lying there in that boat, on that very spot, in the sleep of death. I seemed to be with you at that very place, beholding the mournful company and the peaceful dead, when the beautiful hymn was sung last Sabbath in church, "How blest the righteous when he dies."

Mrs. Nassau's rare excellencies of disposition and character will always be a precious memory to us, to all who knew her. How generous she was, always ready to give away the prettiest and the best. And what a tender heart of pity she had for the weary, the sick, and the sorrowful.

Little children were specially noticed by her. And how skillful and judicious she was in preparing medicine for suffering infants, and how tenderly she would take them in her arms and nurse them, never giving a thought whether they were *clean* or not. We are afraid your dear little boy will fret for his dear mother. . . .

FROM MRS. LOUISE REUTLINGER.

BARAKA, October, 1870.

. . . My heart deeply feels the loss, for she was mother, sister, and friend to me. Great was the gift in her. But our Heavenly Father knows what is best for His children. It is a link more to Heaven. . . . If there is anything I could do for dear little Charley, please, you will let me know. . . .

From the "Foreign Missionary" of January, 1871.

MRS. MARY C. NASSAU.

"She is not dead, but sleepeth." "For so He giveth His beloved sleep." These words of sacred writ came clearly and forcibly to my mind, after the first stunning shock we experienced on hearing of the death of our beloved sister, Mrs. Nassau.

"Death loves a shining mark;" and how is this illustrated in the case before us! Our loveliest, our best, and most devoted sister has been taken. We can say of her, as of but few, she had not an enemy; but, oh, how many friends! Says one, "I never so felt the death of a comparative stranger before." And, indeed, no one felt her long to be a stranger. I can see the tears spring to the eyes of the dark-browed sons and daughters of Ethiopia, for whom she lived and died, as they repeat, in subdued tones, "*Mama Nassâ a wendi*" (Our mother is dead). And well they may feel it, for they are orphans, indeed.

Years ago she turned away from all the allurements of home, friends, position, and influence, and, at her Saviour's bidding, turned her glad and eager footsteps to the darkest of all lands,—and there she lived, loved, labored, and died; and from thence she went to her reward. Ere this she has cast her bright crown at the Saviour's feet, with many jewels. She heard the voice and followed the footsteps of the Good Shepherd, though the path lay through much trial and self-sacrifice; but, when the way became too rugged, and her strength exhausted, He has taken her to His bosom.

Oh, that we were all thus "meet for the inheritance of the saints in light!" And how shall we become so? By following the noble example she has left, and which can never be forgotten by those who knew her. Let this Mary, like Mary of Bethany, be a leading star to guide wise women to Christ,—to teach them, not like the pensive recluse, to live only in and for themselves, but to go forth, as did she, to bless the perishing and unpitied of earth,—to give to the Saviour, as did she, the dew of her youth; and God will accept the sacrifice.

God has taken her from us, and we can only say, as she was wont to, under circumstances of trial, " He doeth all things well."

> " Go, gentle spirit, to thy wished-for rest;
> Thy work was done; thy Saviour's will obeyed;
> His presence was with thee in every scene
> Of duty and of trial, and when He
> Saw fit that thou should'st leave thy toils and come
> To Him, 'twas best, 'twas infinitely best
> To change the dimmer sphere of earth for Heaven."

FROM MRS. ISABELLA S. MACKEY.

NEW LONDON, PA.,
January 24, 1871.

. . . I could weep with you more easily than try to comfort you. What a host of memories crowd upon me when I think of Evangasimba, and the dear ones with whom we had such companionship there! But they are gone, to occupy a higher station. What a happy company they must make in Heaven!—your sainted wife, and my dear, departed husband, and Mr. Paull, and Mr. Ogden, and all the others who have labored and loved in that far-off land. How happy they will be!

It is comforting that any of the natives are qualified to fill stations left vacant. . . .

FROM REV. W. H. CLARK.

PONCA, DIXON CO., NEBRASKA,
Jan. 25, 1871.

. . . It cast a heavy gloom upon us, and vividly recalled the years of unbroken friendship and sweet intercourse with her that we enjoyed. Though Heaven is the richer for her transfer, earth, and especially poor Africa, is sadly poorer. . . . Our hearts go out in sympathy with you and your sister, left so alone, and with so much resting on you. How you must miss her cheerful smile, her words of encouragement in hours of darkness. She knew how to cast her burdens upon the Lord, and her cheerfulness had a real and proper basis. Her faith was not misplaced, for Africa *shall* be redeemed; and her example and influence will, I feel assured, play no mean part in the great work. You, dear brother, especially, and we all, have been highly privileged in being allowed communion so long with such a lovely spirit, such a great and noble heart, so full of charity, or rather so full of "the mind of Jesus." . . .

OBITUARY.

The following outlines are extracted from a sketch of Mrs. Nassau's life and character, in the *Presbyterian* of February 11, 1871.

Gifted with a quick and comprehensive intelligence, she had improved it well by study. At the Academy, as a child, her spelling was perfect. Her letters and other writings, written with flowing pen, and without laborious reference to a dictionary, are marred by few inaccuracies. Geometry was play; languages recreation. With only an imperfect grammar, and slight occasional assistance from a native interpreter and others, she rapidly acquired the Benga by chatting with her little pupils, learning to speak almost as fast as she did to read. One-third of the first edition of the Benga Hymns is her translation or original composition; and it was principally her zeal that incited others to the addition of the other hymns of the second edition. The selection and compilation of the spelling- and small reading-lessons of the Benga Primer are almost entirely her unaided work. She even began the study of Hebrew, that a contemplated translation of Ruth and Jonah might conform to the rule of the Bible Society, requiring a translator to read from the original. This she did at Benita as a recreation, at irregular times, when wearied by other work. With Tregelles and Gesenius in her hand she became able to read fairly.

Teaching never was a tedious work, nor did she do any duty as if it was a *labor*. Everything was entered on in a spirit of light-heartedness. The ease with which her own mind grasped any study, and her love for youth, made her choose a teacher's life at Trenton, and afterward at Chestnut Hill. At the latter place she was particularly successful; the school, without the necessary restrictions of boarding, suited her freedom of manner, and it being her own little dominion, she governed readily by love. Freshness of heart, interest in childhood, vivid presentations of truth, made her apt to "teach." At the Corisco Girls' School her pupils never were "glad to get away from teacher," but on the playground, in the house, and even pursuing her to her own room, and breaking needed rest and privacy, they clung to her lively descriptions of other lands, and Bible scenes and history. At Benita, in the confusion of a first settlement, before there was time to establish a day-school, and where there were but two completed rooms, the evening was taken up by teaching the alphabet and spelling. Scores of young men in church and trade owe their reading to her.

She seemed to move in an atmosphere whose magnetism drew all classes, especially of children and women. None were afraid of her; all were at once at ease in her presence. An affectionate heart, that had been early deprived of the love of parents and brothers, and had never known a sister's, took in its warm embrace all who were thrown into her sphere. Pupils, husband, children—the poor, the afflicted, the oppressed, all rested in a love that was not demonstrative or violent, but sunshiny, deep, constant.

With this gentle tone and manner, there were not wanting firmness and decision. Having had only brothers for home playmates gave her fearlessness; bereft of parents, she had learned, in thought and action, independence. These lent to her manners a piquant simplicity that was exceedingly refreshing in its disregard of forms and conventionalisms; and to her decisions a promptness that was quick, and, for a pupil or other subordinate who would attempt rebellion, could be startling—particularly when accompanied by an unusual tone and gesture of command.

A distinguishing trait of Mrs. Nassau was her generosity; she was perfectly unselfish. She sacrificed herself for any and all. In school recitations, so that an ambitious friend should take the honor which she seemed just to fail to attain. In private the poor and the suppliant received from her hand—not in the charity that gives to get rid of importunity, but because, in the charity in which "judgment hath no part," she pitied. The missionary salary was each year supplemented from her little patrimony, to obtain comforts, conveniences, or a few luxuries, the enjoyment of which helped to stand up against the climate, and without which she would either sooner have fallen or had to return. In her benefactions one hand so literally knew not what the other did, that her memory would be offended if they were detailed. Her excellence in attending the sick, and especially infants, made frequent calls for her help both in the mission and among the natives. A slight acquaintance with her father's medical books, increased by subsequent study, with a desire to help the suffering, and a quick judgment to diagnose and to decide on the indicated remedy, made her a good physician. She read regularly the *Medical and Surgical Reporter*, and studied combinations with clearness. Her babes found in their fond mother a most skillful nurse.

There was a quiet patience in submission to trial, meek endurance of wrong, and a sweet forgiveness that was Christ-like.

With decided views, and a keen sense for and love of justice that made her cordially hate wrong and all meanness, she was tolerant of others, and charitable to the tempted and fallen. Indeed, one sometimes wondered to see her, like her Master, eating with publicans and sinners.

Mrs. Nassau was eminently fitted for the new scenes and emergencies of pioneer life. She adapted herself to circumstances, and, not fastidious, her cultivated tastes did not make necessity bitter. Though not strong in body, she had great self-command. Sudden danger made her calm, and an alert perception suggested resource. When *Ukuku* (the spirit whose oracles govern the native tribes, and whose frown is sometimes death) tried to frighten away the school-girls at Corisco, she quietly locked them in her room, and faced the raging women and drunken men who were pressing into the house. When that same spirit assailed the Benita house, she, pale but calm, sat listening to the musket-shots of the fight outside.

But the mission will most miss her for her judgment—impartial, wise, and, by close observation and long experience among the natives, almost unerring. *Everything* at Benita tells of her. She had a keen interest in all that was done, from the building of a chicken-coop to the cutting of a sail—from the giving of a book to a new pupil to the examination of a candidate before session, she, either as interested spectator or trusted counsellor, knew of everything. She had wonderful insight into character, and was rarely deceived by the fairest pretences of the sharpest natives.

Her piety lay in the deep convictions of the heart, and was realized in her life of devotion to humanity. Though her letters and fond notes are warmed and lighted by her love to the Saviour, she did not in conversation speak of thoughts and feelings—rarely spoke even of religion as a *topic*; but the daily retiring to the closet, the Bible a constant companion in her room, and the often-suffused eye, told of communings with Jesus. Religion was so lived by her, and her peace flowed so like a river absent of tides, that it was unmarked because without fluctuation. This appearance of quiet waiting grew in this last year of her life, 1870, the close of which she, in its beginning, said she did not expect to see. On her death-bed she uttered no fears, nor breathed excited aspirations. She quietly remarked that she understood, by the depression disease makes, how unfit a place a deathbed is for preparation; and this not in the despair of one failing in an attempt to prepare, but in the calm survey of one prepared. Her trust in God was complete, and she had no words of anxiety for her two boys, saying they would be well cared for.

Some who knew Mary Latta as a merry schoolgirl may not recognize this portrait. They did not know her truly. Some did wonder that the witty girl, whose laugh or practical (never unkind) joke had so delighted, was going as a missionary to Africa. Though that cheerful disposition and light heart were chastened by the burdens and weariness of uninterrupted years, they never were crushed. They were the life of the missionary company; were one reason of her so long sustaining herself. A noble woman, a devoted wife and fond mother, a skillful teacher, an accomplished missionary, a sincere Christian.

FROM MRS. GEORGIANNA M. M'QUEEN.

LONGMEADOW, MASS.,
February 26, 1871.

. . . How sudden to you Mrs. Nassau's death; for, although you can look back *now* and see that her health was failing month by month, at the time you could not realize it. . . . God has ordered it otherwise. It is a comfort to you, as you think of her last hours, that they were so free from pain. You needed not dying testimony to be assured that she was ready to go,—that her lamp was trimmed and burning.

What a change for her,—lying down in weakness, awakening in Heaven! As you bore her lifeless body back to her African home, she would not have returned to it and to her husband and children, whom she loved so tenderly, could she have done so, for she had seen her Saviour,—the King in His glory,—which was far better.

But you and your sister, in your loneliness and sorrow, need sympathy; and you have it, not only from your family and friends, from your missionary associates, but from those who, not knowing you personally, love the work in which you are engaged, and are saddened when a beloved laborer falls.

Mrs. Nassau was unusually well qualified for her work,—cheerful, hopeful, and inspired others.

Should the mission be reinforced, it will be a long time before another lady can be competent to do the work Mrs. Nassau could do, or can obtain the influence over the natives which she had. Her cheerful, pleasant words attracted them, and her kind words made them friends. . . .

Mrs. Walker, writing to Miss I. A. Nassau, from Bloomfield, N. J., Nov. 22, 1872, about the two boys' photographs, says,—

"I delight to trace the lineaments of their sainted mother in their dear faces. How precious her memory to us! I love to tell the story of her life to those who love the cause of missions, and love to work for Jesus. But there is no circumstance of her life that impresses me more than that peaceful death, on the open sea, during the silent watches of the night. I seem to see the *very* spot, —the boat gliding along. And that anxious company. *Each one.* The dead; the stricken husband; poor motherly Mrs. Sneed, with Charley; darling Charley, so precious to his mother in life! And that sympathizing company of boatmen.

"Strange that one so tender and delicate as she should cross and recross the ocean, and pass away from earth to her home on high in such a manner! How little those who were training her so carefully in her childhood imagined such a thing! But I have often thought, knowing, as I did, Mrs. Nassau's beautiful character and noble mind, if she could have known or thought there was a *possibility* of her dying just as she did, she would not have hesitated a moment to have entered that path in life's journey, ending as it did. It was sad for the loved ones she left; but, oh, not for her,—not for her. . . ."

Miss Sue F. Campbell,—a schoolmate of Mrs. Nassau,—of Rock Spring, Centre Co., Pa., wrote, February 25, 1873, to Miss I. A. Nassau, of an article in *Woman's Work for Woman:*

"I, too, dear friend, mourned for Africa when, as you say to the ladies of Marion, 'one beloved work after another was abandoned.' I have vivid recollections of earnest seasons at the throne of grace as sickness or death removed the laborers, till you and your brother were the only representatives of the church in America. I rejoice that a brighter day has dawned; new laborers in the field; our dark-browed sisters arousing to the gospel call. . . . An item in the *Presbyterian*, some weeks since, from 'An African Missionary,' respecting 'Woodstock,' moistened my eyes. I can name him, for I know who made 'two mounds in the white sands of Benita.'"

Some verses that I addressed to Mrs. Nassau in America, in 1863, elicited a request for the composition of an extended article, with "Africa" as the theme. Occasion for compliance with her wish was not presented until my own return, in 1872, by a formal invitation to address a literary society, in March of that year. The following extract alludes to the cemetery in which she lies:

> 'Tis chosen well, that little yard
>   Of missionary graves,
> . Just near the house they liked on earth,
>   And by the ocean's waves.
>
> The forest trees are undisturbed
>   By axe or Art's curt style,
> Save where a winding path pursues
>   Nature's own wooded aisle.
>
> The vines may clamber unrestrained,
>   And light fall cheerily
> O'er grass and bush, where birds untamed
>   Still twitter merrily.

But Art its *added* hand has set
   (Not taken aught away)
Where Love has sought, on marble fair
   To save from Time's decay
Dear names, whose lives and mem'ries rare
We cannot willingly forget.

There Infancy was laid to rest,
   And Manhood in his strength,
And patient Womanhood. How blest
   To reach their Home at length!

There, too, beneath the fervid sky,
   Where sunbeams blaze by day;
Or, when the moon is mounted high,
   Cool mystic shadows play;
Where stars so silently look down
   Through vistas of the night,
From Southern Cross and Southern Crown,
   On marble cold and white;
The light of sun and moon and star
   On tablet-sculptured cross rests calm,—
Benita's brave-borne cross of *her*
   Who wears Benita's Crown and Palm.

"Lone midnight hour on the sea, what watchers were with thee?
What step divine walked on the wave? What angel ministry?
Would not our loved have chosen thus, all in the holy night,
Up that star-lighted tropic sky, to pass to realms of light?
Bear back the dear unbreathing clay! Benita's dark-browed band
Will lay it tenderly away in their own Palmy land."

THE END.